SCIENCE OF
DANCE
TRAINING

Priscilla M. Clarkson, PhD
University of Massachusetts
Margaret Skrinar, MS
Dance Kinesiologist

Human Kinetics Books
Champaign, Illinois

4890.

Acknowledgments

We wish to thank our husbands, Ron Pipkin and Gary Skrinar, for their valu-able assistance with the preparation of this manuscript. Also, Francie Joseph, Andrea Watkins, Catherine Royce, and Gail Collins have provided critical reading and/or helpful insight and guidance for which we are grateful.

Library of Congress Cataloging-in-Publication Data

Science of dance training.

    Includes bibliographies and index.
    1. Dancing—Physiological aspects. 2. Dancing—
Accidents and injuries. I. Clarkson, Priscilla M.,
1947–   . II. Skrinar, Margaret, 1944–   .
[DNLM: 1. Athletic Injuries. 2. Back—injuries.
3. Dancing. 4. Leg Injuries. 5. Pelvis—injuries.
WA 487.5.D4 S416]
RC1220.D35S25   1988   617'.1   87-3370
ISBN 0-87322-122-2

Developmental Editor: Sue Wilmoth, PhD
Production Director: Ernie Noa
Projects Manager: Lezli Harris
Copy Editor: Claire Mount
Assistant Editor: Julie Anderson
Proofreader: Linda Purcell
Typesetter: Sonnie Bowman
Text Design: Keith Blomburg
Text Layout: Admakers
Printed By: Braun-Brumfield

ISBN: 0-87322-122-2

The views, opinions, and or findings contained in this book are those of the authors and should not be construed as an official Department of the Army position, policy, or decision unless so designated by other official documentation.

Printed in the United States of America

10 9 8 7 6 5 4 3 2 1

Human Kinetics Books
A Division of Human Kinetics Publishers, Inc.
Box 5076, Champaign, IL 61820
1-800-DIAL-HKP
1-800-334-3665 (in Illinois)

Contents

Foreword

The great masters of dance have an instinctive wisdom for producing artists, one which has been successful throughout the ages. The kinesthetic experience, which is such an integral part of their lives, allows them to feel movement and produce the desired effect through imagery and gesture. Most of the time, the intuitive methods of these gifted teachers are scientifically correct. Unfortunately, these teachers are the exception rather than the rule. Dance in our time is technically more complex than in the past. It has become almost impossible to develop technique safely without a thorough understanding of biomechanical laws.

The current approach to dance education contrasts with the traditional methods of teaching. Today's dancers are more aware of their bodies and more inquisitive than former generations. They demand explanation and logic from their teachers as they analyze and challenge movements. No longer is academic dogmatism permissible. The authority and discipline of the old ballet masters have been swept away from the dance studios and replaced by the methodologies of younger, less experienced innovators.

The popularity and appeal of dance now blooms universally, and individuals of all origins, body types, and ages are attracted to its rhythm and motion as never before. Consequently, the number of injuries has increased. The cause of these casualties is inadequate training and abuses that result from lack of true understanding of the dance technique and physical structures.

The significant number of technique-related dance injuries forced Sparger and Gelabert to found the discipline of Dance Injury Prevention in the early 1950s. *The Science of Dance Training* continues this precedent of concern for dancers' physical problems and contributes valuable information to this growing field.

The Science of Dance Training is the result of important research and studies done by individual authors in various fields related to dance education. This information will be of interest to researchers in Dance Medicine, as well as dancers, teachers, choreographers, and medical professionals who treat dancers. In uniting these multiple aspects of dance pedagogy, Priscilla Clarkson and Margaret Skrinar have opened new frontiers in the academics of dance and have introduced an area for continued research and investigation.

Raoul Gelabert, Ph.D.
Founder/Director of Gelabert Studios
Dance Kinetic Education Institute, NYC

Preface

Less than 10 years ago the areas of dance medicine and dance science did not exist. Up until then the principles of dance training were much the same as they were 100 years ago. Consequently, the training of dancers has evolved from the practice of the past, which many times has been based on superstition and intuition. Few, if any, physicians recognized injuries specific to dance. Often, the medical care of dancers was left to self-treatment or alternative, and sometimes quack, treatments. A dancer's health seemed to range from benign neglect to outright carelessness. Prior to 1976, only a handful of professionals in dance, medicine, and science had questioned these circumstances. As the acceptance of dance medicine and science expands, more professionals are working toward the improvement of dance training.

The development of *The Science of Dance Training* was spawned by a symposium titled "A Widespread Call for Systematic Research in Dance," coordinated by Margaret Skrinar for the 1983 national meeting of the American Alliance for Health, Physical Education, Recreation, and Dance. This book, like the symposium, is based on objective scientific inquiry rather than tradition, intuition, or past experience alone. The goal is to initiate guidelines to promote the safest, most efficient, and most effective training of dancers. It is intended that this book will serve as an important source of information for dancers and their teachers as well as a reference for medical personnel and exercise scientists.

The Science of Dance Training is organized into four sections. The first section presents a perspective on dance training from the point of view of a dancer, a scientist, and a physician. Sections II, III, and IV are organized to present information on scientific, medical, and behavioral aspects of dance training, respectively. All contributors have been actively engaged in research pertaining to dance.

Our own backgrounds in both dance and exercise science facilitated the development of this book. Each of us is a former dancer: Clarkson in classical ballet and Skrinar in modern dance. We have performed, choreographed, and taught dance. Both of us have witnessed first hand, from the professional to the local level, the problems with training dancers. In addition to studying dance, each of us has pursued a career in exercise science. In this book, we believe that we have assembled all of what is objectively known concerning the medical, scientific, and behavioral aspects of dance training.

PART I

Perspectives in Dance Medicine and Science

Scientific studies of dance training have appeared only recently in the literature. In the last few years such studies are becoming more frequent because of the interest of several exercise scientists in the area of dance. Ballet and modern dance companies are now being asked to participate as subjects in research studies. Under the aegis of scientists, dancers have been measured from head to toe, have run on treadmills, and have filled out diet questionnaires.

Many dance companies have now identified a physician and/or a health professional who is knowledgeable about dance injuries and training. Whereas some dancers see these experienced health care professionals when they are in need of treatment, others do not. Many dancers still seek out alternative treatments and rely on the experience and advice of their peers. Much of this advice is unreliable and ill-advised.

When dancers of today began their training, there were no scientists and few medical professionals interested in dance. How do dancers respond to this new interest in them? How do the scientists and medical professionals at the forefront see their role fitting into and promoting the areas of dance science and medicine? In chapter 1, the dancer's perspective is described in the sensitive and practical language of self-experience in the new world of dance medicine and science. In chapter 2, the exercise scientist's perception of the role of science in the study of dance is presented. In chapter 3, the physician's view of dance medicine is brought to light by a physician who has had a long-standing interest in the treatment of dancers.

Chapter 1

What Dance Medicine and Science Mean to the Dancer

Martha Myers
Connecticut College

Throughout history dancers have performed despite injuries, not daring to acknowledge to their directors or teachers—sometimes not even to themselves—the extent of their injury or its pain. "Work it out" and "The show must go on" are phrases that reflect the prevailing response to physical trauma common in the performing arts. Generations of dancers have been victims of this grim theatrical tradition, their plight exacerbated by a medical profession largely ignorant of their special needs as patients and by companies indifferent to their problems. The new disciplines of dance medicine and science are challenging this tradition, promising performers longer, healthier careers.

Although one still hears horror stories of dancers' experiences with treatment for injury, it is less likely that a dancer today will have my experience in seeking treatment in the mid-fifties. I was unable to dance, or even to walk without persistent pain on the medial aspect of the knee. Over a number of months I visited five orthopedists, from New York to Boston. One predicted a life of invalidism without an immediate operation; another suggested cortisone injections. Two offered advice to find another occupation. A fifth, a renowned Boston specialist who had treated many dancers, prescribed a simple exercise for strengthening the vastus medialis. Whether this intervention or simply rest was responsible for the healing, or a combination of both, some ten months later I was able to begin the long road back to performing.

But during that year of recovery, no one thought to look at the movement patterns and limitations of physique that had contributed to this injury. The dance sciences as well as a specialization in dance medicine were unknown then. Operations on knees, backs, feet, and ankles were performed without knowledge of the functional range of motion essential in these limbs for proper execution of dance movement. Also, inadequate rehabilitation and disregard for the etiology of the injury (such as specific techniques performed and poor movement mechanics) further compromised the success of many of these operations and led to reinjury. The results from the dancers' perspective were often disastrous, and careers abruptly ended. With or without surgery, the common prescription of prolonged rest with insufficient rehabilitation allowed muscles to atrophy and kinesthetic proprioception and coordination to decline.

Complementary Systems of Medical Treatment and Rehabilitation

Given this history, it is not surprising that dancers have developed fear and frustration with the efficacy of the medical art in relation to dance. Poverty and ignorance of body sciences have also been factors in turning dancers away from established medicine and science as a means of diagnosis, treatment, and prevention of injury. Many have instead chosen complementary therapies (adjunctive and alternative).[1] Yet others have combined these or added them to established treatment resources.

Alternative Systems

Chiropractic, acupuncture, and nutritional therapies are the more popular *alternatives* to traditional treatment. The body therapy systems and massage are more often *adjunctive* resources. But there is no strict dichotomy to these categories. My experience working with dancers in professional and educational situations suggests a number of reasons for the choice of complementary interventions, particularly the alternative therapies.

1. Frustration with conventional treatment. After weeks or months of unsuccessful medical interventions, patients feel (accurately or not) that medicine has either failed or done as much as it can, and/or that the physician has given up on them. Sometimes the nature

---

[1]Lerner, M. and Remen, N. (1985). Integral cancer therapies, *Advances*, 2 (3), 14–33. The authors distinguish between *established* (medical) therapies and *adjunctive* and *alternative* therapies, grouping the latter two together under *complementary therapies* (p. 15).

of the problem is such that, indeed, little can be done within medical parameters to improve the patient's condition. Drugs to alleviate pain, changes in life-style to prevent further deterioration, and continued physical therapy are common medical options at this stage.

2. Persuasive word of mouth from associates who have had positive experiences with a particular modality or practitioner. The client may or may not have first sought established medical help and may or may not have been dissatisfied with it.
3. The treatment sounds simple, quick, effective, and relatively inexpensive, such as manipulation for a back ailment or megavitamin therapy.
4. There is fundamental dislike of the physician/patient relationship and/or a history of unsatisfactory relationships with a physician. This attitude is often associated with a basic antiestablishment stance, based on philosophical beliefs and aesthetic preferences.
5. Modalities associated with medical treatment such as operations, drugs, and interruption of activity are worse threats than the pain and incapacity of the injury.
6. Lastly, and for many most importantly, there is the problem of expense. The majority of professional students and performers cannot afford insurance and are often forced to delay or avoid medical treatment, especially in large cities where costs have far outstripped their means.[2]

Some of the rationales listed above invite further comment. With reference to ("1") for example, physicians may indeed have exhausted the protocols they consider appropriate to a given patient's condition. If dancers become impatient before this point, or refuse to accept it, they frequently try alternative treatment.

Dancers' fear of invasive medical procedures ("5") is not unreasonable given the high vulnerability of their profession. As physicians admit, no operation is without risk, and some of their colleagues operate more frequently than others. A person's chances of being in the high statistic group can depend on not only geographical locale but the particular specialty of the attending physician. For instance, MacLemson (1976) notes an English study in which orthopedic surgeons were reported to have operated on 10% of the cases referred to them as disc problems whereas the neurosurgeons operated on more than 50%. He also pointed out that, with respect to low back pain, "irrespective of treatment 70% of our patients get

---

[2]Several major cities (e.g., New York and Los Angeles) now have organizations that offer performers access to expert medical advice and treatment at minimal expense.

well within 3 weeks, 90% within two months'' (p. 65). The complementary therapies, with some exceptions, are noninvasive. They do not irrevocably alter joints or soft tissue. As surgical techniques improve and dance medical specialists proliferate, the morbidity of these fears will hopefully diminish.

Antiestablishment bias (''4'') is certainly a motive for some dancers who choose complementary systems of care. They have philosophical, political, and aesthetic aversions to treatment, which is viewed as impersonal, high tech, and materialistic. Integral to the psychodynamics of this stance are different viewpoints regarding the nature of illness; the role of various agents in recovery (the role of the patient being a primary one among these); natural versus mechanical interventions; and treatment of the whole versus part of the person. Some of these choices involve aesthetic preferences as well, not surprising for an art in which the body functions as an aesthetic as well as a physical object.

Adjunctive Systems

The alternative systems of treatment such as chiropractic and acupuncture are generally familiar to the lay public and will therefore not be discussed in detail (Melzack, Stillwell, & Fox, 1977). The adjunctive therapies, however, especially their role in postmedical rehabilitation and injury prevention, are less well-understood and are briefly described in this section.

Body Therapies

Among the older and more familiar of the body therapy systems are The Alexander Technique (F. Mathias Alexander); Bartenieff Fundamentals™ and Labananalysis (Irmgard Bartenieff and Rudolph Von Laban); The Feldenkrais Method (Moshe Feldenkrais); and Ideokinetic Facilitation (Lulu Sweigard). These and numerous, more recently developed systems share certain common principles and goals, such as (a) altering motor programming to increase the body's fluency and efficiency in adapting to environmental forces (gravity, momentum, stress, etc.); (b) analyzing and reorganizing habitual patterns of bodily use to improve function and self-ease in movement (e.g., in alignment, standing and walking or *enchainments* in dance); and (c) believing in a biopsychosocial model that is concerned with the mind/body relationship. Movement is seen as a means of achieving mind/body integration. Clinically many dancers seek to augment medical treatment and rehabilitation in two ways: to maintain noninjured parts of the body in good condition during treatment and to help prepare the body for return to class and performance after injury.

Performers have learned that the distance between the physical therapist's door and the stage door can be long and hazardous. Racing too quickly from one to the other, without taking time to reestablish kinesthetic proprioception in the injured part and recoordination of the whole body, can lead to reinjury. The body therapies can be an important resource in this final process of healing, working in conjunction with the dance medicine specialist.

An example comes to mind from my experience working with a physical therapist in the screening clinic offered at the American Dance Festival's Summer School. The therapist examined students, referring appropriate cases to the orthopedic specialist for the Festival. Weakness of ankle joint musculature was a common finding among the dancers (Villaneuva, 1984). Students were given exercises to strengthen these structures, and the mechanisms of injury were explained to them as well as any individual structural anomalies that might be contributing to the problem. I then addressed faults in the student's technique, such as excessive supination in *relevé* and maladaptive patterns of alignment, which were factors in the etiology of the injury. Various body therapy protocols were used to help the dancer understand and correct these pathomechanics.

The body therapist's approach to treatment and rehabilitation focuses more on internalized mechanisms as opposed to the external approaches of conventional medicine. For example, in my experience, the physical therapist's use of manual manipulation is primarily in stretching and strengthening muscles around a joint in correct patterns of usage (as in proprioceptive neuromuscular facilitation). Postural repatterning also is approached from a muscular point of view with specific exercises to retract a forward head, release a contracted lumbar spine, stretch the pectorals, and so on. It is a more external approach to repatterning than that of the body therapist. The patient is less a partner than a subject to whom a modality is applied. Images, for instance, might be given to the patient in physical therapy; but therapist and client would not spend an entire session on imaging as a primary process in releasing muscular contraction and redirecting neuromuscular pathways (as in the practice of Sweigard Ideokinesis).

The body therapy session, on the other hand, is not a treatment but rather a lesson. The subject is kinesthetic awareness. The therapist does not physically place the patient's head in the desired position. An hour's lesson might be devoted to helping students discover what they do with the head. For example, in Feldenkrais the student might lie supine, sensing where pressure is felt between the floor and the head (whether at the top, center, or base of the skull); which ear lies closer to the ground; which shoulder is closer to the ear; and so on. In an Alexander session the student might sit in a chair, the instructor lightly touching his head with both hands, allowing him to explore through subtle tactile suggestions new positions that feel lighter and more comfortable, allow fuller breathing, and lead to improved posture. In Bartenieff Fundamentals™ the student might learn how the head can initiate movement of the body through space, altering the relationship of body parts; the student can learn also how her spatial preferences can enhance or interfere with the integrated action of these parts.

The emphasis in the systems described is on developing kinesthetic awareness through introspection, leading to physical reeducation. Moreover, the process is as much one of subjective learning as of processing objective information. Its goal is to make the student a self-learner, independent of the teacher. It relies on the authenticity and validation of introspection through self-report. It insists on the student's autonomy and capacity for change. Attending to internal states and asking questions of ourselves as in "How am I feeling?" "What am I feeling?" produces a new internal state. Introspection is basic to both psychotherapy and body therapy.

Therein lies the strength and weakness of these systems. Not all individuals have the same capacity for, or interest in, introspection. They do not wish to engage in a prolonged process whose results cannot be quantified. Clinically, I have found, however, in the numerous dancers with whom I have worked, even those initially resistive, an acknowledgement that the process helped them address old problems in their technique, and remedy minor functional musculoskeletal stress. Such adjustments in technical practice and performance can be important in avoiding injury, especially overuse syndrome, which is often associated with faulty technique. Current research substantiates what dancers have often discovered: By altering factors which contribute to the etiology of an injury, it can be healed. A major study on dance injury among professional performers revealed the importance of some commonsense but hitherto unacknowledged interventions that contributed to their recovery. Among them were changing the technique practiced, correcting poor technical habits, or changing the company with which they performed (Solomon & Micheli, 1985). It is also my experience that the introspective process of body therapy education is most effective in combination with scientific education as well as understanding and applying the principles of kinesiology, neuroanatomy, and motor learning to movement performance at all levels of the training process.

Massage Systems

Dancers have used massage for years as a relaxation aid and a balm for sore muscles. Some performers in major companies consider a massage, like class, part of their daily regimen and even have private masseurs who go on tour with them. Recently it has become a recognized partner of the dance and sports medicine team in treatment, rehabilitation, and injury prevention. According to A. J. Ryan, Editor of *The Physician and Sportsmedicine* (Brody, 1985), massage both before and after exercise can be beneficial. Providing nutrients to muscles enables them to work longer and more efficiently, thus improving performance. He points out that it also reduces muscle tension, relieves tissue edema, and helps prevent soreness following exercise. In injury its capacity to reduce inflammation and pain and relieve muscle spasms can speed recovery. It is a vital component in the prevention and treatment of injury for dancers.

Dancers have become aware that an injury produces changes not only in the affected soft tissue or bone but equally throughout the musculature as the patient copes with pain and restricted motion. These alterations interfere with normal movement patterns and may persist long after the original injury is healed. Deep massage and friction massage can be important aids in maintaining the body's normal functioning. The former increases blood flow and balances muscle tonus; the latter breaks down fascial adhesions which hinder proper healing and motion of ligaments, tendons, and muscles.

The most familiar form of massage in this country is Swedish. Shiatsu and foot reflexology (both Eastern forms), and the Benjamin System are gaining a wider audience. There are also systems such as Rolfing (Structural Integration) that have developed unique massage techniques as part of a more comprehensive program of neuromuscular reeducation. In Rolfing, deep pressure and tissue manipulation are used to break up fascial adhesions and restructure perceived imbalances in the body. It can be perceived by some clients as extremely painful, whereas for others it is an important source of postural realignment and psychological insight. There are massage practitioners in the larger dance centers (e.g., New

York) who specialize in working with artists, and those who combine massage with a variety of exercises in neuromuscular reeducation. Massage prescribed for specific illnesses and trauma should be practiced by medical specialists only. As this treatment has grown in popularity among the general public, the muddying of medical/nonmedical boundaries has become a cause for some concern. Credentials are essential for anyone working with the body. This is crucial for medical management; yet few states, at present, require licensing for practitioners.

Modifying motor patterns in everyday life and dance technique to create more efficient, less iatrogenic ones and to prevent injury seems like a reasonable endeavor. So does the use of lay massage techniques for enhancing the healing process and relieving the musculoskeletal conditions that frequently lead to injury. It is important to note, however, that specific benefits of these adjunctive systems still rest primarily on clinical evidence.[3]

New Concepts and Resources

Medical treatment has taken light-year leaps in the past decade, even the past five years, with concepts of injury prevention advancing on a similar scale. Treatment and prevention of injury as well as new advances in training are of prime importance to a long and healthy dance career.

Treatment of Injuries

Several types of injury that would have irrevocably ended careers thirty years ago, for example cruciate and achilles ruptures, are repaired with return-to performance function today. Factors contributing to this are: (a) earlier recognition of trauma and incipient trauma, with more precise diagnostic tools such as arthroscopy, thermography, CT scanner, and Positron Emission Tomography; (b) high tech treatment options such as arthroscopic and laser surgery and, in rehabilitation, electrical stimulation devices, computerized exercise equipment, air casts, cryotherapy,

---

[3]Irene Dowd, a foremost practitioner of Ideokinesis and Neuromuscular Training in New York City, has completed research on a project directed by Judith A. Smith, Ph.D., R.N., Director of Community Health Nursing Programs, University of Pennsylvania School of Nursing. Preliminary findings have shown significant results in the parameter studied (hip joint mobility). Results are not yet published.

and biofeedback equipment; (c) more sophisticated surgical and rehabilitative techniques which allow more successful repair of soft tissue, bone grafting, and even the possibility of growing new bone from old (Burkholz, 1985); and (d) anti-inflammatory drugs. These interventions speed recovery and reduce the complications that develop from prolonged immobility (adhesions, scar tissue formation, muscle atrophy).

Prevention of Injury

Imagine a world, however, in which traumatic and chronic injury among athletes was the exception rather than the rule. Sports and dance sciences today are providing a data base for new injury prevention and training techniques that may one day make this as near a reality as is possible given the inherent vulnerability of the human body. New training tools such as film (slowed to 10,000 frames per second) and digitized computer analysis of movement reveal a performer's micromotions. These patterns are then compared to those that are optimal to achieve a specific motor task (swinging a bat or executing a *pirouette*). Thus training regimens can be individually focused and the kinds of injuries that result from errors in technical execution minimized. This work has been going on for some time at major sports centers throughout the country.

The traditions of dance training, however, may be more resistant to change than those of athletics, where the financial stakes are higher and the relationship of means to ends more immediately apparent (e.g., change the technique and win the gold medal or double the annual salary). In a performing art the value of dance medicine and science is seen mainly in terms of self-preservation (injury prevention and repair). Dance has lagged behind sports in recognizing science's contribution to achieving a more creditable artistic performance, and its relevance to gaining applause. As medical and scientific resources become increasingly popular, dancers will find in them values important for the aesthetics of performance. They will gain insights that will enhance the *quality* of their performance on stage, a benefit connected with but additional to avoiding injury and surviving a risky profession.

Professional dancers are most often enthusiastic about the technical innovations available to them for injury prevention, including modification of classroom techniques. One faculty member at the American Dance Festival reported from her course in functional anatomy that she did not want to miss a class, because she learned today what *not* to teach in her class tomorrow. A well-known soloist with a New York City ballet company contrasted conditions that prevailed fifteen years ago when he entered the company with those of today. He reported that they never stopped dancing back then, despite the pain. Nor did they receive any physical therapy treatment for common problems—tendonitis, shin splints, muscle spasms—until it was so bad there was just no way to move. Now, when members of the company feel something isn't working right, they can go to the resident physical therapist's office for help before discomfort has time to turn into a serious injury. Some of the older dancers with the company remember when they didn't know about ultrasound treatment, a modality in common use for more than a quarter of a century. Also, muscle testing for possible weaknesses, examinations for structural anomalies that compromise the aesthetic purity of a line and its neuromuscular efficiency, was equally unfamiliar.

I have observed in the therapy office, high above the stage at Lincoln Center's State Theatre, dancers not only being cared for but learning to care for themselves. In addition to the stretch and strengthening manual techniques practiced by the therapist, the dancers stretch achilles and gastrocnemius on slant boards available in the office and studios. After limbs, backs, and feet are scrupulously evaluated, manipulated, massaged, and occasionally pounded in the restorative process, the dancers learn a regimen to follow on their own (exercises, icing, etc.) to continue the improvements made.[4]

Some professional companies are practicing team medicine. The physical therapists for both New York City Ballet and American Ballet Theatre work in association with an orthopedic consultant and podiatrist. The team is often in attendance at performances. They are also doing research that will provide important information for technical training as well as treatment and rehabilitation.

Some professional training schools and educational institutions hold physical examinations (screenings) for students prior to admission to the program or at its beginning. Among the items checked by the consulting orthopedist or physical therapist are degree of turn out, relative muscular balance of limbs, structural and functional abnormalities, and alignment. In some instances, individual programs are provided and students advised of the style of dance for which they are physically best adapted. They may also learn how to work most effectively within their physical limitations and advantages.

All of this scientific scrutiny strikes some artists as a denial of self-determination. It smacks of ''big brother.'' What are the limits beyond

---

[4]Physical therapist Marika Molnar is the first in-house medical practitioner for a major ballet company in the U.S.

which, even in the name of health and self-preservation, such advisement becomes limiting prescription? Skeptics point to the numerous famous dancers whose limitation of physique (turn out, flexibility, proportions) falls far short of the aesthetic and/or functional ideal. These are important issues. They are already being raised in sports training, where scientific technology is used to select teams for particular sports. They will inevitably affect dancers also.

Training Advances

Scientific research is also advancing into the classroom. It is addressing questions such as: What is the optimum execution of a specific step or sequence? What are the wear-and-tear risks? What is the ideal body type for specific styles? How can principles of motor learning help make teaching movement more efficient (e.g., are there faster ways to master a dance style or improve movement quality, and is it possible to overtrain)? How does the psychological profile of the dancer interface with these questions (i.e., what is the effect of an individual's coping strategies on motor learning and performance, quality of movement and expressiveness, or proneness to injury)? The body of literature in these areas is increasing as is evident in the material presented in chapters to follow.

In the past, such questions were often met with disinterest or even scorn from dance artists and teachers. But among young performers today, who often combine educational degrees with professional credentials, there is increasing sophistication. They are aware of correct warm-up techniques, potentially hazardous actions, and the training benefits and deficits of different dance styles for their bodies. Educated dancers evaluate their teachers more critically. Some young professionals and students have complained to the author that it's difficult to find a satisfactory teacher. They believe, however, that their ability to discriminate and to protect themselves will extend their careers.

The scientific information explosion will affect teachers at all levels of the training process. More will be demanded of them. Exceptional teachers have been able to recognize common physical problems and injuries in their students. They have been able to correct alignment and technical faults with intuitive, if not scientific, understanding of the anatomic and neuromuscular organization that produces a particular aesthetic, or injurious result. The quality of their students reflects this. Will a broader base of better educated teachers improve the quality and quantity of elite performers? Will the attrition rate among nonprofessionals who study dance for pleasure be reduced? Will both professionals and nonprofessionals dance more safely?

The cautious scientist can say only "Wait and see" and "Let's provide every means for finding out." There is no question but that advances in dance medicine and science already have made enormous changes in the field. Compared to even the recent past, dancers are performing not only better but more safely. They are increasingly aware of the importance of dance science and medicine to performance and career longevity. As more dancers have access to these specialized resources, a new partnership will be established between dancers and the medical/scientific team that provides their care.

References

Brody, J. (1985, April 10). Personal health, massage: A "treatment" to be selected with care. *New York Times*, p. C-1.

Burkholz, H. (1985, April 5). Redesigning human bones. *New York Times Magazine*.

MacLemson, A.L. (1976). The lumbar spine: An orthopedic challenge. *Spine*, **1**, 59–71.

Melzack, R., Stillwell, D.M., & Fox, E. (1977). Trigger points and acupressure points for pain: Correlations and implications. *Pain*, **3**, 3–23.

Solomon, R., & Micheli, L. (1985). Concepts in the prevention of dance injuries: A survey and analysis. In C. Shell (Ed.), *The dancer as an athlete* (pp. 201–212). Champaign, IL: Human Kinetics.

Villaneuva, E. (1984, June). *Anatomy of the foot and ankle.* Paper presented at the Dance Medicine Seminar, co-sponsored by the American Dance Festival and the Physical Therapy Department of Duke University Medical Center, Durham, NC.

Additional Bibliography

Bartenieff, I., with Lewis, D. (1980). *Body movement, coping with the environment.* New York: Gordon and Breach, Science.

Feldenkrais, M. (1972). *Awareness through movement.* New York: Harper and Row.

Jones, F. (1976). *The Alexander technique, body awareness in action.* New York: Schocken Books.

Myers, M. (1980, Feburary–July). Body therapies and the modern dancer: The "new science" in dance training (Alexander, Bartenieff, Feldenkrais, Sweigard). *Dance Magazine.* [Six articles]

Myers, M. (1985). Perceptual awareness in integrative movement behavior: The role of integrative movement systems (body therapies) in motor performance and expressivity. In C. Shell (Ed.), *The dancer as athlete* (pp. 163–172). Champaign, IL: Human Kinetics.

Sweigard, L. (1974). *Human movement potential: Its ideokinetic facilitation.* New York: Dodd, Mead and Co.

Chapter 2

Science in Dance

Priscilla M. Clarkson
University of Massachusetts

A popular image of dancers has been set forth in the famous paintings of Degas. Ballerinas, a bit overweight for today's standards, leisurely lounge at the ballet *barre*. The dancers are serene and calm—the picture of grace. Degas would paint an entirely different picture today. Ballerinas would not have the luxury to gain such weight nor would "serene" or "calm" ever describe a dancer before, during, or after class. Ballet today is one of the most rigorous forms of physical training. Yet, while the training itself is rigorous and the standards have changed, the actual training of dancers has seen little change.

A ballet class of 100 years ago would be markedly similar to one of today's classes. The exercises, the sequence of the exercises, the terms for the exercises (all in French), and in some cases even the music would be the same. A dancer could easily take a ballet class in any country around the world. Trial and error has found basically one technique that works, and it has remained stable. Generally modern dance classes as well adhere to a set technical style. There are some small exceptions. Recent research has shown that the performance of *grand pliés* (deep knee bends) produces a large stress on the knees. This research was later presented in Dance Magazine and prompted many teachers to delete this exercise from the traditional *barre* work.

Reasons for Lack of Research in Dance Training

One reason dance training has seen so few changes is the lack of research in this area. Most exercise scientists have come from a sports or physical education background, and their interests have remained in those areas. The few exercise scientists who had come from a dance background or who were interested in studying dance had to break the sport study tradition. This was not easy for two reasons: Dance was not popular in the area of sport science, and sport science was not popular in the area of dance. In chapter 1, Myers provides ample evidence and reasons for the dancer's lack of interest in science. Dancers and their teachers saw themselves as artists, not athletes. Why, though, were scientists so reluctant to study dance? The major reason is probably the exercise scientist's inability to understand dance training. Lack of understanding was based on the myth that dance training lacked rigorous physical exercise (the Degas image) and was merely an artistic endeavor, and the fact that dance training has a specific vocabulary of movement terms which is unlike that of any sport. A secondary reason could be the frustration of trying to change the dancer's close-minded approach to training. Those exercise scientists who forged ahead despite the problems found little moral or financial support for their research on dance. Finally, the ground has been broken in dance medicine. Some researchers are choosing to study dance, and more teachers are asking for information on safer, more effective training practices. The systematic study of dance training is still quite new.

Some particular areas of dance training that require further research are a) ballet shoe design, b) biomechanical analysis of movements, c) supplemental forms of training (e.g., aerobic), d) effects of heat stress, e) low body weight, f) overtraining, g) training techniques, and h) training for adolescents. An overview of these research areas is presented below.

Suggested Areas of Further Research

Many research needs in dance can be related to or adapted from sport science research. For example, in the area of biomechanics, several laboratories have studied athletic footwear. In fact, most of the athletic shoe companies have hired biomechanists to operate their research and development laboratories. Studies of footwear have led to the development of a plethora of shoe types, with running shoes being a prime example. Dancers, however, are wearing the same ballet shoe (*pointe* shoe) that has been worn for 75 years. The shoe covering is pink satin, even on the flat surface of the toe where dancers stand. The smooth satin finish on the toe area lasts only as long as the shoe is not worn; once worn, the shoe's toe is frayed and ripped. The inner composition of the toe provides the support needed to stand on pointe (on the toes), but the material used to provide support rapidly breaks down. Consequently, a professional dancer may use one pair of pointe shoes per performance whereas a preprofessional dancer may wear the pointe shoes for one month of classes. Considering that pointe shoes cost $30–$40 per pair in 1986, certainly a better design should be considered. In addition, all pointe shoes have basically the same design even though it is well known that only certain foot and toe shapes can adapt to them easily.

The biomechanical or motor control analysis of dance movement is an interesting endeavor. Dancers use illusion to create the visual impressions. An example of this can be observed in a *grande jete* leap where the dancer seems momentarily suspended in the air. Few studies have analyzed how feats such as these are accomplished. How is "grace" defined in scientific terms? An analysis of segmental timing should provide answers to how the body creates dance illusions.

Most sports require their athletes to supplement practice with other forms of training. It is very common, for example, to see football players training in the weight room or performing endurance activities. Questions as to what type of training could supplement traditional dance training have gone largely unasked. A few dancers have taken up additional strength training, but most of these use the Pilates system, which seems to have a cult following. No scientific studies have been conducted to evaluate the effectiveness of the Pilates system especially as it pertains to dance. In general, supplemental endurance training is rarely considered by dancers. Because many pieces of choreography, by their length and intensity, require the body's aerobic system, dancers should consider adding endurance activities to their training programs. The exercises in dance classes stress the body's anaerobic system, further suggesting the need for aerobic training to better prepare dancers for performance situations.

Heat stress during exercise has received much attention in recent years. Sport training practices have been adapted to minimize heat stress, and equipment has been redesigned to prevent the detrimental effects of overheating. Heat stress in dance is another matter. It is not uncommon for dancers to wear plastic pants to class even in the hottest studios. Recently, my colleagues and I had the opportunity to take some anthropometric measurements on preprofessional dancers at a well-known summer ballet program. The temperature outside was in the low 90's. In the dance studios, which were located in an old factory building, there was no air conditioning, and the temperature was considerably warmer than it was outside. Yet many of the dancers wore plastic pants, leg warmers, and sweaters. Dancers did this to lose weight and to keep their muscles warm. The former is certainly wrong and the latter is dubious. Principles of general heat stress are unknown to dancers and their teachers. As yet, studies to examine the effect of heat stress in these "sweat box" studios have not been conducted.

Thin is in, most notably in the ballet world. This is evidenced by the numerous reports of bulimia and anorexia in ballet dancers. How thin should and can a dancer be and still be healthy and strong? Is there a point where strength is sacrificed for thinness? The low body weight and rigorous training of female ballet dancers have been associated with loss of the menstrual cycle (amenorrhea). The long term effect of amenorrhea in dancers is not known. Several researchers have suggested a possible relationship among amenorrhea, osteoporosis, and dance injuries. Research is only just beginning in these areas.

Overtraining and its avoidance is of particular interest in the area of sports. In dance, however, overtraining is not an issue. In fact, for many preprofessional companies, it is a common phenomena. For these dancers, performances may occur only three to four weekends a year. As the performances near, the choreographers realize that more refinements are needed in the choreography or in the dancers, and the rehearsal times are increased. At the same time, many dancers are trying to rapidly lose weight to appear thinner on stage. Dancers are often in poor physical shape by the time of the dress rehearsal and performance. The extent of this overtraining has never been studied or monitored.

Another potential area of study is a full examination of training techniques. General research questions would include: What is the most effective way to teach dance skills? What is poor technique and how can it be monitored and changed? Teachers are often frustrated by students who come to them from other dance schools with problems developed over years of poor training. It is necessary to determine an effective means to correct chronic conditions. Perhaps the most common among these problems is foot pronation (rolling in of the feet), which, if left uncorrected, can result in serious stress on the ankles and knees. In a recent study we have demonstrated the effectiveness of an augmented feedback system to correct the problem of chronic foot pronation in dancers. The use of augmented feedback is well suited to dance because much of the technique is learned or practiced at the *barre*. During *barre* exercises, dancers isolate small, discrete movements, and the relatively stationary position allows the use of feedback monitors.

A final area of interest for research is dance training in adolescents. Serious young dancers in the 10- to 13-year age group can expect to spend 16 hours per week whereas the 14- to 17-year-olds can expect to spend

22 hours per week in dance training. And although no other sport requires such a commitment at this skill level, little research has been conducted concerning intense training at such a young age. It is not uncommon for talented 15-year-old dancers to leave home and go to New York for their dance training. Many of these young dancers live without direct adult supervision. They are responsible for getting themselves to Professional Children's School for morning academic classes, to the ballet school for afternoon classes, and home to prepare their own meals and do homework. The majority of these young dancers will never make it into a professional dance company. In specific need of scientific study are both the physical and the psychological stress that these adolescent dancers must endure.

I have provided only a brief overview of some areas for research in dance training. Each year large numbers of children begin dance training. Gradually, the elite are selected; only a small fraction ever make it into a professional company. Yet there are numerous college, regional, and preprofessional dance companies. Research in dance would therefore benefit many dancers. Behind the beauty and grace that the audience sees on stage, and underneath the magic of costumes and makeup are bodies that undergo rigorous physical training. To improve a training regimen that has been unchanged for a century is a challenge, but there are unlimited possibilities for research in this area.

Chapter 3

What Is Dance Medicine?
A Physician's Perspective

Allan J. Ryan
The Physician and Sportsmedicine

Dancers at all levels are monitored or treated by physicians engaged in many different fields of medical practice as well as by nonmedical people who come from a variety of backgrounds. To describe such attention properly as dance medicine, the care must be administered by a physician. This is not to decry the possible value of other services, but to limit the use of the term, *dance medicine,* to those aspects that can be clearly described in terms of what the physician is expected to know and do. Medical practice is organized in terms of qualifications based on specific training and interests; physicians organize themselves in particular associations for the purposes of setting and maintaining high standards for care and encouraging research and development in special fields. Dance medicine should be considered as one of these specialties.

Medical Specialties

Medical degrees (M.D., D.O.) are general qualifications for medical practice including surgery. Except in remote rural areas, a great deal of medical practice is oriented directly or indirectly to hospital practice. Physicians are qualified to work in the hospitals only in particular areas, and these areas relate specifically to the recognized medical specialties. As a result all physicians are classified into subspecialties from the most generalized (e.g., general practice) to the most specialized (e.g., ophthalmology). There are many areas or fields of special interest for physicians that are not currently described as recognized specialties. Some of these cut across several specialties because they encompass ideas, knowledge, and methods that are ordinarily found in those specialties. Dance medicine is such a field.

The field of dance medicine involves study of and working with people of both sexes and all ages. It requires a good working knowledge of exercise physiology, biomechanics, kinesiology, nutrition, traumatology, physical medicine, and rehabilitation. Physicians working with dancers may also be surgeons and/or orthopedists, but if they are not they must know the proper indications for surgical management of problems that dancers encounter. Many physicians see dancers casually as part of their particular practices, and frequently for reasons not related to their dancing. Others see dancers on a more regular basis because of their interest in dance, and because dancers are able to identify them as knowledgeable about the field. Some become affiliated with dance programs or companies for these reasons.

Medical Organizations

There is presently no medical organization or association specifically oriented solely to dance medicine. The American College of Sports Medicine, the American Orthopedic Society for Sports Medicine, the American Osteopathic Society for Sports Medicine, and the Podiatric Academy of Sports Medicine all have members who are interested and active in dance medicine.

In some of the large cities there are clinics, programs, centers, or institutes organized in terms of dance medicine. These are free-standing, university-affiliated, or related to particular dance schools or companies. Groups and individuals working with dancers, not including physicians, refer dancers to physicians for medical management.

The definition of dance medicine, therefore, cannot be related to a specific field of practice or a particular group of persons trained professionally in this field. It can be related to the practical experience of physicians who have worked with dancers and who have in some instances recorded these experiences in articles and books. This literature unfortunately is scattered in a variety of publications and cannot be identified currently through indexing systems under this general title. When brought together it comprises a substantial body of knowledge which is growing slowly but steadily. Its foundation is principally based on clinical research because there is a lack of well-conducted and reported basic research regarding the medical aspects of dance.

Establishment of Dance Medicine

Dance medicine properly includes aspects of instruction, performance, and research relating to the health of dancers in their various activities as well as to the prevention and management of injuries. This may involve their nutrition, weight control, physical conditioning, hematology, hormonal function, provision of proper equipment, and control of their environment. The implementation of such measures is complicated by the fact that dancers include all persons involved in dance activities on an informal as well as a formal basis, both amateur and professional, and those who are using dance as a physical fitness activity, such as in aerobic dance.

There are four principal reasons to establish dance medicine as a special field of interest and practice: (a) There are medical conditions that occur characteristically in dancers; (b) dancers' medical problems should not, if possible, be treated by complete cessation of activity; (c) the goal of rehabilitation should be to restore anatomical relationships and function as close to normal as possible; and (d) the tradition of unqualified treatment or avoidance of necessary treatment must be influenced if not changed completely. The achievement of all of these goals is possible today given present knowledge and technology. Major barriers to its accomplishment are the fears of dancers that physicians do not understand the nature and demands of dance, and in the case of the professionals, the financing of proper care when income is directly related to ability to perform and insurance coverage is meager or nonexistent.

Dance Injuries

As with athletes, dancers are subject to injuries and other medical conditions that are related to the specific physical activities involved. Although these conditions and injuries do not occur exclusively in dancers, they are relatively common and may therefore be anticipated and possibly prevented. This can only be done by persons who understand the factors prone to produce them and the precautions that can be taken against them.

Movements in dance often involve exaggerated and even strenuous actions that may exceed normal ranges of motion and tax bone and soft tissues to the extremes of their ability to withstand such stress. Because these movements are repeated many times in class, rehearsal, and performance, the tendency to injury is increased by overuse. Such injuries may occur even when the movements are performed as perfectly as possible, but imperfect or improper execution of the prescribed movement greatly increases the tendency to injury. Studies of the kinesiology and bio-mechanics of dance movements can lead to strategies for the prevention of injuries, which the dancers can learn or otherwise use to their advantage.

When a dancer is injured or ill the medical treatment should allow, if possible, some continuation of physical activity to avoid even temporary loss of the physical and physiological qualities that contribute to successful performance. Muscle strength is lost very rapidly with inactivity and muscle atrophies sometimes to the extent that it may not regain its full former strength even with intensive and extensive retraining. Flexibility is lost when muscles cannot be fully stretched and ligaments contract. Position sense, which is extremely important to the dancer, is controlled through the central nervous system but is dependent on the function of the muscle spindles and Golgi tendon organs, both of which can be seri-ously affected by prolonged immobility. Recovery may be very slow and even incomplete.

Most dance activity is anaerobic rather than aerobic, but a high degree of physical conditioning for the particular activities is important, involv-ing both strength and endurance. This is particularly true when long hours of rehearsal and performance are involved many days of the week. Every effort must be made by therapist and dancer to minimize loss of this over-all body conditioning even if one part of the body must be protected and if the intensity and duration of the activity must be reduced because of physical weakness. The therapist who is familiar with the usual dance activities of the patient is in the best position to decide how much activity is necessary during recuperation.

Injury Rehabilitation

The goal of rehabilitation of the injured dancer is to restore the ability of that dancer to perform as before the injury. This involves not only a return to normal function, but, because dance is a visual art, a restora-tion of normal anatomical relationships. A significant anatomical defect or distortion could terminate a dancer's career just as easily as a signifi-cant loss of function. An elbow stiffened at 90° flexion could be only minimally handicapping in daily living activities but devastating to a dancer. Some people can compensate reasonably well in most activities for a torn anterior cruciate ligament, but it would be virtually impossible for a professional dancer to do so.

As a result of these considerations, it is necessary for the therapist to take particular care to restore functional and anatomical relationships as close to normal as possible, even if this requires more than ordinary measures. The reasons for such measures, if they are necessary, m .st be thoroughly explained to dancers in order to establish their confidc 'ice and motivation to full recovery. The explanation and subsequent measures will be much more acceptable to the dancer when offered by someone who the dancer knows is thoroughly familiar with the demands of dance and the particular dancer's role in meeting these demands.

Educating Dancers

Because there is a long tradition among dancers of treatment for physical problems by nonqualified persons and of self-treatment, it is necessary to educate them regarding the possible results of such treatment in order to change their behavior. This frequently involves familiarizing them with anatomy and physiology as well as the basic principles of the science of movement in terms of biomechanics and kinesiology. This knowledge makes it possible for them to understand how they may be further harmed, if not disabled, by unqualified therapists. It becomes more acceptable to them when it comes from someone whom they can see is experienced in the study and practice of dance.

The successful establishment of dance medicine as a special field of interest depends on the identification of a special body of knowledge, the development of a means of disseminating this knowledge, and the training of qualified educators and practitioners through the use of this knowledge. This requires making available facilities for such training and for research to expand this body of knowledge as well as for the provision of medical supervision and care. Already a significant body of knowledge is available concerning dance medicine, but much of it is not readily available to the practitioner or dancer. Furthermore, this knowledge has to compete for their attention with other information which may be misleading or erroneous because it lacks the recognition of its authenticity, which is conveyed by its being seen as a part of an accepted scientific field of interest.

Articles describing clinical experiences and research in dance medicine appear in a variety of education and medical magazines and journals. There is no journal published in English that is dedicated to dance medicine, and only two newsletters in dance medicine exist. The existence of a professional journal would stimulate the production of such articles and bring the best of them together where they could be more readily identified. There are still relatively few books in English that deal with dance medicine, which may be used as resources for education and reference. There are some audio and video cassettes available. Films of dance deal principally with technique and the recording of performance.

Professional training in dance through college and university programs is concerned principally with the development of conditioning, technique, and other aspects of performance. Only a few deal with education in the area of dance medicine. Where such education exists, it usually occurs after the fact, in the course of a physician's dealing with the medical problems that have arisen among the students but not having the opportunity to help prevent these problems.

Education of physicians in dance medicine has been limited chiefly to the presentation of conferences and workshops by the few who have organized a center of interest or a program in this field, or through the practical experience of working in a clinic or institute where dancers are seen and treated for medical problems. There are still only a few such centers or clinics that have a facility and personnel who devote all or a considerable portion of their time, equipment, and research to dance medicine. This is in part a reflection of the fact that dance medicine does not enjoy a high priority among other fields of special medical interest for funding of facilities or research.

The Future

The present growing interest in sports medicine has made it possible for the interest in and practice of dance medicine to grow along with it in some areas. The two fields can continue to develop together and along parallel lines, but dance medicine must acquire a separate identity in order to be fully accepted by the entire dance community and to accomplish its special goals.

PART II

Scientific Aspects of Dance Training

This section provides an overview of dance training from a scientific perspective. The authors have presented the currently available research in the physiology and biomechanics of dance. Chapter 4 describes how the muscular system functions and how this functioning is influenced by dance training. Particular attention is paid to energy production in the muscle and the relationship of muscle energy to performance capabilities. A comprehensive description of the muscular system responses to strength and flexibility training is presented in chapter 5. This chapter provides current information on the principles of strength conditioning, including overload, reversibility, and specificity and how these principles can be used to enhance the training of dancers. Chapter 6 presents a clear overview of the cardiovascular responses to dance training. These authors have also provided some valuable information and recommendations for better training practices.

Because much of a dancer's success, especially in classical ballet, depends upon having a specific body type, chapter 7 was included to describe how body type is assessed and what is the characteristic body type of a dancer. Chapter 8 describes the biomechanics of dance and presents interesting and useful information on how dance movements are produced and analyzed.

Chapter 4

Energy Production in Dance

Priscilla M. Clarkson
University of Massachusetts

For centuries, audiences have observed dance as an aesthetic collage of movements with seemingly infinite permutations of steps, speeds, and forces. The transformation of movement into art requires a well-trained body. For the finest performance, dancers, dance teachers, and choreographers should base training practices on sound physiological principles as well as aesthetic choices. Such practices will lead to efficiency and ease of training with less risk of injury.

The dancers' muscles are the primary working parts. The brain and spinal cord provide the neural signals for which muscles are to be used, but the muscles themselves must supply the necessary energy for movement to occur. This chapter will provide a brief overview of muscle structure and how energy is produced for muscle work. Such information will enable dancers and dance teachers to understand important principles of efficient and safe training practices. Dancers should not only aspire to perform beautiful movements but also apply physiological principles so they can perform well for many years. To understand how a dancer's muscles move and how energy is produced for dance movements, a basic understanding of muscle structure and energy production is necessary.

Muscle Structure and Contraction

Muscles are composed of many narrow fibers separated by layers of connective tissue (see Figure 4.1). The connective tissue extends beyond the ends of the fibers so that the layers of connective tissue from all the fibers join together to form tendons. The tendons function to attach the muscle fibers to bones. The muscle fibers shorten, or contract, and exert a pull (via the tendons) on the bones to produce movement. A muscle such as the calf muscle may contain thousands of muscle fibers. The large number of fibers makes it possible for a muscle to provide a variety of tension levels. For example, to perform a *saute*, a large number of muscle fibers in the calf muscle would contract for sufficient force to propel the body into the air (see Figure 4.2a). To produce a pointed foot as in a *tendu* position (see Figure 4.2b), fewer muscle fibers would contract.

Each muscle fiber is composed of a series of protein chains organized into tubes called myofibrils. The two major proteins that comprise the myofibrils are myosin and actin. These proteins are organized into basic units called sarcomeres which are delineated by the Z-lines (see Figure 4.3). The actin proteins are connected to the Z-lines, and the myosin proteins occupy spaces between the actin proteins. The myosin proteins have extensions (or crossbridges) projecting towards the actin. Attached to the crossbridges are adenosine triphosphates (ATP), the muscles' energy producing material. At rest, the actin and myosin are prevented from coming in contact with each other. During contraction, however, the myosin crossbridges bind to the actin and exert a pulling effect so that the Z-lines of each sarcomere are drawn toward the center.

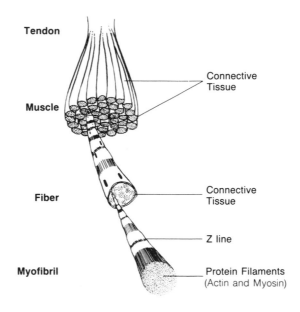

Figure 4.1 Muscle structure. From E.L. Fox, 1984, *Sports physiology*, p. 90. Adapted by permission.

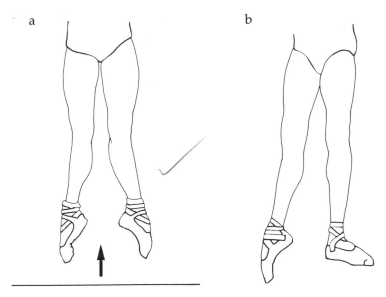

Figure 4.2 Dancer performing (a) a *saute,* from first position: jumping up and pointing the feet; and (b) a *tendu:* pointing one foot on the floor.

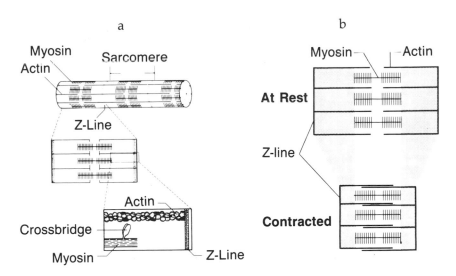

Figure 4.3 (a) Substructure of myofibril, (b) Sarcomere in a rested state and during contraction. From E.L. Fox, 1984, *Sports physiology,* p. 92-93. Adapted by permission.

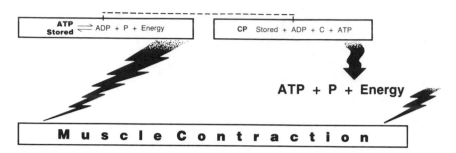

Figure 4.4 The production of energy for muscle contraction. Energy is derived from the immediate energy sources of ATP (adenosine triphosphate) and CP (creatine phosphate). ADP is adenosine diphosphate.

In order for this process to occur, energy must be available. This energy can only be derived from the breakdown of ATP. ATP is made up of the chemical adenosine with three phosphates attached. One of the phosphates is attached by a high energy bond. A chemical reaction breaks this bond which releases energy, and muscle contraction can occur. The end products of this reaction are adenosine diphosphate (ADP) and P. ATP can be broken down by one of three energy systems depending upon the intensity and duration of the dance exercise being performed.

When each muscle fiber contracts or shortens, all the sarcomeres within that fiber shorten using the energy derived from the breakdown of ATP. ATP is stored in and synthesized by the muscle fibers. An overview of energy metabolism during exercise will be presented in this chapter. If more detailed information is desired, several excellent review articles and book chapters are available (Brooks & Fahey, 1984; Fox, 1984; Gollnick & Hermansen, 1973; Gollnick, Piehl, & Saltin, 1969; Havel, 1970; Hermansen, 1969; Holloszy, 1975; Holloszy & Booth, 1976; Holloszy, Oscai, Mole, & Don, 1971; Katch & McArdle, 1977; McArdle, Katch, & Katch, 1981; Saltin & Essen, 1971).

Dance as an Anaerobic Exercise

Each muscle fiber is able to store a small amount of ATP to be used for immediate energy. Also, ATP can be quickly synthesized from another chemical, creatine phosphate (CP) (see Figure 4.4). The stored ATP and CP are classified as immediate energy sources. Any exercise lasting under 30 seconds relies predominantly on ATP and CP for energy production. For example, during a short *allegro* exercise, the ATP and CP system would predominantly supply the needed energy. After the *allegro* exercise, during the rest period between combinations, ATP and CP would be resynthesized. Because many dance exercises, either at the *barre* or in the center (*au milieu*), are short bursts of activity, stored ATP and CP are important energy sources for dance.

If an exercise lasts longer than 30 seconds, more ATP must be produced through a series of chemical reactions, with each series of reactions requiring specific enzymes. These chemical reactions function to break down either carbohydrate or fat. Muscles are capable of both short intense bursts of activity as well as long duration, low- to moderate-intensity activity. The muscle has different ways to produce energy (ATP) from carbohydrate and fat to accommodate these varied energy demands.

After the immediate energy sources are used, the muscle begins to metabolize the carbohydrates stored in the muscle. Muscle carbohydrates are derived from carbohydrates taken in the diet. After the carbohydrates are ingested, they are digested into simple sugars (glucose) which are then carried by the blood stream to the muscles. The muscle fibers take up the glucose molecules and store them in compact units called glycogen. When exercise is performed, specific enzymes in the muscle fiber are activated to break down glycogen and produce ATP. Following the first 30 seconds of a 2-minute dance combination, the muscle fibers begin to metabolize glycogen (see Figure 4.5). This process can occur both anaerobically and aerobically, meaning without and with the use of oxygen, respectively. The initial breakdown of glycogen through a series of chemical reactions results in the end product, pyruvic acid. If pyruvic acid is converted into lactic acid, the process of glycogen breakdown is anaerobic, and the energy system is sometimes referred to as the lactic acid system. During a short burst of intense activity the pyruvic acid will be predominantly converted into lactic acid. If the exercise is of low intensity, the pyruvic acid will be transported into a specialized cellular component, the mitochondria. In the mitochondria, further chemical reactions take place, and ultimately large quantities of ATP will be produced. For this process to happen, oxygen is required. When the breakdown of glycogen includes the chemical reactions in the mitochondria, the process is aerobic.

Therefore the type (intensity and duration) of exercise performed determines whether glycogen will be metabolized aerobically or anaerobically. If the exercise is so intense that it can only be done for three minutes or less, glycogen will be predominantly broken down anaerobically (see Figure 4.5). If the exercise is of moderate intensity and can be continued for over three minutes, the glycogen will be predominantly metabolized aerobically to produce ATP. Generally, dance exercise falls into the former category.

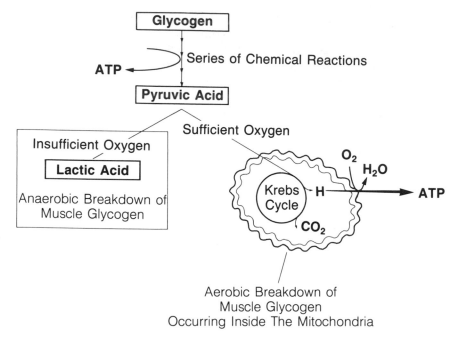

Figure 4.5   Anaerobic and aerobic breakdown of muscle glycogen.

Both *barre* and center exercise are classified as anaerobic. Each barre exercise lasts from 30 seconds to 2 minutes: One leg is exercised while the other leg maintains stability during this phase (Cohen, Segal, Witriol, & McArdle, 1982; Schantz & Astrand, 1984). The stable leg, although not at complete rest, is able to recover from previous use as the working leg. Floor or center exercises last from 15 seconds to 3 minutes with rest between the combinations. These rest periods are generally used for instruction, demonstration, and correction. Dance classes are therefore categorized as intermittent bursts of moderate-to-intense activity. Although a dance class may last 60 to 90 minutes, each exercise bout lasts only 15 seconds to 3 minutes with interbout rests. Therefore, exercise in dance class can be classified as an anaerobic activity; muscle fibers use predominantly stored ATP and stored carbohydrates (glycogen) to produce energy for movement.

Dance as an Aerobic Exercise

Several pieces of choreography do last over three minutes and these would begin to utilize the muscles' aerobic system (Cohen, Segal, & McArdle, 1982; Cohen, Segal, Witriol, & McArdle, 1982; Schantz & Astrand,

1984). The intensity of such an exercise is moderate and the duration is relatively long (generally three to five minutes). The demand for energy production per unit time is not as great as for short-term strenuous exercise. Glycogen in the muscle is therefore broken down by the more complex process which requires oxygen. When pyruvic acid is metabolized in the mitochondria, it enters a series of chemical reactions called the Krebs cycle (see Figure 4.5). In the Krebs cycle, there are two main products formed, CO_2 and hydrogen ions. The CO_2 diffuses out of the mitochondria and out of the muscle cell to be carried by the blood stream to the lungs and expired. The hydrogen ions go through another series of chemical reactions where ATP is generated. In this process, the hydrogen ions finally combine with oxygen and H_2O is formed.

The oxygen that is used in the mitochondria comes from the air we breathe. By measuring the amount of oxygen the body uses, energy production of the aerobic system can be estimated. When oxygen consumption is measured during a maximal intensity exercise, the maximal amount of oxygen consumed by the body can be determined. Maximal oxygen consumption (abbreviated max $\dot{V}O_2$, where V is the symbol for volume) is a reliable indicator of the power of the aerobic system. Endurance exercises require aerobic energy production; thus athletes who perform such exercise as distance running and cycling have high max $\dot{V}O_2$ values. Dancers, both modern and ballet, have been shown to have max $\dot{V}O_2$ levels similar to nonendurance athletes (Clarkson, Freedson, Keller, & Skrinar, 1985; Cohen, Segal, Witriol, & McArdle, 1982; Kirkendall & Calabrese, 1983; Mostardi, Porterfield, Greenberg, Goldberg, & Lea, 1983; Novak, Magill, & Schutte, 1978; Schantz & Astrand, 1984). These data indicate that dancers do not have a well-trained aerobic system which further supports the contention that ballet and modern dance are anaerobic activities. Thus, although some choreographic works may require a dancer to dance for over three minutes, these may not be performed frequently enough to induce a training effect of the aerobic system.

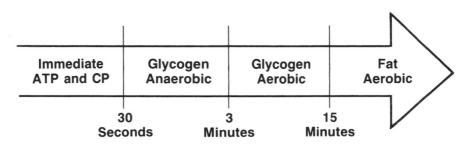

| Immediate ATP and CP | Glycogen Anaerobic | Glycogen Aerobic | Fat Aerobic |

| 30 Seconds | 3 Minutes | 15 Minutes |

Figure 4.6. The predominant energy source used for an intense-effort exercise for each exercise time period.

Aerobic dance has received much attention as a means for cardio-vascular improvement and weight loss (Hooper & Noland, 1984; Watterson, 1985). In an aerobic dance class, a routine will be performed without interruption for 5 to 30 minutes depending on the fitness level of the students. When an exercise is continued for more than five minutes, the muscle slowly begins to use fat as a means to produce ATP (see Figure 4.6). Beyond 15 minutes, the muscle switches from the predominant breakdown of glycogen (aerobically) to the predominant breakdown of fat. The breakdown of fat requires oxygen and is also called aerobic.

Some fat is stored in the muscles, but the bulk of fat is stored and must be mobilized from adipose (fat) tissue. The fats which are taken in the diet are carried through the blood stream to adipose tissue much of which is located beneath the surface of the skin (subcutaneous). It is this fat tissue that one can pinch for the well-publicized "pinch-an-inch" test. The adipose tissue consists of fat cells which function to store fat from the diet. The fat cells release this fat back into the blood stream to be carried to the muscle and used to produce ATP during aerobic exercise. Long duration or endurance type exercises facilitate the mobilization of fat from adipose tissue and promote its metabolism in muscle. Thus dancers who want to lose weight should consider endurance forms of exercise in addition to their regular dance classes.

Muscle Fatigue

When muscles perform intense bursts of activity like jumps, the anaerobic breakdown of glycogen produces ATP and the by-product, lactic acid. The production of lactic acid is associated with a burning sensation and fatigue in the muscles. Special nerve endings located around muscle fibers are stimulated by lactic acid formation in the muscle fibers. These nerve endings are responsible for the sensation of pain or burning. Lactic acid also interferes with muscle contraction and the regeneration of ATP. Recent studies have suggested that a tolerance for lactic acid occurs with anaerobic training. Therefore, in regular classes, a well-trained dancer should not experience the burning sensation as frequently as a novice dancer.

The more intense the exercise, the greater the need for energy hence the greater breakdown of glycogen into lactic acid. One factor involved in discontinuing an exercise due to fatigue is the increased production of this by-product. During periods of rest, lactic acid is metabolized in the muscle or is removed from the muscle into the blood stream. For example, when a dancer is performing *developpes* at the *barre* using the right leg, lactic acid is produced and accumulated in the thigh muscle leading to fatigue. During the end of the exercise the thigh muscle may have a sensation of burning. When the dancer turns to do the *developpes* with the left leg, lactic acid will be metabolized or removed from the right thigh muscle. During this period, the muscles of the right thigh will recover and be able to perform the next exercise.

Each center exercise lasts under three minutes and is generally intense enough to increase lactic acid production in the working muscles. The rest time between combinations serves as recovery time for the muscles when lactic acid is metabolized or removed. The more strenuous the combination, the more glycogen is broken down and the more lactic acid is produced. Thus a waltz combination would require less recovery time than a strenuous combination with multiple jumps.

The removal of lactic acid from the blood (and presumably from the muscle) is facilitated by low-intensity movement such as walking or swinging the limbs (Belcastro & Bonen, 1975). Complete rest, such as sitting down, delays removal of lactic acid and prolongs recovery time. Without adequate recovery, performance of the next combination is adversely affected. The common practice of hanging on the *barre* watching other dancers while awaiting the next turn should be discouraged. Rather, slow, nondisruptive movement should be performed.

Although the fatigue described above is relatively transient, the dancer may also encounter absolute exhaustion due to long hours of rehearsals. The muscle fibers can store only a finite amount of glycogen which is continuously broken down to supply energy. If the breakdown exceeds the replenishment, the glycogen stores eventually become depleted and the dancer experiences exhaustion. When dancers are required to attend long rehearsals for several days prior to and including the day of the performance, their muscles may be in a near glycogen depleted state for the performance, especially if dancers are severely restricting their dietary intake at this time. This may be one factor contributing to the apparent increase in falls and injuries during performances and dress rehearsals.

Dancers, like everyone else, have experienced a special category of fatigue, known as delayed onset muscle soreness. This soreness generally appears 24 to 48 hours after a novel, unaccustomed, or intense bout of exercise. Soreness is considered an indicator of muscle damage (Armstrong, 1984; Byrnes et al., 1985; Friden, Sjostrom, & Ekblom, 1983). If a class is particularly stressful, including intense-effort, novel combinations, myofibrils in the muscle fibers may be damaged, and delayed onset muscle soreness will ensue. A loss of functional strength has been shown to accompany the soreness (Friden et al., 1983), and this strength loss may adversely affect dance performance. Therefore, on the days before a performance, classes should be of moderate intensity and strenuous new combinations should be avoided. Delayed onset muscle soreness is a transient experience which generally subsides within 72 hours. Soreness or pain that lasts longer may indicate serious injury, and a physician should be contacted.

Class and Performance

Training adaptations of the energy systems are specific to the energy system being used. Does classical ballet violate this principle of specificity? Schantz and Astrand (1984) measured blood lactic acid levels of professional dancers from the Royal Swedish Ballet during a regular ballet class and during a choreographic work. During the *barre* or the center work in class, the blood lactic acid concentration increased to 3 mmoles (about a two-fold increase from resting values). However, during rehearsal or performance of a classical choreographic work, lactic acid levels rose to 10 mmoles. Also, heart rates approached maximal levels during rehearsal and performance. In a previous study of professional dancers from American Ballet Theater, heart rates during company class never reached maximal levels (Cohen, Segal, Witriol, & McArdle, 1982). These data show that the intensity of class exercise differs considerably from the intensity of performance exercise.

During a ballet class of the Royal Swedish Ballet, the work to rest ratio for the barre exercises was 60 seconds work and 30 seconds rest. During the center exercises of moderate intensity, the work to rest ratio was 35 seconds work and 85 seconds rest and during center exercises of severe intensity (*allegro*), the ratio was 15 seconds work and 75 seconds rest. In contrast, a principal female part in Act I of Giselle danced for 12 minutes with 5 minutes rest followed by 5 minutes dance, 5 minutes rest, 8 minutes dance, 1 minute rest and 8 minutes dance. During a performance of Pulcinella, a male dancer danced for 12 minutes continuously. During the performance of both these dances, heart rates of the dancers frequently approached maximal levels (Schantz & Astrand, 1984).

Clearly, classes and choreographic works differ considerably in intensity and duration. In this regard dance training violates the principle of specificity. For class exercises, the predominant energy production pathways are the breakdown of stored ATP and creatine phosphate and the anaerobic breakdown of glycogen. For performance of certain choreographic works, the anaerobic breakdown of glycogen is increased. Also, the duration of the performance (over three minutes) suggests that aerobic breakdown of glycogen would take place. Therefore, specific metabolic adaptations which occur during class will not fully prepare the dancer for performance. Because professional dancers are rehearsing on a daily schedule, the rehearsals serve as the training. However, preprofessional or college dancers who rehearse intermittently cannot depend on regular classes to fully prepare them for rehearsals. Dancers who are not trained for the rehearsals will fatigue easily and perform poorly, and this may lead to general ennui and diminished learning efficiency.

Aerobic Exercise and The Sylphlike Image

The dancer must not only move with flawless precision but must also have a pleasing appearance. In dance, especially ballet, the correct body is dictated more by aesthetics than technique. One of the most important factors for the correct body form is a low percentage of body fat. To have this low body fat, a dancer must expend enough energy to prevent excess fat storage. Although many professional dancers have problems with weight control, the preprofessional young dancer often has the greatest problem. Professional dancers are generally able to expend large amounts of energy during several hours of daily classes, rehearsals, and performance. The preprofessional young dancers, who do not attend a performing arts school, are at a severe disadvantage. Because they attend school for the greater part of the day, they may be only able to take one dance class per day. The net caloric expenditure for an average ballet class is only 200 kcal per hour for professional women ballet dancers (Cohen, Segal, Witriol, & McArdle, 1982), which is a relatively low caloric expenditure. Thus, a young dancer with a weight problem will find it difficult to lose weight taking only one dance class per day, and these dancers would surely testify to the frustration in maintaining the sylphlike image.

Because endurance or aerobic exercise is an efficient means of burning calories and using fat to produce energy for the muscles, it is the ideal type of exercise to recommend to dancers with weight problems, particularly the young dancer. In addition to their regular dance classes, these dancers should be encouraged to jog, swim, or even take an aerobic dance class as a means to enhance weight loss along with following a proper diet. Jogging at a fast pace for a continuous 15-minute period can account for another 150 kcal use. Some teachers are fearful that jogging may produce large or tight thigh muscles. Endurance exercise will not result in muscle enlargement, and with proper stretching before and after jogging, no muscle tightness should result.

An important issue to dancers is not only the amount of fat on the body but also the distribution of the fat. Dance, especially classical ballet, requires a lean, linear body type with an equal (proportional) distribution of fat. An unequal distribution of fat can be explained by the composition and function of fat tissue. Fat tissue is composed of thousands of fat cells so that the number of fat cells in a given area will determine the degree of fatness at that site. For example, if a dancer tends to have more fat on the thighs and buttocks compared to other areas of the body, it is probably because there are more fat cells in these areas. One theory suggests that after puberty the number of fat cells a person has is fixed and cannot be changed by weight loss or gain. The fat cells simply reduce or enlarge during weight loss or gain, respectively, but they never disappear.

A common misbelief is that fat can be lost from a given area by exercising that area. This process is referred to as *spot reducing*. For example, if a dancer wanted to lose fat from around the thighs where she has an unequal distribution, she would perform leg exercises to lose the extra fat. Unfortunately this will not happen. Regardless of which muscles are exercising, fat may be mobilized from fat tissue anywhere in the body. Therefore, if a dancer is concerned with excess fat on the thigh and begins to do leg exercises to reduce the thigh fat, fat will be mobilized from all over the body and not just the legs. The net result will generally be a similar distribution of fat as before the weight loss. To lose the desired amount of fat around the thigh, the dancer (through attempted spot reducing and dieting) may actually have to lose so much fat that health is jeopardized. Dancers and dance teachers should realize that spot reducing does not work (Katch, Clarkson, Kroll, McBride, & Wilcox, 1984).

The issue of weight is one of the greatest concerns of dancers. An overweight preprofessional dancer may be given limited casting and be cast only in the less desirable roles. For professional dancers, a gain in weight may mean a loss of their jobs. Most ballet companies require their dancers to meet *contact weights.* If a dancer is not rehearsing or taking class for several hours a day, it may be difficult to maintain the minimum weight standards. Dance is an anaerobic exercise and not an efficient means of using energy; fat is not the primary energy source. Thus dance is a paradox: On the aesthetic level, dance demands a very low body fat, while on the physiological level, dance exercise is inefficient for weight loss.

Summary

This chapter has provided information on how muscles function during dance training. The exercises in dance classes are classified as anaerobic. For energy sources, anaerobic exercise uses the muscle stores of ATP, creatine phosphate, and glycogen. Evidence suggests that the intensity and duration of exercises performed in the dance class are not similar to those in choreographic works, and some choreographic works may stress the aerobic energy systems. Thus, college and preprofessional dancers who do not rehearse on a daily schedule may not be fully prepared for weekend or intermittent rehearsals. The anaerobic nature of dance exercises also explains why weight control is a problem for some dancers. The most efficient way to lose weight is to perform aerobic or endurance exercises which utilize the body's fat stores. Knowledge of proper training practices should enable dancers to perform better, be less prone to injury, and achieve a healthy, more sylphlike body.

References

Armstrong, R. (1984). Mechanisms of exercise-induced muscle soreness: A brief review. *Medicine and Science in Sports and Exercise*, **16**, 529–538.

Belcastro, A.N., & Bonen, A. (1975). Lactic acid removal rates during controlled and uncontrolled recovery exercise. *Journal of Applied Physiology*, **39**, 932–937.

Brooks, G.A., & Fahey, T.D. (1984). *Exercise physiology: Human bioenergetics and its applications*. New York: John Wiley and Sons.

Byrnes, W.C., Clarkson, P.M., White, J.S., Hsieh, S.S., Frykman, P.N., & Maughan, R. (1985). Delayed onset muscle soreness following repeated bouts of downhill running. *Journal of Applied Physiology*, **59**, 710–715.

Clarkson, P.M., Freedson, P.S., Keller, B., & Skrinar, M. (1985). Maximal oxygen uptake, nutritional patterns, and body composition of adolescent female ballet dancers. *Research Quarterly for Exercise and Sport*, **56**, 180–185.

Cohen, J., Segal, K., & McArdle, W. (1982). Heart rate response to ballet stage performance. *The Physician and Sportsmedicine*, **10**, 120–133.

Cohen, J.L., Segal, K.R., Witriol, I., & McArdle, W.D. (1982). Cardiorespiratory responses to ballet exercise and the VO_2 max of elite ballet dancers. *Medicine and Science in Sports and Exercise*, **14**, 212–217.

Fox, E.L. (1984). *Sports physiology* (2nd ed.). New York: Saunders College Publishing.

Friden, J., Sjostrom, M., & Ekblom, B. (1983). Myofibrillar damage following eccentric exercise in man. *International Journal of Sports Medicine*, **4**, 170–176.

Gollnick, P.D., & Hermansen, L. (1973). Biochemical adaptations to exercise: Anaerobic metabolism. In J.H. Wilmore (Ed.), *Exercise and sport science reviews* (Vol. 1, pp. 1–43). New York: Academic.

Gollnick, P.D., Piehl, K., & Saltin, B. (1969). Energy release in the muscle cell. *Medicine and Science in Sports, 1,* 23-31.

Havel, R.J. (1970). Lipid as an energy source. In E.J. Briskey (Ed.), *Physiology and biochemistry of muscle as a food* (pp. 609-622). Madison: University of Wisconsin.

Hermansen, L. (1969). Anaerobic energy release. *Medicine and Science in Sports, 1,* 32-38.

Holloszy, J.O. (1975). Adaptation of skeletal muscle to endurance exercise. *Medicine and Science in Sports, 7,* 155-164.

Holloszy, J.O., & Booth, F.W. (1976). Biochemical adaptation to endurance exercise in muscle. *Annual Review of Physiology, 38,* 273-291.

Holloszy, J.O., Oscai, L.B., Mole, P.A., & Don, I.J. (1971). Biochemical adaptations to endurance exercise in skeletal muscle. In B. Pernow & B. Saltin (Eds.), *Muscle metabolism during exercise.* New York: Plenum.

Hooper, P.L., & Noland, B.J. (1984). Aerobic dance program improves cardiovascular fitness in men. *The Physician and Sportsmedicine, 12,* 132-135.

Katch, F.I., & McArdle, W. (1977). *Nutrition, weight control and exercise.* Boston: Houghton Mifflin.

Katch, F.I., Clarkson, P.M., Kroll, W., McBride, T., & Wilcox, A. (1984). Effects of sit up exercise training on adipose cell size and adiposity. *Research Quarterly for Exercise and Sport, 55,* 242-247.

Kirkendall, D.T., & Calabrese, L.H. (1983). Physiological aspects of dance. In G.J. Sammarco (Ed.), *Clinics in sports medicine* (Vol. 2, pp. 525-538). Philadelphia: Saunders.

McArdle, W.D., Katch, F.I., & Katch, V.L. (1981). *Exercise physiology: Energy, nutrition, and human performance.* Philadelphia: Lea and Febiger.

Mostardi, R.A., Porterfield, J.A., Greenberg, B., Goldberg, D., & Lea, M. (1983). Musculoskeletal and cardiopulmonary characteristics of professional ballet dancers. *The Physician and Sportsmedicine, 11,* 53-61.

Novak, L., Magill, L., & Schutte, J. (1978). Maximal oxygen intake and body composition of female dancers. *European Journal of Applied Physiology, 39,* 277-282.

Saltin, B., & Essen, B. (1971). Muscle glycogen, lactate, ATP, and CP in intermittent exercise. In B. Pernow & B. Saltin (Eds.), *Muscle metabolism during exercise* (pp. 419-424). New York: Plenum.

Schantz, P.G., & Astrand, P.O. (1984). Physiological characteristics of classical ballet. *Medicine and Science in Sports and Exercise, 16,* 472-476.

Watterson, V.V. (1985). The effects of aerobic dance on cardiovascular fitness. *The Physician and Sportsmedicine, 12,* 138-145.

Chapter 5

Principles of Dance Training

Karen Clippinger-Robertson
Seattle Sports Medicine

Training the body involves a systematic use of repetitive and progressive exercises to stress the musculoskeletal, respiratory, cardiovascular, and nervous systems. The goal is to enhance the various components of physical fitness, or conditioning, including strength, flexibility, neuromuscular coordination, and cardiovascular-respiratory function (Roy & Irvin, 1983) such that a given movement can be performed repeatedly, efficiently, with optimal form, and without undue fatigue.

Although all of the components of physical conditioning are important to skill acquisition, many sports emphasize a specific component. For example, Olympic weight lifters require tremendous muscular strength whereas marathon runners require cardiovascular and muscular endurance. Dance, however, demands a high degree of development in many components, which is similar to the demands of gymnastics or figure skating. For example, the aesthetically desired line of many dance movements such as a large jump (see Figure 5.1) or jazz lay-out requires both great flexibility and strength to execute or maintain the position. Other movements such as off-center balances (see Figure 5.2) or a quick and intricate *pointe* section also require fine neuromuscular coordination.

Each of these necessary components should be adequately stressed and developed in dancers' training programs. A common error made by dancers is to emphasize flexibility but neglect strength and the other conditioning components. This lack of balanced training can lead to a failure to see gains in certain skills and a feeling of discouragement in the dancer. It is not uncommon to hear a dancer state "Oh, I am just not a turner," "I just don't have high extensions," or "I am a terrible jumper." Although genetic factors must be considered, a scientifically designed training program can lead to some improvement in any of these areas. In my own experience, the lack of improvement is more commonly due to training errors and misunderstanding rather than a genetically determined limit, which the dancer has reached.

Figure 5.1   A large ballet jump showing the demand for both great strength and flexibility in dance. The dancer is Deborah Hadley, principal dancer of Pacific Northwest Ballet. Photo courtesy of Jack Mitchell.

Figure 5.2   This modern dance movement in which the body parts are not aligned on a pure vertical axis exemplifies the neuromuscular coordination and strength utilized in dance. The dancer is Bill Evans of Bill Evans Dance Company.

The aim of this chapter is to present scientific guidelines for dance training to aid dancers in fully developing their neuromuscular potential. Optimal performance requires development of components in two areas: those which are difficult for the dancer and those in which the dancer may naturally excel.

Training Variables

Fundamental to training is the concept of overload. To achieve the desired improvement, the relevant body system must be progressively and gradually stressed toward the upper limits of its present capacity. If the stress is never beyond that which is normally encountered, there will be no impetus for change and thus no improvement will occur. Overload can be produced by increasing the variables of duration, frequency, or intensity of the exercise session.

Duration

Duration refers to how long an exercise session lasts. An exercise session refers to a technique class, rehearsal, or supplemental conditioning program. The practice of starting with a ballet *barre* only and then taking five more minutes of class per day when returning from an injury would exemplify the use of increased duration to produce overload. Duration is also sometimes used to describe how long a training program is continued (e.g., a 10-week strength training program).

Table 5.1 Hypothetical Student Schedule

TYPE OF EXERCISE SESSION	DURATION	FREQUENCY
Technique Class	90 min	6 times/week
Pointe Class	60 min	2 times/week
Rehearsal	90 min	1 time /week
Aerobic Exercise (e.g., swimming)	30 min	3 times/week
Supplemental Strength Training (Pilates, Nautilus, Free Weights, or Universal)	30 min	3 times/week
Stretching	20 min	3 times/week

Frequency

Frequency refers to how often the training sessions occur. Switching from three to four classes per week is an example of applying overload through increased frequency.

A hypothetical student's schedule is given in Table 5.1 to exemplify the use of duration and frequency. This dancer has a total of 18 exercise sessions per week. Increasing the duration or frequency of any of these exercise sessions would result in greater overload.

Intensity

Intensity refers to how physically demanding or difficult an exercise session is. Intensity is often expressed as a percentage of an athlete's current functional capacity (American College of Sports Medicine, 1980). Intensity can be heightened by increasing the amount of resistance, increasing the distance the load is moved, decreasing the interval of rest, increasing the total number of executions of a particular movement (repetitions), or decreasing the amount of time in which the work is performed (work rate or power).

Figure 5.3 The dancer being lifted becomes the resistance in the partnering shown. The dancers are Deborah Hadley and Don Schwennesson of Pacific Northwest Ballet. Photo courtesy of David Cooper.

Resistance is often associated with an external weight. An example in dance occurs with partnering where the dancer to be lifted becomes the external weight or load (see Figure 5.3). Intensity could be increased by lifting a heavier partner (amount of resistance), lifting the partner higher (distance), or lifting the partner more than one time (repetitions).

Resistance is related also to the effect of gravity on the dancer's own body rather than on an external weight. In doing an extension to the side (see Figure 5.4), for example, the weight of the lifted leg becomes the resistance. Intensity could be increased by lifting the leg with the knee straight versus bent (amount of resistance torque), lifting the leg shoulder high versus waist-high (distance), doing five additional kicks without a rest (repetitions), going from one combination to the next without stopping for feedback (rest interval), or doing an extension combination in double time (power).

Principles of Training

The manner in which these variables of duration, frequency, and intensity are combined to produce overload is very critical in determining the success of a training program. An appropriate combination can be guided by the principles of training including overload, specificity, and reversibility.

Figure 5.4 The weight of the dancer's leg becomes the resistance in the extension to the side that is pictured. Photo courtesy of Jack Mitchell.

Overload

The principle of overload holds that the body system must be challenged above a certain threshold to provide sufficient stimulus to produce improvement. That is, normally encountered stress will maintain but not increase the level of conditioning (Astrand & Rodahl, 1977; Fox, 1984). Furthermore, because the system is continuously adapting, the movements constituting sufficient overload will have to be gradually increased for improvement to continue. However, if too great a stress is imposed over too short a time, the body will be unable to adapt and there will be a decrement in performance or possible injury.

These overload criteria indicate the importance of careful class design to provide the appropriate magnitude and progression of overload. If class demands are too similar from day to day, there will be insufficient overload for the desired improvement. Dance teachers and students, however, are notorious for noticing a weakness or problem and wanting it changed immediately. If, for example, a teacher notes that the students' *grand battements* (high kicks) seem too low, it is not uncommon to double the holds, double the number of times the *battements* are executed, and add several new combinations that utilize this movement for one week. After a week this goal may be forgotten as a new focus is attacked. This approach utilizes too extreme an overload applied for too short a time and is more likely to produce frustration and muscle fatigue or strain. Careful selection of an appropriate mode of progressively increasing overload in small increments over several months is often necessary to achieve the desired gains.

Specificity

Important in the design of a training program is not only the magnitude of the overload but also the specific manner in which the overload is applied. The specificity principle holds that training adaptations are specific to the cells and structural and functional elements which are overloaded. For example, an eight-second section of repetitive stag leaps for maximum height would tend to develop muscular strength and power whereas a section requiring 40 consecutive *releves* (toe raises) would better develop muscular endurance.

According to the principle of specificity, optimal gains require a training overload similar in intensity and duration to the goal movement. In addition, the overload has to be applied to the same muscle groups, with the same type of contraction, and ideally at similar joint angles and velocity (Fox, 1984). As an extreme example, doing slow *tendus* (reaching of the foot in which the toes are in contact with the ground at the end of the movement) would not be very effective in improving fast *grand battements* (high kicks). Although many of the same muscles would be used, the velocity and hip joint angle would be quite different. The principle of specificity necessitates that very careful consideration be given to design exercises that replicate important motor pattern qualities while providing a different and advantageous use of overload.

Reversibility

An unfortunate corollary to the SAID principle is that if the overload is discontinous, a decrement in performance or a detraining effect will occur. This tendency is called the *principle of reversibility*. How quickly decrements will occur appears to depend on the particular conditioning component as well as length of time in training, skill level, age, level of fitness, and extent of imposed detraining.

Of all the conditioning components, cardiovascular conditioning appears to decline most rapidly. Significant decreases in maximum oxygen consumption (aerobic capacity) have been shown to occur within two weeks and a 50% or greater reduction in gains in aerobic capacity with just 4–12 weeks of detraining (Drinkwater, 1973; Pollock, Wilmore, & Fox, 1984). This decrease in aerobic capacity has been shown to occur more gradually in athletes who have engaged in years of endurance training, but, even with these athletes, a 4% decrease with 2 weeks and a 7% decrease with 3 weeks of detraining have still been measured (Coyle et al., 1984; Houston, Bentzen, & Larsen, 1978). Cardiovascular conditioning workouts of moderate intensity performed three times per week are probably necessary to prevent detraining (Brynteson & Sinning, 1973).

In contrast to cardiovascular conditioning, strength and flexibility improvements appear to persist for a longer period of time (DeVries, 1966). However, there is great controversy as to their exact persistence (Clarke, 1973; Thorstensson, 1977). One complicating factor in studying strength detraining is the separation of neural changes from changes that occur within the muscle cell itself (Hutton, 1985). It is obvious that further investigation is required to understand the persistence of different types of strength and flexibility and to determine the minimal stimulus for maintenance. Meanwhile, a common recommendation is to use a workout frequency of one to two times per week for maintenance and three or more times per week for improvement in level of conditioning.

Components of Conditioning

The principles of overload, specificity, and reversibility can be used to guide appropriate structuring of overload to develop the desired components of training. The major components of physical conditioning include strength, power, muscular endurance, flexibility, neuromuscular coordination, and cardiovascular endurance (see Table 5.2) (Roy & Irvin, 1983). Cardiovascular conditioning is discussed in chapter 6. The remaining components, all of which involve muscular training, are covered in the following sections.

Table 5.2 Components of Conditioning

COMPONENT	DEFINITION	EXAMPLE IN DANCE
Strength	Maximum force generated by a muscle against resistance in a single effort	Holding the leg in an extension
Power	The product of the force applied and the speed at which it is applied	Jumps
Muscular Endurance	Ability to produce repeatedly force against a particular resistance	Repeated *relevés*
Flexibility:		
static	Range of motion possible at a joint	Split stretch on the ground
dynamic	Resistance of a joint to motion	*Grand battement*
Neuromuscular Coordination	Synchronous working of muscles during complex movements	
Balance	Maintenance of equilibrium over the base of support	Adagio combination on *pointe*
Agility	Ability to move with quick ease and grace	Modern floor combination with quick changes in level and direction
Kinesthetic Awareness	Developed perception of body movement	Maintaining correct alignment during spiral turns
Cardiovascular Endurance	Capacity for sustained moderate-level exercise	12-min continuous jazz combination

Strength

Strength is the maximum force which can be generated by a muscle against resistance in a single effort. Overload utilizing high resistance such that a limited number of contractions can be completed produces an increase in strength. Although a sometimes unpopular topic in the dance community, strength is important for the correct execution of many dance movements such as holding the leg out in second position (see Figure 5.4), lowering the body to the floor with control (see Figure 5.5), or partnering another dancer (see Figure 5.3). Strength is also a very important factor in injury prevention (Bailey & Bremiller, 1981; Burkett, 1970; Christensen & Wiseman, 1972; Klafs & Arnheim, 1981).

Figure 5.5 Movements using deep knee bending and a controlled lowering of the body to the floor require great thigh strength. The position shown also produces large compression forces behind the kneecap. The dancer is Shirley Jenkins of Strong Wind Wild Horses. Photo courtesy of Betsy Toombs.

Strength gains are due, in part, to an increase in the size of the muscle, or hypertrophy. Hypertrophy results from a greater number of contractile proteins per muscle fiber, more total protein, and increases in connective, tendinous, and ligamentous tissues (Astrand & Rodahl, 1977; Hagerman, 1981). Hypertrophy is of concern to some female dancers, particularly ballet dancers, who are under greater pressure to maintain a sylph-like image. However, although an increase in muscle girth accompanying strength gains has been well-documented in men (Clarke, 1973; DeLorme, 1946; Dons, Ballerup, Bonde-Peterson, & Hancke, 1979), this increase in muscle size is usually very small in women (Brown & Wilmore, 1974; Wilmore, 1974). One study showed a maximum gain of only one fourth of an inch in muscle girth after a 10-week intensive weight training program (Wilmore, 1974). Although similar relative strength gains were made in men and women, the same program resulted in a substantially smaller magnitude of muscle hypertrophy in women.

The difference in hypertrophy between sexes appears to be due partly to the presence of greater amounts of androgens (hormones responsible for the development of male sexual characteristics) and particularly testosterone in men (Brown & Wilmore, 1974; Brynteson & Sinning, 1973; Wilmore, 1974). Testosterone production rates and blood levels are 20–30 times higher in males than in females (Brown & Wilmore, 1974). Thus, despite commonly held beliefs, substantial strength gains can be made in female dancers without the undesired development of big and bulky muscles.

These and other observations that strength gains are more substantial than can be accounted for by changes within the muscle cells suggest that factors other than hypertrophy must be involved (Astrand & Rodahl, 1977; Capen, Bright & Line, 1961; Coyle et al., 1981; Dons et al., 1979; Thorstensson, Holten, Von Dobeln & Karlsson, 1976). The relationship between the nervous system and force production has been well-described during short-term (acute) conditions (Hutton, 1984). Many authorities hold that changes in the nervous system are also involved in long-term (chronic) strength gains (Hutton, 1985). Such changes probably include the ability to use more motor units (increased motor unit recruitment) and to use those motor units recruited more effectively (Eccles, Kozak & Westerman, 1962; Hutton, 1985; Milner-Brown, 1975; Sale, MacDougall, Upton & McComas, 1983). The ability to release some of the inhibition which normally prevents a muscle from producing its full force may also play a role (Ikai & Steinhaus, 1961; Perrine & Edgerton, 1978). Other potential contributing factors to strength gains include refined neuromuscular coordination and development of the elastic potential of muscle (Astrand & Rodahl, 1977; Thorstensson et al., 1976).

Power

Power takes into account not only the amount of force generated but the speed at which it is generated. Power is defined as strength times speed. The faster a particular force is generated, the greater the power produced. Power is important in dance for explosive movements such as jumps (see Figure 5.1). Adequate development of power requires that some class or supplemental exercises demand speed as well as strength (Stamford, 1985).

Muscular Endurance

Muscular endurance is related to how many times a muscle can produce force against a particular resistance. Muscular endurance is trained traditionally with a lower resistance, but higher repetitions than used with strength training. Muscular endurance is needed in dance when performing numerous repetitions of a movement such as *relevés* during *barre.* It is important to know that this type of overload using higher repetitions produces changes in muscle that are different from those associated with strength training and is not a very effective means of producing strength gains (Anderson & Kearney, 1982). If students are required to perform progressively more executions of a particular movement, the teacher should expect an increased ability to perform more repetitions (muscular endurance) but not necessarily an increase in the ability to perform the movement higher, harder (strength), or faster (power).

Neuromuscular Coordination

For neuromuscular coordination, various muscles or muscle groups work together during complex movements (see Table 5.2). Training of neuromuscular coordination involves fine-tuning motor patterns with appropriate force gradation, timing of activation, and accuracy of activation to effect precise and smooth movements (Astrand & Rodahl, 1977; Hutton, 1976).

One important measure of neuromuscular coordination in dance is the ability to perform movements according to the desired aesthetic without noticeable adjustments. When performing a first position *grand plié,* the desire is for a nearly vertical excursion of the pelvis with no noticeable loss of balance of hyperextension of the spine (see Figure 5.6). This ability takes practice and requires harmonious use of the muscles for not only controlling the lowering of the body but also stabilizing the pelvis and trunk. Contraction of specific muscles with appropriate force gradation is needed. This contrasts with the gross overall contraction seen in some beginning-level dancers.

Another example of neuromuscular coordination is a smooth transition between sequential movements. One aspect involves appropriate timing to realize the optimal return of elastic energy. Greater force can be generated by a muscle that has been previously stretched (this is described in detail in the section "Plyometric strength training"). Dance uses a preparatory *demi plié* prior to many movements including turns and jumps. This *plié* applies the needed stretch for the return of elastic energy. Optimal return requires a very rapid stretch (Komi & Bosco, 1978) of a medium magnitude (Asmussen & Bonde-Peterson, 1974; Cavanga, Zamboni, Faraggiana & Margaria, 1972; Ryman, 1978), immediately preceding the concentric phase of the movement (i.e., the up-phase for turns or jumps). Although some dancers seem to have a flawless, intuitive ability to use this quality of muscle, use of elastic energy can be enhanced through training and involves highly developed neuromuscular coordination (Cavanga, 1977; Komi, 1979).

Figure 5.6 A first position *grand plié* is shown with a) correct stabilization of the pelvis and trunk and a near-vertical descent of the pelvis, and b) inadequate stabilization of the pelvis and trunk with the trunk leaning forward and the spine going into hyperextension. The dancer is Maurya Kerr, advanced student at Pacific Northwest Ballet School. Photo courtesy of Karen Clippinger-Robertson.

Flexibility

Flexibility refers to the range of motion possible at a given joint or series of joints (DeVries, 1966). Flexibility is often measured as the angle which is created at a joint as the two adjacent segments are passively approximated. For example, one measure of hamstring flexibility uses the angle formed between the pelvis and thigh when the examiner passively brings the dancer's leg toward her shoulder with the dancer lying on her back.

Dance demands extreme flexibility, and many dancers spend a considerable amount of time stretching in an effort to increase their range of motion. Marked flexibility is not only required to achieve the desired dance aesthetic but also considered important for injury prevention (Klein, 1971; Mirkin & Hoffman, 1978; Schultz, 1979). There is some evidence that a muscle with inadequate flexibility is more prone to injury (Liemohn, 1978; Surburg, 1981). Furthermore, inadequate flexibility may lead to compensations which can be injurious. For example, a dancer with a tight calf (soleus) might roll in (pronate) to get more depth in her *plié*; this repetitive, excessive pronation can cause anterior tibialis strain (shin splints).

Limits on Flexibility. Flexibility is joint-specific and is influenced by both passive and active factors. Passive factors do not involve activation of the muscle(s) being stretched. The most fundamental passive factor influencing joint flexibility is the bony joint architecture or structure. The particular class of joint (e.g., modified hinge at the knee, ball and socket at the hip) will determine in how many different directions or planes movement can occur. Other passive factors include ligaments, tendons, the joint capsule, the quantity and texture of connective tissue within the muscle, fat deposition, and skin thickness and tightness (Hagerman, 1981). Active factors include volitional (conscious) and reflex input which can activate or tighten the muscle.

Passive factors are of varying importance in different joints of the body (Johns & Wright, 1962). For example, although both the shoulder and hip joints are of the same type (ball and socket), there is less flexibility at the hip joint due to the greater limitations imposed by the strong ligaments, restrictive capsule, and the arrangement of the numerous muscles which cross this joint.

Many passive factors can be changed in the young dancer. Although genetics certainly plays a major role, and the fundamental type of joint can not be altered, significant changes can occur. Research has suggested that the angle at which the femur sits in the socket (Sammarco, 1983), or the extensibility of some of the ligaments and capsule of the hip joint (Miller, Schneider, Bronson, & McLain, 1975) can be slightly altered in response to rigorous training and stretching in dancers younger than eleven years of age. Although still controversial, some authorities hold that changes after this age are more limited and may primarily occur in the connective tissues of muscles and tendons (Miller et al., 1975), the muscle tissue itself (Hutton, 1985), and the neural input influencing muscle activation.

Functional Flexibility.   Many dancers can do the splits and yet can not use this range of motion in dance. The actual range which is used during dance movements is called functional flexibility whereas the range of passive motion possible at a joint is static flexibility. Examples of functional range of motion or flexibility include the height the leg can be raised to the side (see Figure 5.7), the degree of hyperextension of the spine and hip used in a lay-out, and the height of the leg to the back when doing an arabesque.

Figure 5.7   A nonclassical ballet extension to second position is pictured to demonstrate extreme functional flexibility at the hip. The dancer is Alaina Albertson, former principal dancer of Pacific Northwest Ballet. Photo courtesy of David Cooper.

In contrast to static flexibility, functional flexibility involves the dancer's active contraction of muscles. The difference in these forms of flexibility is well-exemplified by dancers who can bring their legs up further when lifting with their hands (see Figure 5.8a), than when actively raising their legs with no assistance while doing a *développé á la seconde* (see Figure 5.8b) or an extension to the front (see Figure 5.10).

Figure 5.8 A *développé á la seconde* is shown to demonstrate the difference between static and functional flexibility. a) Static flexibility is demonstrated by the height the leg can be raised passively by using the hand. b) Functional flexibility is demonstrated by the height the leg can be raised actively with muscle contraction. c) The knee can be raised high before beginning to straighten it in order to increase functional flexibility. d) A common error is lifting the hip and letting the leg turn slightly inward, which tends to decrease functional flexibility. Photo courtesy of Karen Clippinger-Robertson.

Functional flexibility is complex, involving many more factors than static flexibility. One factor is dynamic flexibility, or the resistance of a joint to motion. Two additional considerations are strength and optimal biomechanics. Strength is important in order to raise the large weight of the leg in a *développé*, especially considering that, due to their shortening, the hip flexors and abductors decrease their ability to produce force as the leg is raised higher. This may be an important factor for dancers with low *développés* and extensions who also demonstrate marked weakness in hip flexors and abductors in angles above 90° (Clippinger-Robertson, 1986a).

Biomechanics also plays an important role in influencing the height of a *développé*. One aspect involves the appropriate timing of knee extension. A common error is to straighten the knee too early. As the thigh moves to heights above the 90° angle, the weight of the leg exerts an increasingly smaller downward torque. Consequently, the dancer should first raise the knee high before beginning to straighten the knee (see Figure 5.8c). After adequate strength is developed, timing of knee extension can be modified to align with the particular desired aesthetic.

An even more important biomechanical consideration is the correct external rotation at the hip. Dance teachers often instruct students to drop the hip under before lifting up the leg. In other words, dancers must bring the greater trochanter of the femur down closer to the ischial tuberosity. This requires adequate strength in the deep outward rotators, correct timing, and use of these and other muscles at the hip. A common error is to lift excessively the hip and rotate in the upper leg (see Figure 5.8d). Doing this interferes with the necessary drop of the trochanter and the full elevation of the leg (Clippinger-Robertson, 1987).

Programs for Flexibility and Strength Development

It should be clear from the preceding discussion of functional flexibility that all of the components of training work closely together in actual dance movements. Although movements emphasize different components to different degrees, a lack in any one of these components can lessen the quality of performance. Furthermore, a balance between conditioning components, particularly strength and flexibility is important for injury prevention. Some authorities suggest that as flexibility is developed, a comparable amount of strength should be developed in order to support the joints (which become less stable as flexibility increases). Similarly, adequate flexibility is seen as a protective factor whereas excessive flexibility may actually make an individual more prone to injury (Fox, 1984; Marshall et al., 1980; Nicholas, 1970; Nicholas, 1975). More specific guidelines for developing flexibility and strength are presented below.

Stretching Techniques

Static flexibility can be increased by a well-designed weight training program or through various methods of stretching. A stretching routine of 20–30 minutes in duration should be performed three or more times per week. This routine should emphasize muscle groups which are important in dance. Stretches can be performed at the *barre* or on the floor. Common methods of stretching include static, ballistic, and PNF (proprioceptive neuromuscular facilitation) techniques.

Static Stretching. Static stretching involves holding a position which places a particular muscle or muscle group and related connective tissue in a maximally lengthened position. This position is held from 30 seconds to a minute (Kirkendall & Calabrese, 1983; Roy & Irvin, 1983). A slow, gentle stretch is recommended. Because the resistance of many of the passive factors (viscoelastic properties) and reflex active factors to stretch is both rate and magnitude dependent (Hayes, 1980), a low-velocity and medium-magnitude stretch should allow theoretically more effective extensibility. A common error is to apply the stretch too quickly and too hard. This results in injury or greater tightness the next day. It is important to avoid competing with other dancers and to work in an appropriate range where a mild stretch but no pain is experienced. If properly performed, static stretching provides both a safe and an effective way of increasing flexibility (Moore & Hutton, 1980; Schultz, 1979).

Ballistic Stretching. Ballistic stretching involves bouncing movements in which momentum is used dynamically to stretch a muscle group. An example is flat back bounces which were previously used in many jazz classes as a means of stretching the hamstrings. The concern with this technique is that the quick stretch enhances active reflex factors, causing a protective reflex contraction of the muscle which is being stretched. Percussive stretching on this tightening muscle can produce muscle tears. Surprisingly, ballistic stretching may be as effective as static stretching (DeVries, 1962). However, it should be avoided because of the higher risk of injury and the greater associated muscle soreness.

PNF Techniques. PNF techniques were developed originally for rehabilitative purposes in physical therapy (Kabat, 1965; Knott & Voss, 1968;

Stockmeyer, 1967). These techniques have been adapted recently for use with dancers and other athletes (Surburg, 1981). PNF attempts to alter active factors (e.g., descending supraspinal input and local spinal reflex circuitry involving the receptors within the muscle; Moore & Hutton, 1980) to gain more flexibility. A common version (contract-relax) uses a 10-second contraction of the muscle followed by five seconds of relaxation. This is often repeated three times, ending with a static stretch from 30 seconds to 60 seconds in duration. A more effective variation (contract-relax-agonist contract) includes contracting the muscle that causes the stretching of the desired muscle. For example, if the goal is hamstring flexibility, the hamstring is contracted for 10 seconds followed by relaxation as the hip flexors are contracted, producing an additional stretch to the relaxed hamstring. Although the mechanism of this technique is still controversial (Flanagan, 1967; Hutton, 1984; Levine, Kabat, Knott, & Voss, 1954; Moore & Hutton, 1980; Pinkstrom, 1967; Voss, 1967), it appears to offer a very effective method for increasing flexibility (Mogberg & Ljunggren, 1947 [cited in Astrand & Rodahl, 1977] pp. 562–563; Moore & Hutton, 1980; Perez & Fumasoli, 1984; Tanigawa, 1972; Wallin, Ekblom, Grahn, & Nordinborg, 1985). A combination of static and PNF techniques probably would provide the best flexibility gains for the dancer.

Strength Training Guidelines

As with programs for increasing flexibility, effective gains can be made with a strength training program consisting of three sessions per week at 30 minutes per session. If the appropriate criteria are followed, movement sequences within the dance class or a separate workout session can be performed to gain strength. The following is a discussion of a program design that optimizes strength development.

Sets and Repetitions.   The most fundamental criterion of program design is that strength gains require relatively few repetitions against a large resistance. Although significant gains in strength have been shown to occur with anywhere from 1–3 sets of 2–10 repetitions (Berger, 1962b; Clarke, 1973; O'Shea, 1966), greater strength gains occur with 3 sets of 6 repetitions (Astrand & Rodahl, 1977; Berger, 1962b; Clarke, 1973). From the perspective of injury prevention, it is often advisable to begin a strength training program with an easier workout of about 2 sets of 10 repetitions (Fox, 1984). After proper technique is perfected and an initial period of conditioning is completed, the program may be advanced to the more intense 3 sets of 6 repetitions.

Load Magnitude.   In any combination of sets and repetitions the muscle must be overloaded close to its maximal capacity but below the injury threshold. Various procedures for reaching this maximum overload can be used. One of the original techniques developed by DeLorme used 3 sets of 10 repetitions with a load intensity of 50%, 75%, and 100% of a 10 repetition maximum (RM). An RM is the maximum load which can be lifted for the given number of repetitions. A 10RM would thus be the heaviest weight that could be lifted 10 times consecutively. Another common approach is to use a percentage of a 1RM with different sets ranging between 60–90% of 1RM (Baechle, 1984; Klafs & Arnheim, 1981; O'Shea, 1976). If a dance exercise without an external weight is being performed, the aim is to produce marked muscle fatigue by the last repetition of the last set.

Progression and Periodization.   To see continual improvement, the resistance used must be increased progressively. A common recommendation is to increase the resistance when it becomes possible to lift the existing resistance for more repetitions in the three sets. Periodization is another helpful method for assuring continual strength gains (Kulund & Tottossy, 1985). With periodization the volume and intensity of overload are cyclically varied to help prevent a plateau or overtraining (Baechle, 1984; Van Handel & Puhl, 1983).

Muscular Strength Versus Muscular Endurance.   Strength development requires high loads. Dancers sometimes think that if they do many repetitions of a movement they will get much stronger. Unfortunately, this is not always the case. One study using a seven-week strength training program found that 20 repetitions at 50% 1RM resulted in no strength gains whereas 12 repetitions at 80% 1RM resulted in a 42% increase in strength (Dons, Ballerup, Bonde-Petersen, & Hancke, 1979). Another study found a 20% increase in strength with a program of 3 sets of 6–8RM whereas a less than 5% increase in strength occurred with 1 set of 100–150RM (Anderson & Kearney, 1982). It is important to note that in this study 24 repetitions of appropriately chosen overload produced an increase in strength that was four times greater than 100 repetitions with a lighter load. This finding may provide one reason why some dancers are weak in certain ankle muscles despite performing hundreds of *releves.* The overload intensity provided by *releves* may be too low to stimulate strength gains. It appears that high repetitions to fatigue build muscular endurance but are not necessarily very effective for strength development. Furthermore, although somewhat controversial (Berger, 1970; Clarke & Stull, 1970), because high overload tends to produce better strength gains while still producing moderate endurance gains, the trend is to utilize high loads and low repetitions to more effectively develop the combination of muscular strength and muscular endurance (Fox, 1984; Shaver, 1971).

Technique. Although near maximal overload is required for strength development, it is important to resist the tendency to cheat by substituting other muscles as fatigue is approached. This not only is ineffective for achieving the desired strength gains but can start bad habits of compensation which lead to injuries. To avoid this habit, it is essential to maintain good trunk and pelvic stability as well as the correct movement pattern which uses the desired muscle. A subtle change in position such as a minimal hiking of the hip when lifting the leg to the side can have a dramatic effect on muscle use. The dancer should control the movement throughout its range rather than rely on its momentum. Performing less repetitions or using a lower resistance is far better than compromising correct technique.

Muscle Order and Alternation. A recommended strength training format exercises the larger muscles such as the trunk, hip, and thigh first. Because the smaller muscles tend to fatigue more readily, this procedure insures sufficient overload of the larger muscles (Fox, 1984). Beginning with the trunk muscles also serves as a helpful reminder to use these muscles to stabilize the trunk and pelvis in following exercises.

Successive exercises should involve different muscle groups to allow sufficient recovery of previously exercised muscles. With alternating muscle groups each group should be returned to two or three times so 2–3 sets of 6–10 are completed for each muscle group.

Range of Motion. Whenever possible a full range of motion should be used in strengthening exercises so that flexibility is not jeopardized. Doing repetitive strengthening exercises over a small range can lead to being tight. In cases where safety, exercise goals, or type of resistance (e.g., isometrics) do not allow the use of a full range of motion, strengthening exercises should be followed by stretching of the muscles or by movement which uses full range of motion of the involved joints.

Motor Skill Specificity. Another important strength training criterion is motor skill specificity. The principle of specificity requires similar muscle use, joint angles, and movement patterns for the optimal transfer of conditioning gains. The specific demands of the particular dance form must be kept in mind in designing an overall preventative strengthening program or selecting exercises for an injured or weak area. Exercises should be designed to replicate these demands as closely as possible. For most dance forms, strength has to be developed over a much larger range of motion than that demanded by most sports, and lower extremity exercises must be performed with the hips turned out as well as parallel.

Balanced Strength Development.   While keeping in mind the demands of dance, it is also important to consider a balanced development of strength. Strengthening of a particular muscle group should also be accompanied by exercises to strengthen muscles which assist with the desired movement (synergists) and muscles with the opposite action (antagonists) to develop a balance of functional strength. Overdevelopment of one muscle group is sometimes counterproductive. For example, a strength imbalance between the front of the thigh (quadriceps) and back of the thigh (hamstrings) has been implicated in hamstring strains (Bailey & Bremiller, 1981; Burkett, 1970; Christensen & Wiseman, 1972; Klafs & Arnheim, 1981). When a strength imbalance is already present from injury or habit, isolated muscle strength can be useful. However, close monitoring is necessary to be sure that a balance rather than overcorrection is produced.

Types of Resistance Training

Table 5.3 summarizes the guidelines for designing a strength training program. Many methods can be used to develop strength. Resistance can be applied in numerous ways using surgical tubing, body parts, innertube, free weights, or weight apparatus. Strength training methods are often classified according to the type of muscle contraction involved and are designated as isometric, isotonic, or isokinetic. Although the previously described guidelines are particularly applicable to isotonics, most of them are relevant to isometrics and isokinetics with some important adaptations. These guideline adaptations are noted below.

Isometrics.   Isometrics uses a static muscle contraction in which no movement of the joint occurs. A near maximal contraction that is held for five to six seconds (Clarke, 1973) appears to produce optimal gains. One advantage of isometrics is convenience because it requires no equipment. One disadvantage, however, is joint angle specificity. Strength gains are specific to the angle exercised (Bender & Kaplan, 1963; Gardner, 1963), and a strength gain of 18% at the exercised angle may be accompanied by only 4% increase in strength 80° from the exercised angle (Meyers, 1967). Therefore, 5–10 repetitions at 3 different angles are recommended for an isometric strength training program. Chosen angles should place the muscle in a shortened position and include the angle where improvement is desired (DeVries, 1966).

An example of the use of isometrics is shown in Figure 5.9. This exercise is designed for strengthening the hip flexors to increase the height

Table 5.3 Guidelines For a Strength Training Program

- Apply high-intensity overload in a gradual and progressive manner:
    Intensity-2 or 3 sets of 6 to 8 reps providing stress close to the maximum capacity
        of the muscle group
    Frequency-3 to 5 times per week depending on intensity
    Duration-30 minutes per session for 6 weeks or longer
- Exercise larger muscle groups before smaller ones
- Use different muscle groups in successive exercises so that recovery is allowed before
  performing another set on the same muscle group
- Develop balanced strength by exercising synergists and antagonists as well as prime movers
- Exercise a joint through a full range of motion when possible, and maintain a good rela-
  tionship between strength and flexibility
- Apply the principle of specificity by replicating movement patterns of dance as closely
  as possible and stressing muscle groups that are most needed in dance
- Isolate the muscle to be strengthened by carrying out the correct motion in a smooth and
  controlled manner without compensations

---

of front extensions. The weight of the leg serves as the resistance. The dancer raises the leg with the help of the hand and holds it for five seconds without assistance for 1 set of 8 repetitions at 90°, 120°, and 140°. As the dancer becomes stronger, the knee is gradually straightened until it is possible to hold the leg with the knee fully extended at 140°. This static exercise series is particularly helpful for developing the ability to hold the leg out at a higher level in a movement such as a front extension. To increase the ability to lift the leg as in a *grand battement*, however, a dynamic exercise series is more effective (Berger, 1962b).

Isotonics.   Isotonics involves a dynamic muscle contraction with a change in the joint angle. This type of strength training emphasizes concentric (shortening) contractions, eccentric (lengthening) contractions, or both. These two types of contractions differ in the force that can be generated; muscle can maximally produce almost 40% more tension eccentrically than concentrically (Fox, 1984). The isometric contraction produces more force than a concentric contraction and less force than an eccentric contraction at similar angles. Thus isotonic-eccentric and isometric contractions are more effective in working at a higher range of motion or with a heavier resistance than isotonic-concentric contractions.

In a front leg extension, a dancer might be able to work concentrically to 100°, isometrically to 115°, and eccentrically to 135° of hip flexion (see Figure 5.10). An isotonic-eccentric strengthening regimen uses the arms to help raise the leg to 135° and the hip flexors to control the lowering of the leg (eccentric contraction) back to the *barre* (see Figure 5.10a). An isotonic-concentric method involves repetitively raising the leg to 100°

Figure 5.9 An isometric exercise for strengthening the muscles used for front extensions (hip flexors) is pictured. The leg is raised with assistance from the dancer's hand and then held for 5 seconds as the hand is released. Several different angles should be used. Photo courtesy of Karen Clippinger-Robertson.

Figure 5.10 Isotonic strengthening exercises to improve front leg extensions are pictured contrasting eccentric and concentric variations. a) The leg is lowered from 135° to the *barre* in a controlled manner (isotonic-eccentric contraction). b) The leg is raised with the aid of the hand and then held at 115° as the hand is released (isometric contraction). c) The leg is raised up from the *barre* to 100° (isotonic-concentric contraction). Photo courtesy of Karen Clippinger-Robertson.

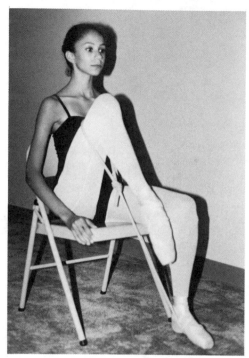

Figure 5-11 An isodynamic exercise for strengthening the hip flexors using surgical tubing to provide resistance is shown. Photo courtesy of Karen Clippinger-Robertson.

alone (see Figure 5.10c), with an ankle weight, or rapidly in a swimming pool (the water provides resistance). The knee can be bent initially to decrease the resistance so that higher angles can be used.

A variation on isotonics is isodynamics, which uses elastic resistance from a tire innertube, surgical tubing, or similar materials. Use of surgical tubing to develop hip flexor strength above 90° can be seen in Figure 5.11. The advantages of this method are low cost and convenience. A piece of tubing can easily be carried in a dance bag and can be used almost anywhere. Another advantage is that dance movements can more easily be replicated in terms of speed, three-dimensional use of space, and discrete muscle use. A drawback is that the more the elastic material is stretched, the greater the resistance. So, overload is not equivalent throughout the range of motion, but rather, is greater toward the end of the range. This shortcoming can be lessened by working at various arcs (e.g., performing one set in each of the following arcs: 0–90°, 80–130°, 120–160°).

Isotonics also traditionally includes the use of free weights, wall pulleys, or guided-weight apparatus (Roy & Irvin, 1983). Although the angle specificity problem is not as extreme as in isometrics, isotonics still does not produce equivalent overload and strength gains throughout the full arc of movement. The resistance load is constant and yet there is a marked shift in mechanical advantage at different joint angles; this provides a maximum resistance only through a small portion of the arc (Thistle, Hislop, Moffroid, & Lowman, 1967). Some isotonic guided-weight apparatuses including the Universal gym and Nautilus machines have attempted to minimize this problem through the use of shifting lever arm lengths or cams to provide variable resistance. Figure 5.12 provides an example of using Nautilus equipment to strengthen hip extensors. Modifications of standard circuits are often helpful for closer replication of dance movements. To avoid injury, however, a qualified instructor should be consulted before making these modifications.

Another type of apparatus, the Pilates system, is popular with many dancers because it uses multiple muscle groups and movement sequences that are more closely aligned to dance. For example, the use of turnout and large ranges of motion can be easily included in a multitude of movement patterns. The Pilates system, however, uses springs for resistance, thus having the same shortcomings as isodynamics, in which greater resistance is generated in restricted portions of the movement arc. Although this disadvantage may be overridden by its motor-skill specificity, there is no research available to indicate this system's effectiveness for developing strength which can be transferred to dance movements. Research in this area would be very valuable to the dance community.

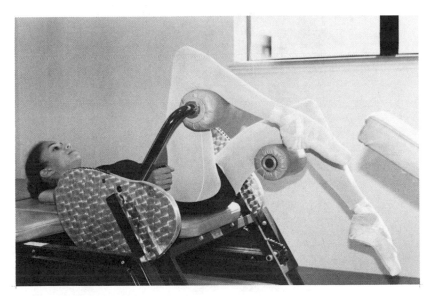

Figure 5.12 A Nautilus machine for strengthening the hip extensors is pictured. This equipment uses cams in an effort to provide a more even percentage of maximal overload throughout the full range of hip extension. Photo courtesy of Karen Clippinger-Robertson.

Isokinetics.   Isokinetics represents a further attempt to solve the problem of uneven resistance and strength gains inherent to isotonics and isometrics. With isokinetics the speed of movement is controlled and accommodating resistance is used to develop maximum tension throughout the entire range of motion. Isokinetics requires the use of special equipment such as that developed by Cybex (see Figure 5.13). In addition to a wider range of maximal overload, this particular system also provides the advantage of being able to work at a faster speed which more closely approximates that used in dance. Some authorities consider that this combination of properties makes isokinetics valuable for developing power (Pipes & Wilmore, 1975). If properly used, isokinetics can be a valuable rehabilitation tool (Thistle et al., 1967) for helping in the progressive return to dance after injury. The prohibitive cost as well as the inconvenience of resetting the equipment for each particular exercise make this method an unlikely choice for a preventative total body strength program. However, future developments may make isokinetics training a viable option.

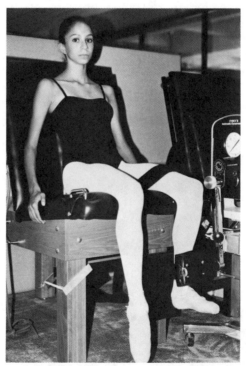

Figure 5.13   A Cybex apparatus being used for strengthening the knee extensors and flexors is shown. This isokinetic equipment utilizes fixed velocity to provide a more even percentage of maximal overload throughout the full range of bending and straightening the knee. Photo courtesy of Karen Clippinger-Robertson.

Plyometrics. Plyometrics are rigorous exercises using hops, bounds, depth jumps, and jumping with weights to develop explosive power (Dollard, 1985; Kulund & Tottossy, 1985). These exercises are based on the muscle's ability to generate more work after an immediately preceding stretch (Cavanga & Critterio, 1974). Muscle contraction involves elastic or spring-like components (Bosco & Komi, 1979; McMahon & Greene, 1979) as well as contractile components (Hill, 1950; Huxley, 1974). During an eccentric (lengthening) contraction the elastic component stretches and stores elastic energy which can then be used partially in the proceeding concentric (shortening) contraction. The stretch also may increase force production through its influence on receptors within the muscle, which can increase activation of the muscle (i.e., alpha motoneuron activation via the stretch reflex) (Bosco et al., 1982a; Grillner, Nilsson, & Thorstensson, 1978).

The phenomenon of storage and utilization of elastic energy is commonly applied in alternating human movement such as running (Asmussen & Bonde-Peterson, 1974; McMahon & Greene, 1979), jumping (Asmussen & Bonde-Peterson, 1974; Bosco et al., 1982a; Komi & Bosco, 1978), and Olympic weight lifting (Enoka, 1979). This application can serve to markedly increase the mechanical efficiency of movement (Bosco et al., 1982a; Grillner, Nilsson, & Thorstensson, 1978; Morgan, Proske, & Warren, 1978) and enhance performance (Komi, 1979). The common use of counter-movements in dance such as a lunge before a weight shift or a plié before a turn or jump suggests that development of the ability to use elastic energy might prove beneficial. The ability to utilize elastic energy appears to improve with training (Komi, 1979) and plyometrics offer one method of trying to achieve this improvement. Some authors believe that plyometrics train the nervous system for an instantaneous switch from eccentric to concentric contraction, which helps optimize utilization of elastic energy and force production (Cavagna & Critterio, 1974; Dollard, 1985; Kulund & Tottossy, 1985).

Although plyometrics may be potentially very useful for dance, the advanced versions of these drills can cause injuries very readily and must only be done after an adequate strength base has been developed (Kulund & Tottossy, 1985) and under close supervision by highly qualified teachers. Beginning plyometric drills could be easily included in dance class by modifying timing of movements such as skips, hops or jumps to emphasize a rapid stretch immediately preceeding the up-phase and by using consecutive repetitions. With advanced level students of sufficient strength and maturation, these drills could be very gradually advanced to include more traditional drills such as jumps from a greater depth of plié (depth jump) or jumping from a box followed by an immediate rebound up to the next box (box rebounding).

Comparing Types of Resistance Training

Isometric, isotonic, or isokinetic resistance training will all increase strength, but at this time there is no clear evidence that one type produces greater gains than another (Clarke, 1973; Johnson, 1972; Johnson, Adamczyk, Tennøe, & Strømme, 1976; Marino & Glein, 1984; Shields, Beckwith, & Kurland, 1985). Probably the most important factor is finding a program which will work within the constraints of the often very busy schedules and restrictive budgets of most dancers. When convenience is the priority, isometrics, tubing, or using a dance bag for resistance might be the best solution. For other dancers, having the social reinforcement of working out at a club is essential for motivation. The important point is to find some type of training program that will be consistently performed.

Another important consideration is the type of contraction required by the goal movement. It is known that strength gains are specific to the type of muscle contraction, and that static (isometrics) yield the greatest static strength increases, dynamic (isotonics) the greatest dynamic strength increases, and isokinetics the greatest increases in isokinetic strength (Berger, 1962b). Thus an attempt should be made to replicate the particular type of contraction used in the movements where improvement is desired.

When the aim is a preventative, general strength training program, a combination of various types of resistance training would probably yield the best results. This contention is supported by the principle of periodization (Baechle, 1984; Van Handel & Puhl, 1983) as well as the observation that dance can be characterized by its use of both static and dynamic components (Cohen, Segal, Witriol, & McArdle, 1982). Isometrics and isotonics can be combined easily by adding a five-second hold to a dynamic contraction which was produced by isotonic resistance training. The hold is applied at the end of the range of motion when the muscle to be strengthened is in a shortened position. Other types of training, such as plyometrics, can be added after a firm base of strength has been established.

Injury Prevention

The development of the dancer's artistic and technical skills is a slow process, and many dance teachers claim that it takes ten years to build a dancer. Throughout this training process there is often a subtle distinction between overload that optimizes the desired conditioning gains and overload that causes injury. The appropriate progression of overload over time and within each class, the development of biomechanically sound technique, and the use of protective equipment and appropriate floor surfaces are all important considerations for injury prevention in dance.

Training Curves

The way that overload is progressed over time is often referred to as a training curve. The goal is to see continuous gradual improvement in training. A training curve that is too steep to allow the various body systems to adapt will generally result in performance decrements or injury. Particular care must be taken to avoid steep training curves with lay-offs, summer workshops, growth spurts, or changes in technique demands.

Lay-offs.   Lay-offs commonly occur because of lack of work, pregnancy, or injury. Due to the principle of reversibility, lay-offs will result in training decrements unless overload is somehow maintained. Unfortunately, this detraining occurs very rapidly, and a level of conditioning that took several years to build can take only weeks to erode substantially. To minimize these losses, the dancer should attempt to stay in the best condition possible.

One approach to an extended lay-off is to take one technique class daily and also participate in supplemental workouts stressing strength, flexibility, and cardiovascular conditioning three times per week. Several weeks prior to return, the amount of dance can be gradually increased to meet the demands of full return. The number of weeks allowed to increase dance to full return would vary according to the length of the lay-offs.

If injury prevents class participation, much can still be done to maintain conditioning. A strength training program stressing muscle groups important in dance should be performed at least three times per week. Riding the stationary bike or swimming can be performed to maintain cardiovascular conditioning and prevent undesired weight gains. If the attending physician permits, a modified *barre* or other dance movements can often be performed pain-free in a pool using floats for resistance. It is also important to maintain flexibility.

The more closely the program can replicate the demands of dance, the less stress will be associated with a return to dance. However, there will still be differences due to the specificity of some dance movements and the increased impact associated with working on land versus in the pool. Therefore, resumption should be gradual. When these precautions are not taken, it becomes easy for a dancer to get caught moving from one injury to another and never fully recovering.

Summer Workshops.   Dance injuries are quite prevalent in summer workshops. It is not uncommon in workshop situations to find dancers who have gone from taking five classes per week to fifteen classes per week. This dramatic increase in overload is exacerbated by the fact that students often take a couple of weeks off prior to the workshop for vacation or because the dance school is closed. Ideally, dancers should gradually increase their number of hours in class before the workshop to make the transition more gradual.

Technique Variations. Another inappropriate training curve occurs when a change in schools or the performance of a new style of choreography lead to a change in technique demands. This problem relates to the principle of specificity. Even though a base of conditioning is present, technique variations may produce quite different stresses on specific areas. For example, a piece with an extended section of deep knee flexion (see Figure 5.5) might produce knee-cap problems whereas a piece with extensive jumping might produce ankle and foot stress. Another piece might place extreme demands on the back through the use of complex partnering (see Figures 5.3 and 5.14) or spinal rotation (see Figures 5.2 and 5.15).

Figure 5.14 An example of modern partnering involving bending and rotation stresses to the spine is pictured. Adequate strength and proper technique are important for injury prevention. The dancers are Gail Heilbron and Jesse Jaramillo of Co-Motion Dance. Photo courtesy of Betsy Toombs.

Figure 5.15 The movement shown utilizes extension and rotation of the spine on an off-vertical axis. Adequate abdominal and back strength as well as proper technique are necessary for the desired aesthetic and injury prevention. The dancer is Wade Madsen, independent choreographer and performer. Photo courtesy of Betsy Toombs.

Figure 5.16 The choreography of today demands tremendous versatility of the dancer as exemplified by the pictured use of *pointe* shoes by a male dancer. Photo courtesy of Betsy Toombs.

The demand for extreme versatility in the dancer has intensified in recent years as many dance companies' repertoires have expanded to draw from classical ballet, modern dance, jazz, and tap. *Pointe* shoes are no longer the exclusive domain of classical ballet (see Figure 5.16), and floorwork is no longer the hallmark of modern dance.

When students and teachers anticipate a novel piece, they should try to prepare for the new demands. This is not possible, however, in the setting of a new piece or the bringing in of an outside choreographer. Even in these situations, some protection could be afforded if more dancers used supplemental strength and conditioning programs to gain a broader foundation from which to work. Some dancers work so close to their limits that a very small change can precipitate injury.

Growth Spurts. The changes in length of the limbs associated with growth spurts in children have been shown to have marked effects on the resistance of the body part to movement and so can also effect coordination (Jensen, 1981). As changes in bone length precede changes in the surrounding muscles, strength and flexibility have been found to temporarily decrease (DeVries, 1966). Some authorities hold that during this state of transition, especially preceding adolescence, overload progression should be more gradual in order to avoid injury.

Overtraining. When excessive overload is sustained over an extended period of time, a condition called overtraining can result. Early indicators of overtraining include sudden weight loss, elevated heart rate (greater than five beats per minute elevation in morning resting pulse), and lack of desire to train (Starnford, 1983). Other common signs include insomnia, muscle soreness, chronic fatigue, mental depression, and declining performance (Dressendorfer, Wade, & Scaff, 1985). Overtraining appears to make athletes more susceptible to injuries including stress fractures (Ryan, Burke, Falsetti, Brown, & Frederick, 1983). For dancers, rigorous schedules, lack of structured seasons of rest and peaking, and increased workload (Costill, King, Thomas, & Hargreaves, 1985) prior to performances make overtaining a noteworthy consideration. It is important to prevent overtraining because, in its advanced stages, reduction or cessation of training for several months may be necessary to allow recovery (Ryan et al., 1983).

Class Format

A gradual progression of overload is important for injury prevention; this includes short-term (individual classes) and long-term training. Warm-up should be used to ready the body for movements requiring speed, power, or complex neuromuscular coordination. Similarly, cool-down should be used to return the body to a resting equilibrium.

Warm-Up. The desired physiological effects of warm-up are linked to the elevation of body temperature. The goal of an effective warm-up should be to elevate internal temperatures one to two degrees so that sweating occurs (DeVries, 1966). This temperature elevation is associated with increases in metabolic rate, enzyme activity within the muscle, blood flow to the muscle, and oxygen reaching the muscle and released within the muscle (Fox, 1984; Ingjer & Strømme, 1979). All of these effects aid in the efficient production of energy for fueling muscle contractions.

Elevating the internal temperature also has these effects: decreased muscle viscosity, increased flexibility of tendons and ligaments, greater speed and force of muscle contraction, increased muscle elasticity, increased speed of transmission of nerve impulses, and decreased contraction and relaxation times of the muscle (DeVries, 1966; Shellock, 1983). It has been suggested that many of these factors are beneficial for injury prevention by increasing neuromuscular coordination or by making the tissue itself less susceptible to damage. The influence of temperature on muscle relaxation time is particularly important in dance because of the common use of reciprocal motion in which the inability of a muscle to relax fast enough may cause the antagonist muscle to produce a tear.

Lastly, warm-up may be beneficial for allowing adequate blood flow to the heart. One study found that, among a group of healthy subjects, 70% showed abnormal electrical activity of the heart with sudden strenuous exercise. These abnormal changes were reduced or eliminated with a prior warm-up (Barnard, Gardner, Diaco, MacAlpin, & Kattus, 1973).

Warm-Up Characteristics. Appropriate warm-up design is important to reap the potential physiological benefits for enhanced performance (Astrand & Rodahl, 1977; Franks, 1972; Grodjinovsky & Magel, 1970; Muido, 1946) and decreased injury. A minimum of 10–15 minutes (Fox, 1984; Franks, 1972) of vigorous activity of sufficient intensity to elevate body temperature without developing fatigue is recommended (Astrand & Rodahl, 1977). Passive warm-up (e.g., shower, bath, massage, diathermy) to increase temperature does not appear to be as effective as active muscle contraction (Falls, 1972; Injger & Strømme, 1979), and the local heating of a part (e.g., submersion of a foot with tendonitis in a bucket of hot water) may actually produce earlier fatigue (Clarke, Hellon, & Lind, 1958; DeVries, 1966; Grose, 1957).

One example of a warm-up is a section of continuous movement of increasing difficulty, which involves large muscle groups and is done at the *barre* or center floor. The range of motion should be limited at first and increased as body temperature rises. An alternative warm-up is a brisk walk or jog followed by dance combinations which build to replicate those needed in class, rehearsal, or performance. Warm-up is more beneficial when it is specific (i.e., when it uses the muscles and movement patterns required for a given activity) as well as active. The combination of specificity and action increases the temperature of the body parts to be used and provides a slight rehearsal effect (Shellock, 1983).

Most dance classes include some kind of warm-up in their formats. It is not always true that the movement is continuous enough to achieve the necessary increase in body temperature. Many warm-ups also fail to involve large muscle groups. It is important to include elements in the warm-up that prepare the student for later dance combinations which demand a large range of motion and force production, or result in high impact. Teachers should use caution when the needed correction of their students often leaves the instructor insufficiently warmed-up to demonstrate difficult combinations safely.

Another important consideration in effective warm-up design is timing. The effects of warm-up are transient, and, ideally, a warm-up should precede a rigorous performance by no more than 15 minutes (Astrand & Rodahl, 1977). The beneficial physiological effects of warm-up appear to be abolished with 45 minutes of rest. Thus a company class is not sufficient for a performance one or two hours later, and a morning class is inadequate preparation for an afternoon rehearsal. This means that it is often necessary for individual dancers to go through a brief warm-up before the performance, taking into account the specific demands of the individual part.

Cool-Down.   Cool-down entails the reverse procedure of a warm-up (Fox, 1984). Following the last rigorous combination of a class or performance, the dancer should continue moving easily for 5–10 minutes until the heart rate drops to about 100 beats per minute (60% of maximum heart rate). Continuous light use of the involved muscles returns the blood to the heart (Pollack et al., 1984) and allows the removal of metabolic waste products to occur more rapidly (Bonen & Belcastro, 1976; see also the Hermansen Study, 1975 [cited in Fox, 1984, pp. 77–78]).

Following a class or performance is an appropriate time to stretch. In general, the dancer can stretch further (DeVries, 1966) and with greater comfort and less risk of injury (Shellock, 1983) after activity when the muscles are warm.

Figure 5.17   A properly performed *grand jeté* reflects a summation of many of the components of conditioning, including power, flexibility, and neuromuscular coordination. Very large forces are generated on take-off and absorbed on landing, making proper technique essential for both optimal form and injury prevention. Photo courtesy of David Cooper.

Technique

A majority of injuries in dance are chronic, relating to over-use, rather than traumatic, the latter of which are more commonly seen in contact sports. This makes proper technique (Bergfield et al., 1982; Gelabert, 1980; Howse, 1972) as well as appropriate overload progression critical for injury prevention in dance. Subtle inaccuracies in technique can place excessive stress on muscles and joints and lead to earlier fatigue and injury. Common errors in alignment technique include excessive arching of the lower back, lifting the hip, hyperextending the knees, rolling-in at the foot (pronation), and forcing turnout from the knee down. The latter three errors have been implicated in knee-cap problems (Clippinger-Robertson, Hutton, Miller, & Nichols, 1986; Howse, 1972), and the habit of lifting the hip (see Figure 5.8d) can be associated with hip flexor strains or tendonitis (Clippinger-Robertson, 1986).

Besides altering alignment, errors in technique influence effective force production and absorption. For example, the timing and depth of the preparatory *plié* are very important for force development in the take-off phase of jumps. Similarly, "working through the whole foot" and the depth of the *plié* are important for force absorption during landing. Dancers with inadequate *pliés* or other such poor landing mechanics may be more prone to injuries such as shin splints and stress fractures.

Although the differences between biomechanically sound and unsound techniques appear quite subtle, the associated differences in force production and absorption are quite profound. One study found that, in dancers performing second-position *grand pliés*, electrical activity of the thigh (*vastus medialis*) ranged from 25% to 128% of maximum voluntary contraction (Clippinger-Robertson et al., 1986). Similarly, in landing from *grand jetés* (see Figure 5.17) dancers exerted downward forces which ranged from three to six times body weight (Clippinger, 1981). Considering the number of *pliés* and jumps performed by a dancer, it seems likely that such differences are important for injury predisposition and longevity. Further investigation into the technique variations that minimize the risk of injury while staying within the desired dance aesthetic would be very useful.

Protective Equipment

Some sports rely on protective equipment such as shoes, pads, and helmets to reduce dramatically physical stress; however, dancers receive little help from equipment. Modern dancers rarely wear shoes, and ballet or jazz dancers wear slippers that offer few protective qualities. However, felt pads, arch supports, sorbithane inserts, or taping can sometimes be helpful when returning from a foot or ankle injury. In special cases, when the type of injury necessitates such protection, an aerobics shoe can be worn temporarily in jazz or modern dance classes.

Occasionally, knee pads are helpful when pieces require a lot of floor work. Unfortunately, some dancers hesitate to wear pads if they won't be worn during the performance. However, knee irritation can often be avoided if dancers wear knee pads, at least during the initial learning of the piece when the section is repeated several times.

Environmental Factors

The most important environmental concern for the dancer is the dance surface; the floor should have appropriate resiliency and surface friction (Seals, 1983). Although economics play a decisive role, the importance of a resilient surface in injury prevention should not be underestimated, and good surfaces should be a high priority. When hard floors can not be avoided (such as on tour), careful choices of class and concert content should be made in an attempt to minimize stresses. For example, pieces or combinations with lots of large jumps should be avoided on floors lacking in resiliency. If jumping is necessary, decreasing the height of the jumps, using proper landing mechanics, adding sorbithane inserts, and wearing aerobics shoes can help to lessen the forces absorbed by the body.

Similarly, if floors are too slippery, dancers should avoid or modify pieces with fast changes in direction, lots of turning, or fast and complex *pointe* work. Modifications include attempting less revolutions in turns, slightly slowing the tempo at critical weight shifts, or more protective partnering. When shoes are worn, dancers can increase the friction between the sole of the shoe and the floor through the use of such substances as rosin.

Summary

Dance is a demanding, intricate form of movement, which involves tremendous versatility and requires development of each of the components of training. The most obvious important components are flexibility, neuromuscular coordination, and strength. However, closer examination reveals that certain dance movements also require power, muscular endurance, and cardiovascular endurance.

Development of these components of training generally requires that progressive overload be applied at least three times per week. The magnitude of this overload is critical for producing an appropriate training curve which will result in gains rather than injury. Overload can be manipulated to achieve the desired gains in specific training components by altering frequency, duration, and intensity. To be effectively transferred, this overload should involve the same muscles used in the actual movement and movement patterns similar to that required by the goal movement.

In a class format, it is difficult to meet all the criteria for optimal development of each of the training components while developing the technical and artistic skill of the dancer. This difficulty suggests the possible need for supplemental programs for such components as strength, flexibility, and cardiovascular conditioning. Ideally, screening procedures could be used to evaluate individual dancers, and specific recommendations for supplemental programs could be prescribed.

An obvious example from dance is strength development: It is difficult within the class format and without external weights to apply sufficiently intense overload to produce gains in muscular strength. This need is supported by findings of relatively low strength levels in tested muscles of female ballet dancers (Kirkendall et al., 1984; Kirkendall & Calabrese, 1983; Mostardi, Porterfield, Greenberg, Goldberg, & Lea, 1983). Many authorities believe that supplemental strength training is primarily responsible for the current upswing of record breaking performances in athletes. As with dancers, many other athletes were originally resistant to supplemental programs, believing that their sport alone was sufficient training. Prior to World War II, swimming coaches forbade supplemental training and discouraged their stars from even walking excessively out of fear that they would develop "bunchy" muscles (DeVries, 1966). The fallacy of these prior beliefs has been well demonstrated in recent Olympic performances.

An application of scientific principles of training to dance is needed. Close work among the dance, scientific, and medical communities is necessary to evaluate old methods and develop new methods. There is much work to be done to sort out the valuable dance principles which have been passed down through generations from the myths. Such a process can only yield better methods of dance training and provide a beginning for more effective injury prevention.

References

American College of Sports Medicine. (1980). *Guidelines for graded exercise testing and exercise prescription.* Philadelphia: Lea and Febiger.

Anderson, T., & Kearney, J.T. (1982). Effects of three resistance training programs on muscular strength and absolute and relative endurance. *Research Quarterly for Exercise and Sport, 53*(1), 1–7.

Asmussen, E., & Bonde-Peterson, F. (1974). Storage of elastic energy in skeletal muscles in man. *Acta Physiologica Scandinavica, 91*(3), 385–392.

Astrand, P., & Rodahl, K. (1977). *Textbook of work physiology.* New York: McGraw-Hill.

Baechle, T.R. (1984). Women in resistance training. *Clinics in Sports Medicine, 3*(14), 791–807.

Bailey, W., & Bremiller, W. (1981). *Factors precipitating hamstring strains in track athletes.* Unpublished thesis.

Barnard, R.J., Gardner, G.W., Diaco, N.V., MacAlpin, R.N., & Kattus, A.A. (1973). Cardiovascular responses to sudden strenuous exercise. *Journal of Applied Physiology, 34,* 833.

Bender, J.A., & Kaplan, H.M. (1963). The multiple angle testing method for the evaluation of muscle strength. *Journal of Bone and Joint Surgery, 45A,* 135–140.

Berger, R.A. (1962a). Comparison of static and dynamic strength increases. *Research Quarterly, 33,* 329–333.

Berger, R.A. (1962b). Effect of varied weight training programs on strength. *Research Quarterly, 33,* 168–181.

Berger, R.A. (1970). Relationship between dynamic strength and dynamic endurance. *Research Quarterly, 41,* 115–116.

Bergfield, J.A., Hamilton, W.G., Micheli, L.J., Clippinger, K., Weiker, G.C., Hadacek, L.A., Sammarco, G.J., Molnar, M., & Calabrese, L.H. (1982). Medical problems in ballet: A round table. *The Physician and Sportsmedicine*, **10**(3), 98–112.

Bonen, A., & Belcastro, A. (1976). Comparison of self-selected recovery methods on lactic acid removal rates. *Medicine and Science in Sports*, **8**, 176–178.

Bosco, C., Ito, A., Komi, P.V., Luhtanen, P., Rahkila, P., Rusko, H., & Viitasalo, J.T. (1982). Neuromuscular function and mechanical efficiency of human leg extensor muscles during jumping exercises. *Acta Physiologica Scandinavica*, **114**, 543–550.

Bosco, C., & Komi, P.V. (1979). Potentiation of the mechanical behavior of the human skeletal muscle through pre-stretching. *Acta Physiologica Scandinavica*, **106**, 467–472.

Brown, C.H., & Wilmore, J.H. (1974). The effects of maximal resistance training on the strength and body composition of women athletes. *Medicine and Science in Sports*, **6**, 174–177.

Brynteson, P., & Sinning, W.E. (1973). The effects of training frequencies on the retention of cardiovascular fitness. *Medicine and Science in Sports*, **5**, 29–33.

Burkett, L.N. (1970). Causative factors in hamstring strains. *Medicine and Science in Sports*, **2**, 39–42.

Capen, E.K., Bright, J.A., & Line, P.A. (1961). The effects of weight training on strength, power, muscular endurance and anthropometric measurements on a select group of college women. *Journal of the Association of Physical and Mental Rehabilitation*, **15**, 169–173.

Cavagna, G.A. (1977). Storage and utilization of elastic energy in skeletal muscle. *Exercise and Sport Science Reviews*, **5**, 89–129.

Cavagna, G.A., & Critterio, G. (1974). Effect of stretching on the elastic characteristics and the contractile component of frog striated muscle. *Journal of Physiology*, **239**, 1–14.

Cavagna, G.A., Zamboni, A., Faraggiana, T., & Margaria, K. (1972). Jumping on the moon: Power output at different gravity values. *Aerospace Medicine*, **43**, 408–414.

Christensen, C.S., & Wiseman, D.C. (1972). Strength, the common variable in hamstring strains. *Athletic Training*, **7**, 36–40.

Clarke, D.H. (1973). Adaptations in strength and muscular endurance resulting from exercise. *Exercise and Sport Science Reviews*, **1**, 73–102.

Clarke, D.H., & Stull, G.A. (1970). Endurance training as a determinant of strength and fatigability. *Research Quarterly*, **41**, 19–26.

Clarke, R.S., Hellon, R.F., & Lind, A.R. (1958). The duration of sustained contractions of the human forearm at different muscle temperatures. *Journal of Physiology*, **143**, 454–473.

Clippinger, K., & Novak, M. (1981). *Comparison of ground reaction forces in landing from a grand jeté with barefeet versus pointe shoes.* Unpublished manuscript, University of Washington, Seattle.

Clippinger-Robertson, K. (1985, July). Increasing functional range of motion in dance. *Kinesiology for Dance,* 8(3), 8-10.

Clippinger-Robertson, K. (1987). A unique challenge. Biomechanical considerations in turnout. *Journal of Physical Education, Recreation and Dance,* 58(5), 37-40.

Clippinger-Robertson, K.S., Hutton, R.S., Miller, D.I., & Nichols, T.R. (1986). Mechanical and anatomical factors relating to the incidence and etiology of patellofemoral pain in dancers. In C. Shell (Ed.), *Proceedings of The International Symposium on the Scientific Aspects of Dance* (pp. 53–72). Champaign, IL: Human Kinetics.

Cohen, J.L., Segal, K.R., Witriol, I., & McArdle, W.D. (1982). Cardiorespiratory responses to ballet exercise and VO₂max of elite ballet dancers. *Medicine and Science in Sports,* 14(3), 212–217.

Costill, D.L., King, D.S., Thomas, R., & Hargreaves, M. (1985). Effects of reduced training on muscular power in swimmers. *The Physician and Sportsmedicine,* 13(2), 94–107.

Coyle, E.F., Feiring, D.C., Rotkis, T.C., Cote, R.W., III, Roby, F.B., Lee, W., & Wilmore, J.H. (1981). Specificity of power improvements through slow and fast isokinetic training. *Journal of Applied Physiology,* 51(6), 1437–1442.

Coyle, E.F., Martin, W.H., III, Sinacore, D.R., Joyner, M.J., Hagberg, J.M., & Holloszy, J.O. (1984). Time course of loss of adaptations after stopping prolonged intense endurance training. *Journal of Applied Physiology,* 57, 1857–1863.

DeLorme, T. (1946). Heavy resistance exercises. *Archives of Physical Medicine and Rehabilitation,* 27, 607–630.

DeLorme, T., & Watkins, A. (1948). Techniques of progressive resistance exercise. *Archives of Physical Medicine and Rehabilitation,* 29, 263–273.

DeVries, H.A. (1962). Evaluation of static stretching procedures for improvement of flexibility. *Research Quarterly,* 33, 222–229.

DeVries, H.A. (1966). *Physiology of exercise for physical education and athletics.* Dubuque, Iowa: Wm C. Brown.

Dollard, M.D. (1985). Plyometric ballistic conditioning. *Aerobics and Fitness,* 3(2), 33–35.

Dons, B., Ballerup, K., Bonde-Petersen, F., & Hancke, S. (1979). The effect of weightlifting exercise related to fiber composition and muscle cross-sectional area. *European Journal of Applied Physiology,* 40, 95–106.

Dressendorfer, R.H., Wade, C.E., & Scaff, J.H. (1985). Increased morning heart rate in runners: A valid sign of overtraining? *The Physician and Sportsmedicine,* 13(8), 77–86.

Drinkwater, B. (1973). Physiological responses of women to exercise. *Exercise and Sports Science Reviews*, **1**, 91–95.

Eccles, R.M., Kozak, W., & Westerman, R.A. (1962). Enhancement of spinal monosynaptic reflex responses after denervation of synergic hind-limb muscles. *Experimental Neurology*, **6**, 451–464.

Enoka, R. (1979). *The second knee bend in Olympic weightlifting: Rationale and analysis.* Unpublished manuscript, University of Washington, Seattle.

Falls, H.B. (1972). Heat and cold applications. In W.P. Morgan (Ed.), *Ergonic aids and muscular performance* (pp. 140–158). New York: Academic.

Flanagan, E. (1967). Methods for facilitation and inhibition of motor activity. *American Journal of Physical Medicine*, **46**, 1007–1011.

Fox, E.L. (1984). *Sports physiology.* New York: CBS College.

Franks, D.B. (1972). Physical warm-up. In W.P. Morgan (Ed.), *Ergogenic aids and muscular performance* (pp. 159–191). New York: Academic.

Gardner, G.W. (1963). Specificity of strength changes of the exercised and nonexercised limb following isometric training. *Research Quarterly*, **34**, 98–101.

Gelabert, R. (1980). Preventing dancers' injuries. *The Physician and Sportsmedicine*, **8**(4), 69–76.

Grillner, S., Nilsson, J., & Thorstensson, A. (1978). Intra-abdominal pressure changes during natural movements in man. *Acta Physiologica Scandinavica*, **103**, 275–283.

Grodjinovsky, A., & Magel, J.R. (1970). Effect of warm-up on running performance. *Research Quarterly*, **41**(1), 116–117.

Grose, J.E. (1957). Depression of muscle fatigue curves by heat and cold. *Research Quarterly*, **29**(1), 19–31.

Hagerman, F. (1981, March). *The physiological basis of strength flexibility training.* The fourteenth annual sports medicine and conditioning seminar, conducted by the Northwest Sportsmedicine Foundation, Seattle.

Hayes, K. (1980). The physiological basis of stretching. *Kinesiology for Dance*, **11**, 2–5.

Hermansen, L., et al. (1975). Lactate removal at rest and during exercise. As cited in E.L. Fox, *Sport physiology* (pp. 77–78). New York: CBS College Publishing.

Hill, A.V. (1950). The series elastic component of muscle. *Proceedings of the Royal Society of London*, **137B**, 273–280.

Holt, L.E., Travis, T.M., & Okita, T.A. (1970). A comparative study of three stretching techniques. *Perceptual Motor Skills*, **3**, 611–616.

Houston, M.E., Bentzen, H., & Larsen, H. (1978). Interrelationships between skeletal muscle adaptations and performance as studied by detraining and retraining. *Acta Physiologica Scandinavica*, **105**, 163–170.

Howse, A.J.G. (1972). Orthopaedists aid ballet. *Clinical Orthopaedics and Related Research*, **89**, 52–63.

Hutton, R.S. (1976). Introductory remarks: Changing concepts of motor control. *Psychology of Motor Behavior and Sport*, **1**, 161–169.

Hutton, R.S. (1984). Acute plasticity in spinal segmental pathways with use: Implications for training. In M. Kumamota (Ed.), *Neural and mechanical control of movement* (pp. 90–112). Kyoto, Japan: Yamaguchi Shoten.

Hutton, R.S. (1985). Neuromuscular physiology. In R.P. Welsh & R.J. Shephard (Eds.), *Current therapy in sportsmedicine* (pp. 1–4). St. Louis: C.V. Mosby.

Huxley, A.F. (1974). Muscular contraction. *Journal of Physiology*, **243**, 1–43.

Ikai, M., & Steinhaus, A.H. (1961). Some factors modifying the expression of human strength. *Journal of Applied Physiology*, **16**, 157.

Ingjer, F., & Strømme, S.B. (1979). Effects of active, passive or no warm-up on the physiological response to heavy exercise. *European Journal of Applied Physiology*, **40**, 273–283.

Jensen, R.K. (1981). The effect of a twelve month growth period on the body moments of inertia of children. *Medicine and Science in Sports and Exercise*, **13**(4), 238–242.

Johns, R.J., & Wright, V. (1962). Relative importance of various tissues in joint stiffness. *Journal of Applied Physiology*, **17**, 824–828.

Johnson, B.L. (1972). Eccentric versus concentric muscle training for strength development. *Medicine and Science in Sports*, **4**, 111–115.

Johnson, B.L., Adamczyk, J.W., Tennøe, K.O., & Strømme, S.B. (1976). A comparison of concentric and eccentric muscle training. *Medicine and Science in Sports*, **8**(1), 35–38.

Johnson, L.C., Fisher, C., Silvester, L.J., & Hofheins, C.C. (1972). Anabolic steroid: Effects on strength, body weight, oxygen uptake and spermatogenesis upon mature males. *Medicine and Science in Sports*, **4**(1), 43–45.

Kabat, H. (1965). Proprioceptive facilitation in therapeutic exercise. In S. Licht (Ed.), *Therapeutic exercise* (pp. 327–343). Baltimore: Waverly.

Kirkendall, D.T., Bergfield, J.A., Calabrese, L., Lombardo, J.A., Street, G., & Weiker, G.G. (1984). Isokinetic characteristics of ballet dancers and the response to a season of ballet training. *Journal of Orthopaedic and Sports Physical Therapy*, **5**(4), 207–211.

Kirkendall, D.T., & Calabrese, H. (1983). Physiological aspects of dance. *Clinics in Sports Medicine*, **2**(3), 525–536.

Klafs, C.E., & Arnheim, D.D. (1981). *Modern principles of athletic training*. St. Louis: C.V. Mosby.

Klein, K. (1971). Incidence of knee injuries related to flexibility and strength imbalance. In American College of Sports Medicine, *Encyclopedia of sports science and medicine*. New York: Macmillan.

Knott, M., & Voss, D.E. (1968). *Proprioceptive neuromuscular facilitation*. New York: Harper & Row.

Komi, P.V. (1979). Neuromuscular performance factors influencing force and speed production. *Scandinavian Journal of Sports Science, 1*, 2–15.

Komi, P.V., & Bosco, C. (1978). Utilization of stored elastic energy in leg extensor muscles by men and women. *Medicine and Science in Sports, 10*(4), 261–265.

Kulund, D.N., & Tottossy, M. (1985). Warm-up, strength, and power. *Clinics in Sports Medicine, 4*(1), 137–158.

Levine, M., Kabat, H., Knott, M., & Voss, D. (1954). Relaxation of spasticity by physiological techniques. *Archives of Physical Medicine, 35*, 214–223.

Liemohn, W. (1978). Factors related to hamstring strains. *American Journal of Sports Medicine, 18*, 71–76.

Marino, M., & Glein, G. (1984). Muscle strength and fiber typing. *Clinics in Sports Medicine, 3*(9), 85–97.

Marshall, J.L., Johanson, N., Wickiewicz, T.L., Tischler, H.M., Koslin, B.L., Zeno, S., & Meyers, A. (1980). Joint looseness: A function of the person and the joint. *Medicine and Science in Sports and Exercise, 12*(3), 189–194.

McMahon, T.A., & Greene, P.P. (1979). The influence of track compliance in running. *Journal of Biomechanics, 12*, 893–904.

Meyers, C.R. (1967). Effects of two isometric routines on strength, size, and endurance in exercised and nonexercised arms. *Research Quarterly, 38*, 430–440.

Miller, E.H., Schneider, H.J., Bronson, J.L., & McLain, D. (1975). A new consideration in athletic injuries: The classical ballet dancer. *Clinical Orthopaedics, 3*, 181–191.

Milner-Brown, H.S. (1975). Synchronization of human motor units: Possible roles of exercise and supraspinal reflexes. *Electroencephalography and Clinical Neurophysiology, 38*, 245–254.

Mirkin, G., & Hoffman, M. (1978). *The sportsmedicine book*. Boston: Little Brown and Co.

Moore, M.A., & Hutton, R.S. (1980). Electromyographic investigation of muscle stretching. *Medicine and Science in Sports and Exercise, 12*, 322–329.

Morgan, D.L., Proske, V., & Warren, D. (1978). Measurements of muscle stiffness and the mechanism of elastic storage of energy in hopping kangaroos. *Journal of Physiology, 282*, 253–261.

Mostardi, R.A., Porterfield, J.A., Greenberg, B., Goldberg, D., & Lea, M. (1983). Musculoskeletal and cardiopulmonary characteristics of the professional ballet dancer. *The Physician and Sportsmedicine,* **11**(12), 53–61.

Muido, L. (1946). The influence of body temperature in performance in swimming. *Acta Physiologica Scandinavica,* **12**, 102–109.

Nicholas, J.A. (1970). Injuries to knee ligaments: Relationship to looseness and tightness in football players. *Journal of the American Medical Association,* **212**, 2236–2239.

Nicholas, J.A. (1975). Risk factors, sports medicine and the orthopaedic system: An overview. *Journal of Sports Medicine,* **3**, 243–259.

O'Shea, J.P. (1966). The development of strength and muscle hypertrophy through selected weight programs. *Research Quarterly,* **37**, 95–107.

O'Shea, J.P. (1976). *Scientific principles and methods of strength fitness.* Reading, MA: Addison-Wesley.

Perez, H.R., & Fumasoli, S. (1984). Benefit of proprioceptive neuromuscular facilitation on the joint mobility of youth-aged female gymnasts with correlations for rehabilitation. *American Corrective Therapy Journal,* **38**(6), 142–146.

Perrine, J.J., & Edgerton, V.R. (1978). Muscle force velocity and power velocity relationships under isokinetic loading. *Medicine and Science in Sports and Exercise,* **10**, 159–166.

Pinkstrom, D. (1967). Analysis of traditional regimens of therapeutic exercise. *American Journal of Physical Medicine,* **46**, 713–731.

Pipes, T.V., & Wilmore, J.H. (1975). Isokinetic versus isotonic strength training in adult men. *Medicine and Science in Sports,* **7**, 262–274.

Pollock, M., Wilmore, J., & Fox, S.M. (1984). *Exercise in health and disease.* Philadelphia: W.B. Saunders.

Rack, P.M.H., & Westbury, D.R. (1974). The short range stiffness of active mammalian muscle and its effect on mechanical properties. *Journal of Physiology,* **240**, 331–350.

Roy, S., & Irvin, R. (1983). *Sports medicine: Prevention, evaluation, management, and rehabilitation.* Englewood Cliffs, NJ: Prentice-Hall.

Ryan, A.J., Burke, E.R., Falsetti, H.L., Brown, R.I., & Frederick, E.C. (1983). Overtraining of athletes: A round table. *The Physician and Sportsmedicine,* **11**(6), 93–110.

Ryman, R. (1978). A kinematic analysis of selected grand allegro jumps. *Dance Research Annuals,* **9**, 231–242.

Sale, D.G., MacDougall, J.D., Upton, A.R.M., & McComas, A.J. (1983). Effect of strength training upon motoneuron excitability in man. *Medicine and Science in Sports and Exercise,* **15**(1), 57–62.

Sammarco, G.J. (1983). The dancer's hip. *Clinics in Sports Medicine,* **2**(3), 485–498.

Schultz, P. (1979). Day of the static stretch. *The Physician and Sports-medicine,* **7**(11), 109–117.

Seals, J.G. (1983). A study of dance surfaces. *Clinics in Sportsmedicine,* **2**(3), 557–561.

Shaver, L.G. (1971). Maximum dynamic strength, relative dynamic endurance and their relationships. *Research Quarterly,* **42**, 460–465.

Shellock, F.G. (1983). Physiological benefits of warm-up. *The Physician and Sportsmedicine,* **11**(10), 134–139.

Shields, C.L., Beckwith, V.Z., & Kurland, H.L. (1985). Comparison of leg strength training equipment. *The Physician and Sportsmedicine,* **13**(2), 49–56.

Stamford, B. (1983). Overtraining. *The Physician and Sportsmedicine,* **11**(10), 180.

Stamford, B. (1985). The difference between strength and power. *The Physician and Sportsmedicine,* **13**(7), 155.

Stockmeyer, S. (1967). An interpretation of the approach of Rood to the treatment of neuromuscular dysfunction. *The American Journal of Physical Medicine,* **46**, 900–956.

Surburg, P.R. (1981). Neuromuscular facilitation techniques in sports medicine. *The Physician and Sportsmedicine,* **9**, 114–127.

Tanigawa, M.C. (1972). Comparison of hold-relax procedures and passive mobilization on increasing muscle length. *Physical Therapy,* **52**, 725–734.

Thistle, H., Hislop, H.J., Moffroid, M., & Lowman, E.W. (1967). Isokinetic contraction: A new concept of resistance exercise. *Archives of Physical Medicine and Rehabilitation,* **48**, 279–282.

Thorstensson, A. (1977). Observations in strength training and detraining. *Acta Physiologica Scandinavica,* **100**, 491–493.

Thorstensson, A., Hulten, B., Von Dobeln, W., & Karlsson, J. (1976). Effect of strength training on enzyme activities and fibre characteristics in human skeletal muscle. *Acta Physiologica Scandinavica,* **96**, 392–398.

Van Handel, P.J., & Puhl, J. (1983). Sports physiology: Testing the athlete. *Clinics in Sports Medicine,* **2**(1), 19–30.

Voss, D.E. (1967). Proprioceptive neuromuscular facilitation. *American Journal of Physical Medicine,* **46**, 838–898.

Wallin, D., Ekblom, B., Grahn, R., & Nordinborg, T. (1985). Improvement of muscle flexibility: A comparison between two techniques. *The American Journal of Sports Medicine,* **13**(4), 263–268.

Wilmore, J.H. (1974). Alterations in strength, body composition and anthropometric measurements consequent to a ten week weight training program. *Medicine and Science in Sports,* **6**, 133–138.

Acknowledgments

The author wishes to thank Maurya Kerr of the Pacific Northwest Ballet School for modeling for photographs and to express appreciation to all the other modern and ballet dancers who generously allowed the use of their photographs. Gratitude is also due to Pacific Northwest Ballet for their kind donation of company photographs and to Robert S. Hutton, PhD, for his generous assistance with references.

Chapter 6

Cardiovascular Aspects of Dance

Steven Chatfield
University of Hawaii

William C. Byrnes
University of Colorado

Frequently, dance training methodologies are the result of the transmission of venerable teachings. This traditionalist approach has met with undeniable success and will probably become recognized, for the most part, as physiologically appropriate and efficient. In this chapter, a variety of published scientific research has been used to facilitate an evaluation of the cardiovascular (CV) demands of dance. A scientific analysis of the CV adaptations to dance as an artform is used to generate recommendations about the purposefulness of the varying phases of dance training. Other forms of dance-like activities that have recently been popularized and whose health and fitness benefits have been extolled, such as aerobic dance and dancersize, will not be addressed.

Anatomy and Function of the Cardiovascular System

The cardiovascular system consists of the heart and associated blood vessels (the vascular system). The fluid transport medium within this closed system is blood. The cardiovascular system performs a number of functions that are essential to life-support and health. Included among these general functions are: supplying oxygen to and removing carbon dioxide from the cells of the body; transporting essential nutrients and waste products to and from metabolically active tissues; controlling pH (i.e., the acid-base balance of the body); and, serving as an intermediary for various metabolic and endocrine functions.

The cardiovascular system can be divided into the systemic and the pulmonary circuits. The systemic circuit includes the chambers of the heart and conducting vessels associated with transport to and from all organ systems except the lungs. The pulmonary circuit includes the chambers of the heart and conducting vessels associated with transport to and from the lungs.

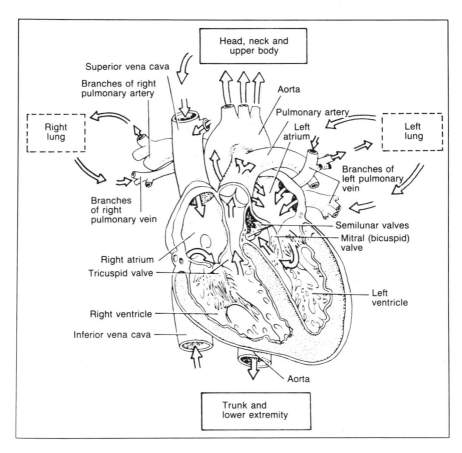

Figure 6.1   The heart: direction of blood flow is indicated by arrows. From *Exercise Physiology: Energy, Nutrition and Human Performance* by W.D. McArdle, F.I. Katch, and V.L. Katch, 1981, Philadelphia: Lea and Febiger. Reprinted by permission.

The heart is a four-chambered muscular pump (see Figure 6.1) designed to be the driving force behind the movement of blood through the vascular system. The right atrium receives venous blood returning from the systemic circulation and channels it into the right ventricle which pumps deoxygenated blood to the lungs via the pulmonary artery. The left atrium receives oxygenated blood from the lungs via the pulmonary veins and channels it into the left ventricle which then pumps it into the systemic circulation via the aorta.

As described earlier (chapter 1), exercise such as dance requires an increase in energy production by the active skeletal muscle mass. Regardless of whether this energy production occurs aerobically (prolonged work of low to moderate intensity, e.g., an *adagio*) or anaerobically (brief periods of high-intensity work, e.g., a 60-second *allegro*), an increased blood flow to the active muscle site or sites occurs. In the case of predominantly anaerobic energy production, the cardiovascular system provides a means of partially eliminating metabolic by-products, such as lactic acid, and provides the materials required for replenishment of anaerobic energy sources. During aerobic energy production, an increased blood flow serves to maintain the oxygen supply necessary to meet the energy requirement of the exercise task and remove the increasing amount of carbon dioxide resulting from aerobic energy production.

An increase in blood flow to the active muscle mass during exercise can occur by redirecting the distribution of blood within the systemic circulatory system and/or by increasing blood flow through the whole cardiovascular system. A redistribution of blood flow is possible because of the structure of the systemic circulatory system. The systemic circulatory system is arranged in parallel rather than in series (see Figure 6.2) (i.e., arteries to each organ system branch off a central distributing vessel, the aorta). Flow through a given organ is mainly regulated by a specialized set of vessels known as *arterioles*. Arterioles are blood vessels that possess a high degree of smooth muscle in their walls and are located between arteries and capillaries. The muscularity of arterioles permits precise control over the size of the opening (*lumen*) through which blood flows. Increasing the smooth muscle activity decreases the size of the lumen (*vasoconstriction*) and increases the resistance to blood flow. Decreasing the smooth muscle activity increases the size of the lumen (*vasodilation*) and decreases the resistance to blood flow. Regulation of the arterioles is under both central (central nervous system) and local (metabolic events occurring at the tissue level) control so that blood flow can be efficiently redistributed under a variety of conditions such as exercise.

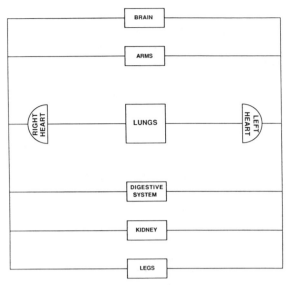

Figure 6.2 Schematic representation of the parallel arrangement of the cardiovascular system.

An increase in blood flow throughout the whole cardiovascular system is accomplished by increasing the amount of blood propelled by each contraction of the heart (stroke volume) and by increasing the frequency of contractions of the heart muscle (heart rate). The product of stroke volume and heart rate represents the quantity of blood pumped by the heart per minute (cardiac output). Cardiac output increases with exercise as a result of increases in both stroke volume and heart rate. Some authors (Astrand & Rodahl, 1977; Mathews & Fox, 1976; McArdle, Katch, & Katch, 1981) have suggested that the stroke volume reaches maximal values during exercise at around a heart rate of 140 beats per minute and that further increases in cardiac output are accomplished solely by increases in heart rate. Next, we will examine acute and chronic cardiovascular responses to dance and dance training.

The Cardiovascular System of Dancers

Data on the cardiovascular effects of dancing and dance training have been acquired by the use of echocardiography, electrocardiography, and indirect calorimetry. In the following section, a brief overview of each measurement technique will be presented followed by a summary of experimental data and its relevance to the understanding of the cardio-vascular responses to dance.

Echocardiography

Echocardiography uses ultrasound echoes to create video images and strip chart recordings of the structures of the heart as it contracts and relaxes. The information that can be calculated by echocardiography includes measurements of stroke volume and thickness of the ventricular walls of the heart. These two measurements have been used as indicators of adaptations of the heart (myocardium) to exercise. Several studies (Cohen & Segal, 1985; Longhurst, Kelly, Gonyea, & Mitchell, 1980a, 1980b; Morganroth, Naron, Henry, & Epstein, 1975) have suggested that cardiovascular adaptations to exercise may follow two patterns. Endurance (aerobic) exercise results in an increase in an individual's maximal stroke volume and therefore an increase in maximal cardiac output. This adaptation seems to be connected to an increase in maximal endurance (aerobic) capacity. Resistive exercise like weight training results in no change in maximal stroke volume but an increase in the thickness of the left ventricle's muscular wall (left ventricular hypertrophy, LVH). This adaptation seems to be a modification resulting from the high blood pressure responses generated by resistive (anaerobic) exercises.

Cohen, Gupta, Lichstein, and Chodda (1980), via echocardiographic examination of professional ballet dancers from the American Ballet Theatre, concluded that ballet training, rehearsal, and performance result in myocardial adaptations resembling both aerobic and anaerobic training. When compared to a normal group of untrained subjects, the myocardial adaptations of the ballet dancers showed characteristics of both endurance and strength athletes. The dancers' hearts demonstrated an increased maximal SV when compared to the untrained normals. This adaptation is in the direction of, but of a lesser magnitude than, endurance athletes, such as distance runners, who demonstrate an enhanced aerobic capacity as a result of training. In addition, the dancer's hearts showed LVH on the order of what has been seen in athletes trained for strength, such as shot-putters and wrestlers, who demonstrate an enhanced anaerobic energy capacity from their training. Finally, Cohen and colleagues observed that total lifetime dance hours and intensity of training correlated significantly with LVH and maximal SV. These authors submit that although these correlations were statistically modest, a definite trend was evident.

It is plausible that total lifetime hours dancing plays a role in aerobic and anaerobic adaptations of the CV system. However, relatively rapid adaptations of the CV system have been demonstrated. Ehansi, Hagberg, and Hickson (1978) found that echocardiograms could detect rapid changes in left ventricular posterior wall thickness (LVH) and in SV. Significant increases could be seen following nine weeks of training while significant decreases occurred following only three weeks of detraining. Dance training varies from instructor to instructor, and performing dancers constantly adapt to new choreographic demands. It is probable that the CV dimensions and functions of dancers reflect some combination of both long-term and short-term adaptations to variable aerobic and anaerobic energy requirements.

Heath et al. (1982) studied ten predominantly recreational female ballet dancers who were matched with runners for training frequency, duration, and relative training intensity. Their data indicated that the myocardial adaptations to dance were similar to those observed with endurance (aerobic) training. These researchers mentioned that myocardial adaptations to anaerobic training were minimal, yet they admit that their dancers were not of an elite caliber and that their dancers maintained a recreational involvement with dance classes, rehearsals and performances that was not comparable to the schedules or rigors of full-time professional dancing.

Electrocardiography

Defining the cardiovascular responses to dance classes, rehearsals, and performance can also be used to determine the myocardial adaptations to dance. Because heart rate increases generally indicate increases in blood flow through the cardiovascular system, this measurement can be used to quantify the cardiovascular response to exercise. Heart rate can be determined by palpation of a major artery (pulse rate) or by means of electrocardiography. An electrocardiogram (ECG or EKG) is a linear representation of the electrical activity in the heart during its contraction and relaxation phases.

A typical ballet or modern dance technique class or rehearsal is composed of a series of work intervals (dance phrases) alternating with rest intervals. During these rest intervals, aesthetic or technical feedback is given by the instructor to the students, and the next dance phrase is presented and learned. These work and rest intervals probably vary a great deal from one dance instructor to the next, from day to day, and from beginning to advanced classes. Therefore, quantifying exercise intensity to dance training via the monitoring of heart rate can be difficult. It should be noted that the relationship between heart rate and blood flow is altered with isometric (static holding) work. Isometric work results in blood pressure and heart rate increases that are greater than would be expected for the amount of work being done. Because dancing incorporates isometric work such as support mechanisms for high extensions and sustained gestures, interpretation of heart rate responses following dance exercise should be made with caution. Heart rate determinations, however, can provide an index of the intermittent nature of dance training.

Chatfield (1984) monitored the heart rate response of intermediate collegiate dancers throughout a 14-week academic semester. Each class period (90 minutes) involved an eclectic combination of modern dance training procedures in a traditional modern dance classroom progression. The progression consisted of two work periods (I and II) separated by a stretching period. The second work period was followed by a five-minute cool down. Figure 6.3 is a schematic representation of the typical heart rate response to this procedure. During work period I, heart rate response was between 60–75% of maximum heart rate reserve (MHRR is the difference between max HR and resting HR) during the exercise interval and between 30–45% of MHRR during the rest interval. During the stretching, exercise heart rate averaged 51% of MHRR. Corresponding values for work period II for exercise and rest intervals were 69% and 48% of MHRR, respectively.

Although different in magnitude, the pattern of heart rate response to dance training observed by Chatfield (1984) in intermediate dancers is consistent with the data of Cohen, Segal, and McArdle (1982) and Selliger, Glucksman, Paehlopnik, and Pachlopnikova (1970) concerning professional dancers. The difference in magnitude may be related to the psychological stimulation of performance, a greater skill level for the professionals, and/or choreography that results in greater physiological demands. In these studies, performance demands as monitored by ECG elicited near maximal heart rates for short periods in alteration with heart rates of 120 beats per minute or less. In one instance, a 23-year-old female soloist dancing the lead in Delibes' Coppelia was on stage for 51 minutes during which time her heart rate ranged from 116 to 181 beats per minute (Selliger et al., 1970). Throughout her continuous performance, interrupted by one intermission, her heart rate averaged 144 beats per minute. Cohen et al. (1982) found similar heart rate responses for members of the American Ballet Theatre during on-stage performance. The highest recorded heart rate was 197 beats per minute on stage while off-stage heart rates often recovered to below 80 beats per minute. Heart rates recorded for professional ballet classes for the American Ballet Theatre (Cohen, Segal, Witriol, & McArdle, 1982) and the Royal Swedish Ballet (Schantz & Astrand, 1984) have varied between resting and near maximal levels.

Data on the HR response to dance class, rehearsal, and performance confirm the intermittent, burst-like, anaerobic nature of dance training and performance, suggesting that endurance (aerobic) myocardial adaptations might not be expected from this form of training. At the same time, continuous repetitions of the work/rest intervals seen during classes, rehearsals, and performances may in some instances provide an adequate stimulus for aerobic myocardial adaptations. Fox and Mathews (1974) have suggested that interval training with the proper combination of work to rest intervals can result in an improved endurance (aerobic) capacity.

Indirect Calorimetry

Exercise physiologists have traditionally measured aerobic capacity by means of a graded exercise test. A graded exercise test involves placing an individual on an exercise device (usually a bicycle, treadmill, or step bench) and progressively increasing the work intensity until the subject reaches volitional exhaustion. During the test, various measurements such as heart rate and blood pressure are determined at regular intervals. A key parameter evaluated by this test is the subject's maximum aerobic capacity ($\dot{V}O_2$max): the maximum amount of oxygen that an individual can utilize to produce the energy required for work. $\dot{V}O_2$max is usually expressed per unit of body weight and incorporates metric units (i.e., milliliters of oxygen per kilogram of body weight per minute—mlO_2/kg/min). Typical values for sedentary individuals and athletes are presented in Figure 6.4. $\dot{V}O_2$max seems to be limited by the ability of the cardiovascular system to deliver oxygen to the working muscle and therefore has achieved acceptance as a measure of cardiovascular function.

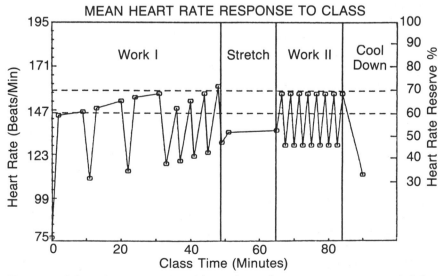

Figure 6.3 Schematic representation of dancers' mean heart rate response to a typical class progression.

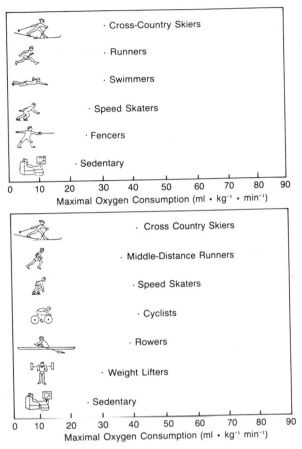

Figure 6.4 Maximal oxygen consumption of male and female olympic-caliber athletes and healthy sedentary subjects. From *Exercise Physiology: Energy, Nutrition and Human Performance* by W.D. McArdle, F.I. Katch, and V.L. Katch, 1981. Philadelphia: Lea and Febiger. Reprinted by permission.

To date, none of the training studies utilizing dance technique class as the training medium have found significant posttraining changes in $\dot{V}O_2$max. Even in instances where pretraining $\dot{V}O_2$max values were representative of the sedentary individual (35–40 $ml0_2$/kg/min), beginning and intermediate level modern dance training did not result in significant gains in $\dot{V}O_2$max (Chatfield, 1984; DeGuzman, 1979). Yet, when advanced and professional female dancers were evaluated, $\dot{V}O_2$max values above the sedentary female and similar to female speed skaters and swimmers have been reported (Saltin & Astrand, 1967; Schantz & Astrand, 1984). These values are below the well-trained female endurance athlete but indicate a modest change in cardiovascular function associated with dance training. In fact, when reviewing the literature, a trend seems to emerge when the $\dot{V}O_2$max data of dancers from beginning students to professionals are analyzed. Values range from 36 ml0_2/kg/min for collegiate females who were beginning dance students (DeGuzman, 1979) up to 51 ml0_2/kg/min for female professional dancers (Schantz & Astrand, 1984). Data obtained for intermediate and advanced female collegiate dancers (Chatfield, 1984; Novak, Magill, & Schutte, 1978) fall roughly in line with a trend of increasing $\dot{V}O_2$max with greater expertise.

The research presented here suggests that dancing may stimulate myocardial adaptations resembling both aerobic and anaerobic exercise. The magnitude of these adaptations is probably related to the total lifetime hours of involvement with dance, the intensity of that involvement, and the particular repertoire. Evidence in support of moderate aerobic adaptations include

- an increased maximal stroke volume when compared to normals;
- HR responses to rehearsal and performance that may provide the minimum required interval training stimulus that Fox and Mathews (1974) suggest will result in increases of all energy systems;
- the apparent trend that emerges from the literature suggesting that $\dot{V}O_2$max values of dancers are roughly in line with their skill level.

Evidence in support of anaerobic energy release playing a dominant role in the energy yield to support dance includes

- predominant left ventricular hypertrophy in dancers;
- the intermittent near-maximal bursts of heart rate resulting from some dancing;
- the highest $\dot{V}O_2$max values for elite dancers being comparable to nonendurance, speed-oriented athletes;
- the near maximal levels of blood lactate seen as a result of dance rehearsals and performances (Astrand, 1973 [cited in DeGuzman, 1979a] Chatfield, 1984; Schantz & Astrand, 1984).

These data suggest, but do not provide conclusive evidence, that dance results in chronic cardiovascular adaptations similar to both aerobic or anaerobic training. Interestingly, a further suggestion of the research is that the CV adaptations to dance are stimulated more by rehearsals and performances than by technique classes.

Research comparing the differing demands of dance class and performance indicates that exertional levels and the duration of intense bursts of activity are lower for class than for performances (Cohen, Segal, & McArdle, 1982; Cohen, Segal, Witriol, & McArdle, 1982; Kirkendall &

Calabrese, 1983; Schantz & Astrand, 1984; Selliger et al., 1970). Intensity and duration along with frequency and specific activity are the factors that must be considered for CV training adaptations.

It is possible that class could involve more work than performance for dancers who are not used on stage very frequently. It is probably safe to assume, however, that in general, the cumulative work involved in a performance is greater for dancers than cumulative work in class. It is also probable, depending on the repertoire, that performance intensities are greater for longer durations and are more frequent than in class. In addition, performance work-to-rest ratios are probably greater than class work-to-rest ratios.

Unfortunately, rehearsal demands, which could provide a link between class and performance demands, are relatively unresearched. What little data does exist indicates that rehearsal demands, in terms of intensities, fall somewhere in between the demands of class and performance (Cohen, Segal, & McArdle, 1982; Schantz & Astrand, 1984). It is reasonable to assume that while intensities would be similar for the same work done in rehearsal and performance, performance may result in slightly higher intensities due to the all-out effort associated with performance. Schantz and Astrand (1984) found that although dancers perceived that they pushed themselves as hard during rehearsal as during performance, their rehearsal HRs were lower than their performance HRs. It is also reasonable to assume that cumulative durations of work for rehearsals would be greater than for performance. This is probably true because rehearsals, generally, are longer than performances and involve numerous repetitions of the performance material. Of course this would vary with the stage of the rehearsal process. As rehearsals for a new piece begin, the work would probably be more similar to class. Near the final stages, before the premier performance, one would expect work demands during rehearsal to more closely mimic performance demands. With established repertory that is rehearsed for maintenance, work demands would be expected to be similar to performance. A key difference in this instance might be the frequency of the demands. Very few dancers perform daily or even five days per week, yet rehearsals are commonly that frequent among active groups. Performances are more commonly clustered on a periodic basis.

In conclusion, it appears that the physiological demands of dance follow a trend of increase from class to rehearsal to performance, at least in terms of intensity. The intensities of rehearsals are probably near those of performances but slightly lower. However, for the performing dance artist, more cumulative work is probably accomplished in rehearsals.

Opinions and Recommendations

Dance is a highly specialized activity. The physical demands of dance as an artform are secondary to the aesthetic intentions of the dance instructor, director, choreographer, and performer. There are as many aesthetic preferences as there are individuals. A variety of physiological demands and adaptations could possibly result, depending upon the individual, in control.

The most consistent physiological demands among styles, instructors, and choreographers are probably those placed on the musculoskeletal system of the dancer, particularly the lower extremities, the pelvis, and the spine (Nicholas, 1975; Schneider, King, Bronson, & Miller, 1974; Washington, 1978). These musculoskeletal stresses are due primarily to the demands to create and maintain a given external appearance of the body in addition to the exaggerated forces that can be involved in dancing, including those forces involved in landing from aerial maneuvers. Because control and alignment are essential factors in the prevention of dance injuries, it seems prudent that the major portion of dance classes, even at the advanced levels, be devoted to developing biomechanically correct movement techniques. In other words, in the classroom, proper dance technique would seem to be the obvious prerequisite to any emphasis on cardiovascular conditioning. Without the foundation of biomechanically safe technique, there can be no long-term involvement with dance.

Biomechanically correct movement is beautiful movement (Hays, 1979; Sweigard, 1974). The qualities of aesthetic intentions expressed through dance can range from the sublime to the grotesque and can be amply stated via biomechanically correct movement. The burden is on both the performer and the choreographer to use and know the principles of biomechanically safe movement techniques. Choreography should not violate the kinesiological principles of the human body. Training the dancer as a performing artist in a physiologically efficient and biomechanically correct manner promotes the development of knowledgeable and adept dancers and choreographers.

Dance as a performing art places heavy demands on movement technique and aesthetic expression. Dance is burst-like in nature. The primary physiological and biomechanical demands of dance are connected to flexibility, agility, spatial cognition, balance, power, and movement control (Nicholas, 1975; Sweigard, 1974). The traditional format of dance technique classes provides an ideal model for developing the capacity to perform high-intensity bursts of movement in a biomechanically correct manner. At the same time, recovery periods between the actual physical activities are used to refine aesthetic principles and intentions.

Whereas dance technique classes can prepare dancers in some ways for the physiological rigors of rehearsal and performance, the final training ground for a dance performance is in rehearsal for that specific performance. During rehearsals the neuromuscular and CV requirements for an aesthetic performance of any given piece of choreography become conditioned to the appropriate intensities and durations for that performance. Although some transfer of conditioning from class may occur, rehearsals provide the fine-tuning needed for diverse repertoire.

If so desired, dance technique classes could be structured to involve some degree of aerobic CV overload. Even beginning classes could use simple, repetitive movements or movement combinations to create aerobic overloads. Aerobic dance classes do this. The emphasis, however, for training a performing artist should be more on aesthetics apprehension and skills acquisition than on aerobic conditioning.

As in-class dance experiences progress, it is advisable to incorporate intermittent, near-maximal bursts of activity as preparation for involvement in rehearsals and performances. However, it seems that the most appropriate and concentrated time for the performing dancer to attain the cardiovascular adaptations necessary to perform difficult physical feats with a designed, controlled, and projected aesthetic appearance is during rehearsals for that performance. This approach solves a number of training problems. Most significantly, using rehearsals of the performance itself as the conditioning program assures that the energy systems involved in the performance will be targeted in the training, and that the specific muscles and reflex patterns used for the performance will be selectively trained so that maximal transfer from training (rehearsal) to performance will occur. To clarify this point, let's look at two contrasting examples.

First, imagine a 20-minute piece that requires all dancers to be on-stage for the entire time. This piece is a series of quickly paced weight shifts and steps which elicits a steady state heart rate near 160 beats per minute. Second, imagine a piece that is 10-minutes long and, again, that requires all dancers to be on stage the entire time. In the second piece there are two contrasting dynamics: One is explosive, utilizing jumps, leaps, kicks, lifts, and throws which elicit heart rates of up to 200 beats per minute for 30–45 seconds; the contrasting dynamic lasts 60–135 seconds and is a smooth calm series of sustained, stationary, slow motion gestures allowing the dancers' heart rates to recover to below 100 beats per minute. These two dynamics continually alternate throughout the piece. The cardiovascular demands of these two pieces are antithetical. Rehearsing for one piece would not condition a dancer to perform in the other, and it is unlikely that any given class would contain a progression of training stimuli adequate to provide conditioning for both of these pieces.

Anyone who has ever experienced rehearsals progressing towards performance can attest to the following progression. At first, learning the material and making mistakes will slow down the process. Once the material has been learned, cardiovascular endurance and/or muscle endurance will limit the desired all-out performance energy. Finally, in the culminating phase of the rehearsal process, an appropriate level of physiological adaptation will result in the ability to accomplish the choreography and transcend the physical aspects of the performance so that the intended aesthetic can be concentrated on and projected. The three stages of physiological adaptation through rehearsal describe the professional dancer's situation. For nonprofessionals it is not uncommon to skip the third stage. Frequently, at that level, dances are completed only days (sometimes hours) before initial onstage performances.

Frequently, dance artists including Martha Graham, Jose Limon, and Erick Hawkins have incorporated phrases from performance repertory as training material for technique classes. Appropriate degrees of difficulty of movement excerpts from repertory can be used at every level of training from beginning to professional. This method of designing training progressions maximizes transfer of physiological adaptations from class to rehearsal and performance. At the same time, this approach provides an excellent format for emphasizing skills and aesthetics used for performance.

Should dancers supplement their dance training with other forms of physical conditioning? It certainly seems advisable for a dancer to maintain an above average rating for $\dot{V}O_2$max. From the existing data, it would appear that beginning and intermediate student dancers could benefit from additional aerobic training. However, advanced and professional dancers seem to have $\dot{V}O_2$max values that are above average and adequate for a reasonable level of cardiovascular health. Perhaps this is due to their involvement in rehearsals and performances.

When an individual is approaching full-time involvement with dance, there is a further concern: overwork. Overwork can result in a feeling of unrelieved fatigue and a sense that, "I just don't have enough energy to run this piece one more time." Even after a good night's sleep, these symptoms persist. In such an instance, the commitment and devotion to dance are probably excessive, and even dance activities need to be monitored and regulated. One of the disturbing consequences of overwork is that it predisposes the individual to injury resulting from loss of muscle control.

In conclusion, the traditional approaches to ballet and modern dance classes and rehearsals seem to provide appropriate and adequate preparation for the demands of performance. Technique classes provide the necessary foundation of aesthetics apprehension and skills acquisition whereas rehearsals provide the specific physiological stresses needed to stimulate necessary adaptations to given performance demands. However, it is likely that, if more scientific information on the effects of dance training were available, training methodologies could be enhanced. Possible benefits include injury prevention and optimal physiological gains from minimal work. Ideally, scientific investigation of dance could contribute to the furtherance and betterment of training methodologies for dance as an art form.

References

Astrand, P.O., & Rodahl, K. (1977). *Textbook of work physiology*. New York: McGraw-Hill.

Chatfield, S.J. (1984). *Selected aesthetic and physiologic changes associated with fourteen weeks of intermediate dance training*. Unpublished master's thesis, University of Colorado, Boulder.

Cohen, J.L., Gupta, P.K., Lichistein, E., & Chadda, K.D. (1980). The heart of a dancer: Noninvasive cardiac evaluation of professional ballet dancers. *American Journal of Cardiology*, **45**, 959–965.

Cohen, J.L., & Segal, K.R.. (1985). Left ventricular hypertrophy in athletes: An exercise echocardiography study. *Medicine and Science in Sport and Exercise*, **17**, 695–700.

Cohen, J.L., Segal, K.R., & McArdle, W.D. (1982). Heart rate response to ballet stage performance. *The Physician and Sportsmedicine*, **10**, 120–133.

Cohen, J.L., Segal, K.R., Witriol, I., & McArdle, W.D. (1982). Cardiorespiratory responses to ballet exercise and the VO_2max of elite ballet dancers. *Medicine and Science in Sports and Exercise*, **14**, 212–217.

DeGuzman, J.A. (1979a). Dance as a contributor to cardiovascular fitness and alteration of body composition. *Journal of Physical Education and Recreation*, **50**, 88–91.

DeGuzman, J.A. (1979b). *The effects of a semester of modern dance on the cardiovascular fitness and body composition of college women*. Unpublished doctoral dissertation, Teachers College, Columbia University, New York.

Ehsani, A.A., Hagberg, J.M., & Hickson, R.C. (1978). Rapid changes in left ventricular dimensions and mass in response to physical conditioning and deconditioning. *The American Journal of Cardiology, 42,* 52-56.

Fox, E.L., & Mathews, D.K. (1974). *Interval training.* Philadelphia: W.B. Saunders.

Hayes, J. (1979). Back to the basics in physical education and dance. *Journal of Physical Education and Recreation, 50,* 33-35.

Heath, G.W., Love, M.A., Baker, M., Perry, W.C., Owens, G.W., & Muse, S.A. (1982). Cardiovascular function in ballet dancers. *Medicine and Science in Sports and Exercise, 14,* 149.

Kirkendall, D.T., & Calabrese, L.H. (1983). Physiological aspects of dance. *Clinics in Sports Medicine, 2,* 525-537.

Longhurst, J.C., Kelly, A.R., Gonyea, W.J., & Mitchell, J.H. (1980a). Cardiovascular responses to static exercise in distance runners and weight lifters. *Journal of Applied Physiology, 49,* 676-683.

Longhurst, J.C., Kelly, A.R., Gonyea, W.J., & Mitchell, J.H. (1980b). Echocardiographic left ventricular masses in distance runners and weight lifters. *Journal of Applied Physiology, 48,* 154-162.

Mathews, D.K., & Fox, E.L. (1976). *The physiological basis of physical education and athletics* (2nd ed.). Philadelphia: W.B. Saunders.

McArdle, W.D., Katch, F.I., & Katch, V.L. (1981). *Exercise physiology: Energy, nutrition, & human performance.* Philadelphia: Lea & Febiger.

Morganroth, J., Naron, B.J., Henry, W.L., & Epstein, S.E. (1975). Comparative left ventricular dimensions in trained athletes. *Annals of Internal Medicine, 82,* 521-524.

Nicholas, J.A. (1975). Risk factors, sports medicine and the orthopedic system: An overview. *Journal of Sports Medicine, 3,* 243-259.

Novak, L.P., Magill, O., & Schutte, J.E. (1978). Maximal oxygen uptake and body composition of female dancers. *European Journal of Applied Physiology, 39,* 77-282.

Rimmer, J.H., & Rosenswieg, J. (1981-82). The maximum O_2 consumption dance majors. *Dance Research Journal, 14,* 29-31.

Saltin, B., & Astrand, P.O. (1967). Maximum oxygen uptake in athletes. *Journal of Applied Physiology, 23,* 353-358.

Schantz, P.G., & Astrand, P.O. (1984). Physiological characteristics of classical ballet. *Medicine and Science in Sports and Exercise, 16,* 472-476.

Schneider, H.L., King, A.Y., Bronson, J.L., & Miller, E.H. (1974). Stress injuries and developmental change of lower extremities in ballet dancers. *Diagnostic Radiology, 113,* 627-632.

Selliger, V., Glucksmann, J., Paehlopnik, J., & Pachlopnikova, I. (1970). Evaluation of state artist's activities on the basis of telemetrical measurements of heart rates. *Internationale Zeitschrift für Angewandte Physiologie Einschliesslich Arbeitsphysiologie,* **28**, 86–104.

Sweigard, L.E. (1974). *Human movement potential: Its ideokinetic facilitation.* New York: Dodd, Mead, & Co.

Washington, E.L. (1978). Musculoskeletal injuries in theatrical dancers: Site, frequency, and severity. *American Journal of Sports Medicine,* **6**, 75–98.

Chapter 7

Body Composition Characteristics of Female Ballet Dancers

Patty Freedson
University of Massachusetts

The recent development of a new scientific discipline in exercise science called kinanthropometry has been defined as "the application of measurement to the study of human size, shape, proportion, composition, maturation and gross function" (Ross, Drinkwater, Bailey, Marshall, & Leahy, 1980, p.3). This field has relevance to assist in describing optimum physique, structure, and composition characteristics of the classical female ballet dancer. That is, one of the purposes of this newly emerging discipline is to improve understanding of human performance via precise quantification of body morphology, shape, size, composition, and proportion. From a subjective, visual-appraisal perspective, the ideal physique characteristics for the classical female ballet dancer may include such descriptions as tall, lean, and very thin. Over the last several years a few studies have appeared in the literature that have begun to quantify some of the physical attributes of ballet dancers (Calabrese et al., 1983; Clarkson, Freedson, Keller, Carney, & Skrinar, 1985; Cohen, Potosnak, Frank, & Baker, 1985; Dolgener, Spasoff, & St. John, 1980; Frisch, Wyshak, & Vincent, 1980; Novak, Magill, & Schutte, 1978). To be successful in classical ballet performance, it seems that the female must conform to specific morphological standards.

Because body form and physique are of utmost importance to classical ballet dancers, this review will first describe some of the techniques that are traditionally used to quantify body composition, form, and structure. The second part will focus on reviewing studies from the scientific literature that describe selected body composition characteristics of the female classical ballet dancer. For comparative purposes, this information will be presented in conjunction with body composition characteristics of other female athletes.

Methods for Body Composition Analysis and Anthropometric Evaluations

Scientists use many techniques today to measure body composition and to evaluate physique. Techniques that assess body composition are generally noninvasive and provide an estimate of an individual's amount of body fat and lean body mass. Underwater weighing and skinfold measurements are examples of body composition analysis techniques. Other techniques that involve physical measurements of the body can be used to describe an individual's physique. An example of such a technique is the somatogram analysis. These techniques will be described in the following sections.

Underwater Weighing

In 1942, Albert Behnke (Behnke & Wilmore, 1974) described the composition of the body as a two-component system that is comprised of a fat component and a lean component. Using this two component model, it is possible to *estimate* the relative proportion of fat and lean weight of the body using a procedure called underwater weighing where a person completely submerges underwater and the weight of the individual is obtained. Underwater weighing is the most common method employed today to estimate body fat and lean body weight. However, it is an indirect procedure that requires the use of constants. These constants assume that density or mass per unit volume of fat tissue is .9007 gm/cc and the density of the lean tissue is 1.10 gm/cc (Sady & Freedson, 1984). Although it is well known that the density of lean tissue is affected by such factors as hydration state, age, sex, physical activity level, bone density, and health status, the estimation of body fat from underwater weighing does not account for these variations. Thus the technique of underwater weighing assumes that fat tissue and lean tissue densities are the same for all individuals. Nevertheless, it remains as the procedure most often used for evaluating body composition of ballet dancers as well as other athletes.

There are three basic formulas that are used to estimate body fat from underwater weighing. The first formula determines an individual's total body volume which is the actual parameter being measured during the underwater weighing:

$$(1) \quad \text{Body Volume} =$$

$$\frac{(\text{Body Weight in Air} - \text{Body Weight in Water}) - (\text{Residual Volume})}{\text{Water Density Correction Factor}}$$

Body weight in air is simply one's body weight obtained on a scale (in kilograms where lbs/2.205 = kg). Body weight in water (in kg) is obtained by weighing a person who is completely submerged underwater and has maximally expired as much air from the lungs as possible. The scale for the underwater weighing is suspended out of the water above the person being weighed. It is recommended that at least 7–10 trials of the underwater weight be obtained because there is a learning effect that takes place over trials with improvement in the underwater weighing measurement occurring as the individual becomes more familiar with the procedure (Katch, Michael, & Horvath, 1967). The residual volume, which is the volume of air remaining in the lungs following a maximal expiration, can be measured out of the water or in the water during the underwater weighing using sophisticated techniques. Residual volume can also be estimated from vital capacity or various other equations that consider gender, height, and age (Goldman & Becklake, 1959). The water density correction factor is obtained from a standard table (Weast, 1969) and is strictly dependent on the temperature of the water.

The second formula is the standard formula for density of an object; in this case, the density of the human body:

$$(2) \quad \text{Body density} \atop \text{gm/cc} = \left(\frac{\text{Body weight (kg)}}{\text{Body volume (1)}}\right) \times 1000$$

The third formula is one used to estimate body fat from body density and, as discussed earlier, assumes no individual differences in the density of the fat and lean components of the body. This formula was derived by Siri (1956):

$$(3a) \quad \text{Percent body fat} = \frac{495}{\text{Body density (gm/cc)}} - 450$$

Another equation that can be used to estimate percent fat from body density is the Brozek formula (Brozek, Grande, Anderson, & Keys, 1963):

(3b)   Percent body fat $= \dfrac{4.57}{\text{Body density}} - 4.142 \times 100$

These equations give similar percent fat values and correlate very highly with one another. The equation that is most frequently used in body composition research presently is the Siri formula. Fat weight and lean weight can be calculated as follows:

Fat weight = Body weight × Percent body fat

Lean body weight = Body weight − Fat weight

The detailed explanation of underwater weighing methodology is presented so that the reader understands the limitations associated with the technique. This information allows the reader not only to be informed about the topic but also to become educated about issues so that the information learned is more meaningful.

Skinfold Assessment

Other indirect methods that have been used to measure percent fat include potassium 40, total body water, arm x-ray, bioelectrical impedance, ultrasound, and computed tomography. The most popular field estimate of body composition is the skinfold assessment in which skinfold measurements (regional subcutaneous fatfold thicknesses) are obtained from selected standard sites on the body (see Appendix for a summary of the types of skinfold calipers available and where they can be purchased). These measurements are subsequently used in a multiple regression equation to estimate percent fat. Table 7.1 presents selected skinfold prediction equations from the literature for both females and males. Also included in Table 7.1 are the correlations obtained when comparing underwater weighing estimates of percent fat, the criterion measure, with the skinfold estimate of percent fat.

The landmarks defining the specific sites for obtaining the skinfold measurement must be standardized in order to minimize errors. Moreover, careful attention is required in the techniques employed in the skinfold measurements. Pollock, Wilmore, and Fox (1984) give an excellent and thorough description of these measurement considerations.

Table 7.1   Skinfold Prediction Equations for Estimation of Body Density

STUDY	SEX	AGE RANGE	EQUATION	r	SE
Pollock et al. (1984)	F	18–55	D_b = 1.0994921 − .0009929 (Σ 3SF) + .0000023 (Σ 3SF)^2 − .0001392 (Age in years)	.84	.009
Pollock et al. (1984)	M	18–61	D_b = 1.1093800 − .0008267 (Σ 3SF) + .0000016 (Σ 3SF)^2 − .0002574 (Age in years)	.91	.008
Thorland et al. (1984)	F	11–19	D_b = 1.0987 − .00122 (Σ 3SF) + .00000263 (Σ 3SF)^2	.82	.006
Thorland et al. (1984)	M	14–19	D_b = 1.1136 − .00154 (Σ 3SF) + .00000516 (Σ 3SF)^2	.81	.006

Pollock et al. (1984) skinfold sites
  females: Σ 3SF = triceps, suprailiac, thigh
  males: Σ 3SF = chest, abdomen, thigh

Thorland et al. (1984) skinfold sites
  females: Σ 3SF = triceps, subscapula, suprailiac
  males: Σ 3SF = triceps, subscapula, midaxilla

D_b = body density

The following example will clarify how to use Table 7.1:

Subject: 25-year-old female ballet dancer
  1. Triceps skinfold = 15 mm
     Suprailiac skinfold = 17 mm
     Thigh skinfold = 10 mm
  2. Sum of 3 skinfolds = 15 mm + 17 mm + 10 mm = 42 mm
  3. Estimate body density using Equation 1 in Table 7.1
     Body density = 1.0994921 − .0009929 × (42) +
                 .0000023 × (42)^2 − .0001392 (25 years) =
                 1.0994921 − .0417018 + .0040572 − .00348
                 = 1.0583

$$\% \text{ Fat} = \frac{495}{\text{Body Density}} - 450 \qquad \text{(Formula 3a)}$$

$$= \frac{495}{1.0583} - 450 = 17.7\%$$

It should be noted that the adult equations (Pollock et al., 1984) presented in Table 7.1 were not derived from an athletic population. For example, the average percent fat values were 24.1% and 17.7% for the females and males, respectively. On the other hand, the Thorland, Johnson, Tharp, Haush, and Cisar (1984) equations were derived from samples of national caliber adolescent athletes (track and field, gymnastics, diving, and wrestling) and are probably applicable to the adolescent ballet dancer. Pollock et al. (1984) argue that the adult equations are valid for the general population and can even be applied confidently to extremes of a population (e.g., low body fat groups such as ballet dancers) because the quadratic function more accurately models the curvilinear association between body density and the sum of skinfolds at both low and high body fat levels.

Somatogram

Body shape and body segment proportionality are also important body composition parameters that can be used to characterize the ballet dancer's physique. The somatogram, developed by Behnke (Behnke & Wilmore, 1974), uses regional segment circumferences and height to compare the shape of an individual to that of a reference individual. The method requires the use of reference K constants for each body circumference that were derived from a reference population. It should be noted that the K constants employed by Behnke are from his definition of the reference individual. Specifically, the reference woman defined by Behnke is 27% fat and weighs approximately 57 kg (126 lbs). Of course, the reference female ballet dancer is less fat and weighs less than the average reference woman. Thus, in order for the somatogram analysis to be validly applied to the ballet dancer, constants specific to this population need to be used. A recent study by Clarkson et al. (1985) presents a somatogram analysis that used K constants generated from a group of 83 highly trained adolescent female ballet dancers. The somatogram for 14 other highly trained adolescent ballet dancers that used the ballet dancer K constant revealed that symmetry and body segment proportions were closer to the '0' line ($\pm$ 4%) than the somatogram that used Behnke's reference (adult) female K constants (see Figure 7.1). Table 7.2 presents Behnke's reference female K constants (Behnke & Wilmore, 1974) and the K constants generated from the adolescent ballet dancer (Clarkson et al., 1985).

To generate a somatogram, obtain the circumference (c_i) measurements (in cm) given in Table 7.2. Extremity circumferences are the average of the right and left sides of the body. Each circumference (c_i) is divided by its respective K constant ($c_i/K = d_i$). Sum the individual circumference measurements and divide by 100 ($\Sigma\ 11\ c_i/100 = D$). The percentage deviation of each d_i from D is integrated into a pattern, the somatogram, which is a quantitative representation of body shape:

$$\frac{d_i - D}{D} \times 100 = \% \text{ deviation}$$

The following example represents the calculations performed to obtain the shoulder deviation in Figure 7.1 (solid line):

a) Shoulder circumference = 96.6 cm = c_i

b) Shoulder K constant from ballet reference = 17.99 = K

c) c_i/K = 96.6/17.99 = 5.37 = d_i

d) Sum of eleven circumferences/100 = 5.16 = Σ 11 $c_i/100$ = D

e) % deviation = $\dfrac{5.37 - 5.16}{5.16} \times 100 = 4.1\%$

The specific landmarks for the circumference measurements are described in detail in Pollock et al. (1984).

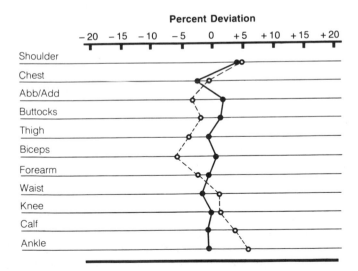

Figure 7.1 Somatograms of adolescent using reference woman (dashed line) and adolescent (solid line) K constants. From "Maximal Oxygen Uptake, Nutritional Patterns and Body Composition of Adolescent Female Ballet Dancers" by P.M. Clarkson et al., 1985, *Research Quarterly for Exercise and Sport, 56*, p. 182. Reprinted by permission.

Table 7.2 Somatogram K constants for the reference female and the elite adolescent female ballet dancer

Circumference	$K_{reference}$	K_{ballet}
Shoulder	17.51	17.99
Chest	14.85	15.34
Abdomen	12.90	12.24
Buttocks	16.93	16.56
Thigh	10.03	9.70
Biceps	4.80	4.47
Forearm	4.15	4.11
Wrist	2.73	2.79
Knee	6.27	6.35
Calf	6.13	6.47
Ankle	3.70	3.97

The somatograms from Calabrese et al. (1983) and Dolgener et al. (1980) obtained from professional dancers are quite similar to the somatograms from Clarkson et al. (1985) obtained from elite adolescent dancers. These data suggest that there are specific body segment girth proportions that define an ideal body type for the female classical ballet dancer.

The value of the somatogram technique for assessment of body physique is that it provides the dancer with a quantitative method to evaluate specific body segments in relation to each other. Moreover, if the K constants employed have been derived from the ideal ballet dancer's physique, it will provide a standard which an aspiring dancer can use for comparative purposes. The method may be used for all types of athletes and can be employed to quantify body segment proportionality and physique. Thus measurable standards may then be applied to define ideal form for selected athletes. For example, it may be possible to identify specific form characteristics that discriminate the adolescent gymnast and ballet dancer quantitatively rather than simple visual appraisal differentiation (see Figure 7.2). It should be noted, however, that more data obtained from the elite athlete are necessary prior to defining this optimal standard.

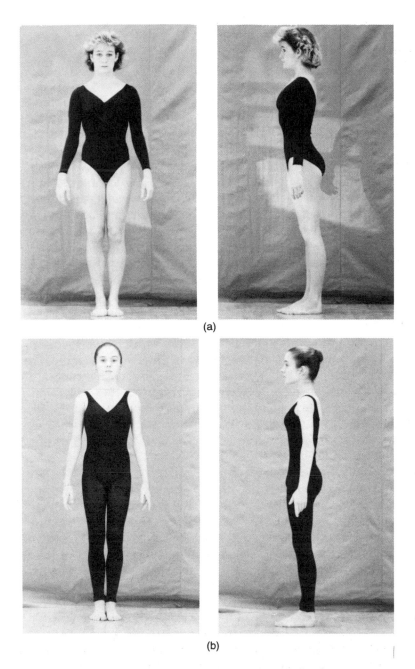

Figure 7.2 (a) 17-year-old Class 1 gymnast (b) 15-year-old ballet dancer.

Body Composition Characteristics of Female Ballet Dancers

Recognizing the importance of body composition in complementing the skill and technical artistry associated with classical ballet has led researchers to characterize the body composition characteristics of classical female ballet dancers. The earliest investigation by Frisch and colleagues (1980) used height and weight to estimate total body water. The estimated total body water was expressed as a percent of body weight employed as a measure of relative body fat. The results of their investigation revealed that for ballet dancers, their height, average body weight, and total body water as a percent of body weight were well below the norm. Using height and weight to estimate body fat has received widespread criticism because it has been shown to grossly overestimate percent fat for low body fat populations such as ballet dancers. Moreover, the basis for their research was to identify factors associated with the high incidence of delayed menarche and amenorrhea seen in these dancers rather than to profile body composition characteristics.

Table 7.3 presents a summary from the research literature of percent body fat and lean body weight estimates (underwater weighing) of various levels of classical ballet dancers. As can be seen, percent fat ranges from 16.4% (high-level adolescent dancers) to 22.1% (professional and college modern dance majors). Even though 2 of the 4 studies reported a mean body fat percentage of greater than 20%, these data were from college dancers rather than professionals. Thus it can be concluded that % fat for the female ballet dancer is lower than what is typically seen for the average female.

To date only one study has evaluated body composition characteristics of male classical ballet dancers. Using the sum of three skinfolds to estimate percent fat (Pollock et al., 1984) (male adult equation in Table 7.1), Cohen et al. (1985) reported a mean percent fat of 7.8% for 10 professional male ballet dancers. Using the adult female skinfold prediction equation presented in Table 7.1 (Pollock et al., 1984), the mean percent fat for the 12 female dancers was 12.9% which is 3–4 percentage units lower than what was reported by Calabrese et al. (1983) and Dolgener et al. (1980).

It is not possible, however, to recommend the optimal body composition profile for three primary reasons: (a) There is a limited amount of data; (b) of the data available, the subject population is from several age groups and represents a wide range of abilities; and (c) the optimal composition should reflect a balance between performance and health. Nevertheless, Katch and McArdle (1983) recommend that, in general, 12% fat represents the lower limit for women to maintain health.

For practical purposes, a simple procedure that can be employed to define desirable weight that requires an estimate of body fat (e.g., underwater weighing or skinfold assessment) is described by Katch and McArdle (1983). The desirable weight for an individual is calculated as follows:

a) desirable body weight $= \dfrac{\text{lean body weight}}{1.0 - \% \text{ fat desired}}$

For example, a 130 lb ballet dancer who is 25% fat wants to know how much weight she needs to lose to be 15% fat.

b) fat weight $= 130 \text{ lb} \times .25 = 32.5 \text{ lb}$

c) lean body weight $= 130 \text{ lb} - 32.5 \text{ lb} = 97.5 \text{ lb}$

d) desirable body weight $= \dfrac{97.5 \text{ lb}}{1.0 - .15}$

$$= \dfrac{97.5}{.85}$$

$$= 114.7$$

e) desirable weight loss $= 130 \text{ lb} - 114.7 \text{ lb}$
$$= 15.3 \text{ lb}$$

Thus recommended weight loss range for this individual to attain 15% body fat should be 13–17 lbs.

It is of utmost importance that the so-called ideal physique for the classical ballet dancer not only should consider maximizing thinness to complete the necessary visual aesthetic qualities but must also be related to maintenance of health and well being. If a parent, dance teacher, or choreographer suspects excessive thinness or fatness, it is recommended that body fat level be assessed so that appropriate recommendations can be made. Most universities and colleges that have exercise physiology, physical education, and/or nutrition departments have the facilities and expertise to measure body fat.

Table 7.3 Underwater Weighing Estimates of Percent Body Fat and Lean Body Weight of Female Classical Ballet Dancers

STUDY	QUALITY OF DANCER	N	AGE (years)	HEIGHT (cm)	WEIGHT (kg)	RELATIVE FAT (%)	LEAN BODY WEIGHT (kg)
Novak et al. (1978)[1]	college undergrad and grads	12	21.2	162.7	51.2	20.5	40.7
Dolgener et al. (1980)[2]	professional or university dance majors	19	22.7	164.1	51.1	22.1	40.0
Calabrese et al. (1983)[1]	professionals	20	21.9	168.0	54.5	16.9	45.3
Clarkson et al. (1985)[2]	elite adolescent	14	15.0	161.1	48.4	16.4	40.4

[1]Percent fat = $\left(\dfrac{4.57}{\text{Body Density}} - 4.142 \right) * 100$ (2)

[2]Percent fat = $\dfrac{495}{\text{Body Density}} - 450$ (15)

Table 7.4 Percent Fat of Selected Female Athletes

Athletic Group	Reference	Age (years)	Height (cm)	Weight (kg)	Percent Fat	Lean Body Weight (kg)
Divers	18	21.1	160.4	52.3	11.5	46.3
Gymnastics	18	22.7	157.0	52.0	14.7	44.4
Distance Running	18	32.4	169.4	57.2	15.2	48.5
Cross-Country Skiing	18	20.2	163.4	55.9	15.7	47.1
Ballet Dancers	3	21.9	168.0	54.5	16.9	45.3

Comparison With Other Female Athletes

Table 7.4 presents average body composition characteristics (underwater weighing) for selected elite female athletic groups that are probably most similar in overall physique to ballet dancers. For comparative purposes, the adult ballet dancer data of Calabrese et al. (1983) are also included. The range of % fat is from 11.5% for divers to 16.9% for the ballet dancers. Lean body weight ranges from 44.4 kg (gymnasts) to 48.5 kg (distance runners).

The National Center for Health Statistics 50th percentile norms for height and weight for 18- to 24-year-old women are 163.0 cm and 58.0 kg. Using these data as a frame of reference, the professional ballet dancer is 5.0 cm taller and 3.5 kg lighter than the average American woman (18–24 years). This is not surprising if one considers the thin, lean, and linear characteristics typically associated with the successful elite female ballet dancer.

Summary

The physical fitness components that relate to optimal ballet performance have only recently been studied. In addition to cardiorespiratory, metabolic, and flexibility considerations, body composition and anthropometric factors also play an important role in ballet performance. Body type often times is the ultimate determinant of success. Even though relatively high rates of injury and abnormal menstrual cycles may be associated with the female ballet dancer's extreme body composition characteristics, it remains the ideal to meet the perfect aesthetic qualities of a sylphlike body. A female dancer may have superb skill and technique but will probably only reach the apex of success if she conforms to a very specific body type and physique.

References

Behnke, A.R., & Wilmore, J.H. (1974). *Evaluation and regulation of body build and composition.* Englewood Cliffs, NJ: Prentice-Hall.

Brozek, J., Grande, F., Anderson, T., & Keys, A. (1963). Densitometric analysis of body composition: Revision of some quantitative assumptions. *Annals of the New York Academy of Science,* **110**, 113–140.

Calabrese, L.H., Kirkendall, D.T., Floyd, M., Rapoport, M.S., Williams, G.W., Weiker, G.G., & Bergfeld, J.A. (1983). Menstrual abnormalities, nutritional patterns, and body composition in female classical ballet dancers. *The Physician and Sportsmedicine,* **11,** 86–98.

Clarkson, P.M., Freedson, P.S., Keller, B., Carney, D., & Skrinar, M. (1985). Maximal oxygen uptake, nutritional patterns and body composition of adolescent female ballet dancers. *Research Quarterly for Exercise and Sport,* **56,** 180–184.

Cohen, J.L., Potosnak, L., Frank, O., & Baker, H. (1985). A nutritional and hematologic assessment of elite ballet dancers. *The Physician and Sportsmedicine,* **13,** 43–54.

Dolgener, F.A., Spasoff, T.C., & St. John, W.E. (1980). Body build and body composition of high ability female dancers. *Research Quarterly for Exercise and Sport,* **51,** 599–607.

Frisch, R.E., Wyshak, G., & Vincent, L. (1980). Delayed menarche and amenorrhea in ballet dancers. *New England Journal of Medicine,* **303,** 17–19.

Goldman, H.I., & Becklake, M.R. (1959). Respiratory function tests: Normal values of medium altitudes and the prediction of normal results. *American Review of Tuberculosis & Respiratory Disease,* **79,** 457–467.

Katch, F.I., & McArdle, W.D. (1983). *Nutrition, weight control and exercise* (2nd ed.). Philadelphia: Lea & Febiger.

Katch, F.I., Michael, E., & Horvath, S. (1967). Estimation of body volume by underwater weighing: Description of a simple method. *Journal of Applied Physiology,* **23,** 811–814.

Novak, L.P., Magill, L.A., & Schutte, J.E. (1978). Maximal oxygen uptake and body composition of female dancers. *European Journal of Applied Physiology,* **39,** 277–282.

Pollock, M.L., Wilmore, J.H., & Fox, S.M. (1984). *Exercise in health and disease.* Philadelphia: W.B. Saunders.

Ross, W.D., Drinkwater, D.T., Bailey, D.A., Marshall, G.W., & Leahy, R.M. (1980). Kinanthropometry: Traditions and new perspectives. In M. Ostyn, G. Beunen, & J. Simons (Eds.), *Kinanthropometry II* (pp. 3–27). Baltimore: University Park.

Sady, S.P., & Freedson, P.S. (1984). Body composition and structural comparisons of female and male athletes. *Clinics in Sports Medicine,* **3,** 755–777.

Siri, W.E. (1956). Gross composition of the body. In J.H. Lawrence & C.A. Tabias (Eds.), *Advances in biological and medical physics* (Vol. IV, pp. 239–280). New York: Academic.

Thorland, W.G., Johnson, G.O., Tharp, G.D., Haush, T.J., & Cisar, C.J. (1984). Estimation of body density in adolescent athletes. *Human Biology,* **56,** 439–448.

Weast, R.C. (Ed.). (1969). *Handbook of chemistry and physics* (50th ed.). Cleveland: The Chemical Rubber Company.

Wells, C.L. (1985). *Women, sport and performance: A physiological perspective.* Champaign, IL: Human Kinetics.

Appendix

Skinfold Calipers	Source
1. Lange	Cambridge Scientific Industries 68 Dysiar Street Cambridge, MD
2. Harpenden	Quinton Instruments 3051 44th W. Avenue Seattle, WA 98199
3. Lafayette	Lafayette Instrument Co. P.O. Box 5729 Lafayette, IN 47903
4. Slim Guide	Creative Health Products 5248 Saddle Ridge Road Plymouth, MI 48170
5. Fat-O-Meter	Health and Education Services 80 Fairbank Street Unit 12 Addison, IL 60101
6. Adipometer	Ross Laboratories 625 Cleveland Avenue Columbus, OH 43216

Chapter 8

Biomechanics of Dance

Donald Ranney
University of Waterloo

Dance is an art form whose purpose is to communicate ideas and feelings; but because it is a type of body movement, that movement can be studied in the same way as any body movement, using the principles and techniques of biomechanics. This biomechanical analysis is often misunderstood by those dancers who think that it somehow reduces the art of dancing to a mechanical act: This is not so. The biomechanical analysis looks at only *one aspect* of dance, in the same way that an X ray of a broken leg gives information only about the bones and not about the leg as a whole. There is far more to dance than the physical movement. Ultimately dance must be perceived from the heart. The tools of science are inadequate to measure that perception.

Before examining biomechanical studies of dance movement, it is helpful to consider what biomechanics is, the language it uses, the principles on which it is based, and the tools used in biomechanical analyses. In the early days, many valuable inferences were made about dance through the study of similar movements in other athletes. Although recently a few studies have concerned dancers specifically, much more research is needed if this kind of analysis is to be used in injury prevention.

Kinesiology and Biomechanics

Kinesiology, the science of human movement, began in the 4th century B.C. with the astute observations of Aristotle. He applied geometrical principles in his study of movements such as walking, running, and jumping. Five centuries later, Galen, the "Father of Anatomy," not only studied the muscles producing movement but even suggested the importance of neural activity in muscle contraction. He treated the gladiators and is credited with being the first team physician (Morehouse & Rasch, 1963).

The Dark Ages brought a halt to all scientific progress, but a new age dawned with the birth of Leonardo da Vinci in 1452. His interest in the structure and function of the human body is well-known (O'Malley & Saunders, 1952; Seireg, 1969). A century later Galileo sought to understand movement through mathematics. His pupil Borelli considered the body divisible into segments, with each segment having a center of gravity. He stated that the bones act as levers; then, by considering the size of the forces acting upon these segments and the length of the lever arms, it became possible to develop the kinds of equations that are so useful today in kinetic analysis of complex movements. He has been called by Steindler the "Father of Biomechanics" (1935).

Biomechanics is defined in *Webster's New World Dictionary* as "the application of the principles and techniques of mechanics to the structure, functions, and capabilities of living organisms." It generally involves the collection of numerical data (quantitative analysis) and their manipulation through mathematical formulas as envisaged by Borelli. *Kinesiology* is a broader term, defined by Webster as "the science or study of human muscular movement." Kinesiology, then, does not restrict itself to the interpretation of mathematical data in the light of biomechanical laws. There is not complete agreement on this distinction, but most authorities conducting research in the field would agree with Webster. Contini and Drillis (1966) have defined biomechanics even more clearly as "the science which investigates the effect of internal and external forces on human and animal bodies in movement and rest" (p. 162).

In the 17th century, Isaac Newton formulated three natural laws regarding inertia, momentum, and interaction of forces which formed the initial principles of biomechanics (Cajori, 1946). A clear statement of these and other biomechanical principles as applied to dance appears in this chapter. Following this, some of the commonly used techniques of data collection, which were only possible in the last century, will be examined. For an interesting and more informative treatment of the history of biomechanics the reader is referred to the first chapter of Rasch and Burke's *Kinesiology and Applied Anatomy* (1978).

The Language of Biomechanics

Every discipline has its own language. Each is valid within its own sphere. Certain definitions in biomechanics are essential to understanding the application of biomechanical analysis to dance. These include *movement, forces, energy, work,* and *power.*

(a)

(b)   (c)

Figure 8.1 (a) Linear movement = translation; (b) Rotation = angular motion; (c) Translational movement followed by angular movement.

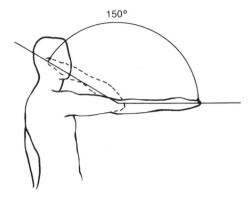

Figure 8.2 Joint motion is angular movement

Movement

Movement may be one of two types: linear or rotational. As a dancer moves across the stage following an imaginary line, whether curved or straight, the body is translated from one place to another. For this reason, linear movement is also called *translational movement* (see Figure 8.1a). If the dancer rotates the body (e.g., in a *pirouette*), this is called *angular movement,* and the angle through which the dancer moves can be expressed in terms of degrees (see Figure 8.1b). In the *grand jeté en tournant* both translational and angular motions occur (see Figure 8.1c). All joint motion is angular; for example, when the flexed elbow extends there is angular motion of about 150° (see Figure 8.2).

Forces

Forces may be external or internal. Gravity is an external force which is proportional to the mass of the body or body part under consideration. An applied load is an external force which may be applied to the body as a whole, as when the dance teacher pushes a reluctant pupil onto the stage, or to the arms and shoulders of the male dancer during the performance of a lift.

Internal forces operate totally within the body and may be active or passive. Active force is generated by muscle when it contracts; energy is necessary to produce an active muscle force. All tissues resist elongation; such resistances in muscle, tendon, skin, and other soft connective tissue provide passive forces resisting movement when muscles contracting (active forces) on the opposite side of a joint are trying to move it (see Figure 8.3). Slow (static) stretching makes muscles longer and more easily stretched (i.e., the passive force is reduced). This makes it easier to perform the movement without fatigue and reduces the risk of tearing these muscles when they are quickly stretched during very rapid movements. A passive force absorbs energy that is transferred to it by the active force which is trying to move the joint. Because all tissues have some elasticity, they store up this energy like a spring that is stretched.

Energy, Work, and Power

The capacity to do work is called *energy*. It is necessary to produce an active muscle force. Energy is best generated by muscles that have been well prepared through strength training, endurance training, and good nutrition. *Work* is force acting through a distance. This is easy to appreciate in translational movement, but it is just as real in angular movement, where the distance the body or body part moves is measured in degrees of rotation. *Power* is the rate of doing work and involves force, distance, and time.

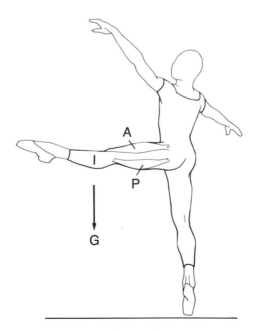

Figure 8.3 Active force (A), in this case the quadriceps muscle, must overcome the passive force (P), where P is the resistance to stretch primarily in the hamstrings. In this illustration, the weight of the limb acted on by gravity (G) also resists the desired movement.

The Principles of Biomechanics

A "principle" is defined by Webster as "a law of conduct." In biomechanics such laws describe the nature of movement and the mathematical relationship between forces and movement. This chapter will consider only those most pertinent to dance.

Leverage

The effectiveness of a force in causing rotation depends on the length of its *moment arm*. A small child sitting at the end of a teeter-totter can balance a larger child sitting closer to the center. The distance from the center of rotation, or pivot point, is called the moment arm. The effectiveness of any force causing angular motion is equal to the size of the force times the length of its moment arm. This product is the *moment of force*. It is sometimes called the *torque*, but biomechanists now tend to reserve the word torque for moments of force when a body rotates through its long axis, as in a *pirouette*.

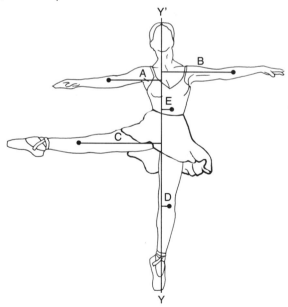

Figure 8.4 Moment of inertia of body parts around the vertical axis YY'. Moment arm lengths are *approximately* as indicated: the distances A and B for the upper limbs, C and D for the lower limbs, and E for the trunk.

Inertia

Things only begin to move when they are pushed. This is a simplification of Newton's first law. This resistance to movement when a force is applied is called *inertia*. Inertia implies an unwillingness to change. Resistance to stopping is also inertia. Because it is harder to move or bring to rest a larger object than a smaller one, inertia varies according to the mass of the object. This is true of both angular and translational movement. Whether lifting a limb or a partner, the greater the mass, the greater the energy required.

Moment of Inertia.   With angular motion, the distribution of the mass must also be considered. Body segments that are closer to the pivot point can be moved more easily. For analytical purposes the body is divided into parts: hand, foot, forearm, thigh, lower leg, and so on; and each part has a mass and a moment arm relating to that mass.

As the dancer spins in a *pirouette*, she rotates about a vertical axis passing through the tip of her toe shoe. For each body segment there is a horizontal distance from the center of its mass to the axis of rotation. Figure 8.4 shows the approximate distance of certain body segments from the axis of rotation in a *fouetté*. Because all parts of her body (except those in the very center) are travelling in a circle, and because the circumference of a circle is related to the square of its radius, the moment of inertia of any part will vary according to not only the mass of that part but also the square of its distance from the center of rotation. There is a complex mathematical formula used in calculating the moment of inertia. What is important to the dancer about the formula is that the moment of inertia for the whole body is the sum of that for all the constituent parts, and that by moving parts toward or away from the center of rotation, the body's moment of inertia can be altered. Because these distances are squared, a small change in the location of body parts can have a great effect on velocity of rotation.

The force required to initiate the spin will need to overcome the inertia of the whole body and all resistance force (e.g., floor friction). Then, there must be enough additional force to impart a significant acceleration. The push-off force also acts through a moment arm. Placing the foot well away from the center of rotation will therefore be more effective than placing the foot closer to it.

Conservation of Momentum

Momentum is the quantity of motion. If there were no resistance, a dancer could spin indefinitely because of the law of conservation of momentum. Momentum is determined (like the moment of inertia) by mass and its distribution around the axis of rotation; but momentum is also related to velocity. The quantity of motion in a rotating body is its speed multiplied by its moment of inertia. Newton's second law states that the speed of rotation times the moment of inertia is constant, unless of course, some force is applied to add or subtract momentum.

This law allows the dancer to alter her rate of spin. Every dancer knows that by moving the arms in toward her body she spins faster and by reaching outward she slows down. By bringing the outstretched arms and legs closer to the body (e.g., moving the arms from second position to first position) the mass of each limb is brought closer to the center of rotation (see Figures 8.5d through 8.5f). Internal manipulation of the body has thus reduced the moment of inertia, so the law of conservation of momentum dictates that velocity must increase. She can do this repeatedly until friction eventually decreases the momentum and she slows down permanently.

Reaction

Whenever a force acts, Newton's third law of motion states that there is an equal force acting in the opposite direction. To jump into the air it is necessary to push against the ground (see Figure 8.6). It is only because the *ground reaction force* is strong enough to oppose the thrust of the feet that the dancer can rise in the air. This is why it is so difficult to jump or even stand on thin ice. The ground reaction force is an example of an external reaction force.

Reaction forces also occur inside the body (internal reaction forces). When a muscle contracts, unless it is pulling at right angles to the bone, some of the force travels along the bone and across one or more joints (see Figure 8.7). The underlying bone resists compression, and the result is an internal reaction. Between these two equal and opposite forces the cartilage lining the joint is compressed by what are called bone-on-bone forces. This compression is necessary for its nutrition. The cartilage acts like a sponge; intermittent compression allows it to soak up joint fluid which brings it nutrients as well as making it more slippery. Excessive or prolonged compression, however, can also damage the cartilage. Too many jumps can be expected to make the feet sore and eventually produce arthritic changes.

Figure 8.5 In this *fouetté*, dancer varies her speed by varying the moment arm lengths for the masses of her upper limbs and right leg.

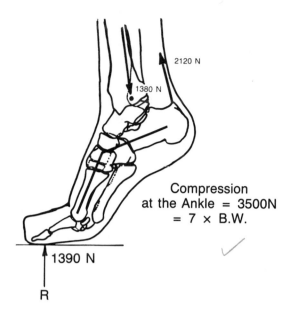

2120 N

1380 N

Compression
at the Ankle = 3500N
= 7 × B.W.

1390 N

R

Figure 8.6 The ground reaction force is represented by R.

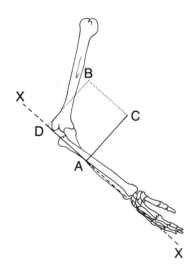

Figure 8.7 Joint reaction force. When the biceps contract along the line AB there is movement along the line AC and compression force across the elbow joint along the line AD. The internal reaction force resisting the force along the line AD is of the same magnitude and in the opposite direction: D to A.

Optimization

Optimization is one of the objectives of biomechanics. It is determining the most efficient and effective way to complete a physical act: how to kick higher, how to turn in the air more times, how to appear motionless in space. While dance is far more than technique, good technique is the foundation on which we build the aesthetic. According to Hays (1981): "Biomechanically efficient movement is beautiful movement and is the only viable approach to teaching dance in the schools today" (p. 35). This attitude has been growing among dance educators in the eighties.

The Tools and Techniques of Biomechanics

Scientific analysis may require information concerning several or all of the following, depending on the complexity of the analysis (Grieve, Miller, Mitchelson, Smith, & Smith, 1975):

- *Movement:* type of movement, direction, body parts involved, speed of movement, and changes in any of these
- *Muscles acting:* which ones, when they act, how strongly they act, whether they are lengthening or shortening, and what changes occur in moment arm length
- *Forces generated* by such activity: their magnitude, direction, timing, and duration

Cinematography

Cinematography allows the movement to be recorded for later analysis. The relevant body segments are first marked as illustrated in Figure 8.8. Usually a high-speed, 16 mm movie camera is employed to record the movement of these segments. As 25-frames-per-second is fast enough for analysis of walking (Winter, 1982), a speed of 100-frames-per-second is more than adequate for running and jumping activities (D.A. Winter, personal communication, 1984). The position of the body segment markers in selected frames is noted, and the information is input into a computer which has been programmed to analyze the motion.

The frame-by-frame analysis is very time-consuming, and, although automatic input to the computer is much faster, it requires a much more expensive infrared-sensitive camera in conjunction with heat reflective markers. Alternatively, simple measurements of joint angles may be made by using strips of flourescent tape placed along the axis of body parts and taking pictures while the dancer is illuminated with stroboscopic lighting (Merriman, 1975). Electrogoniometers may also be useful; these are rods attached to limbs and joined together across a joint (e.g., the knee). Movement of the joint causes electrical signals to be generated, and these flow automatically into the computer. Unfortunately, dancers often find that the apparatus and/or the wires running from them interferes so greatly with performance that the movements studied are no longer natural ones. The equipment used in a particular research project should be determined by the nature of the study and the resources available.

Electromyography

Electromyography records the electrical activity generated by selected muscles. Electrodes placed on the body surface are most often used to detect such activity. The timing of muscle activity is related to the movement by means of a *synchronization pulse* which is simultaneously displayed on the records of movement and muscle activity. The electromyographic (EMG) signal may be calibrated and manipulated electronically to estimate the force output, but this is only a very rough approximation and, in itself, is largely qualitative. Change in muscle length and moment arm is determined with reference to the cinematography and measurements on cadavers.

Force Plates

Force plates are used to determine the exact amount and direction of ground reaction forces. This will be of the same magnitude and in an opposite direction to forces generated by body activity. These data are necessary to quantify the muscle forces. Equipment which directly measures force by attachment to the limbs is not useful because it interferes with dance movement.

Computers

Computers are useful in the analysis of biomechanical data as indicated in the discussion of cinematography. A second possible use is in computer simulation of movement, which has been used in dance notation (Savage & Officer, 1978). To date, nothing has been published on computer simulation of movement in the biomechanical study of dance. This is a fruitful method of research in dance that has yet to be explored.

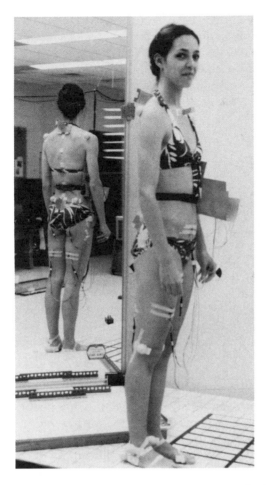

Figure 8.8 Body markers at joints divide the body into segments. Surface electrodes are also shown which record EMG signals and transmit them by means of a radio transmitter fastened to the waist.

Movement Studies in Dance

This survey of the literature reveals that much of the analysis of dance movement reported is not truly biomechanical. Skilled observers have made observations about the nature of movement in the manner of Aristotle and have drawn conclusions about the mechanism of dance movement or the origin of forces. However, the tools of biomechanics have not been employed and analysis in the light of biomechanical principles has not been done (Atwater, 1980; Glassow, 1966; Hays, 1981;

Nichols, 1979; Sweigard, 1974; Todd, 1920a, 1920b, 1973; Wilson, 1977). Such studies are often quite useful. The term *qualitative biomechanics* can be applied to some of these, but the vast majority are more correctly called kinesiological studies, according to the definitions given above. Space does not permit a full treatment of this subject, and anything less would be misleading. In general, the theories such studies have advanced are a fruitful source of ideas for future research of a biomechanical nature.

Inferences From Athletics

The vast majority of biomechanical studies have not concerned dance specifically. This includes most research articles and text materials listed in published dance bibliographies. The word *dance* may appear in an article (Mott, 1977) or a paper may have been presented at a dance conference (Basmajian, 1973); however, these references invariably do not involve actual studies of dance movement. The majority of biomechanical statements made about dance, especially in textbooks, are inferences based on similar movements in athletics. Often, these are not well-referenced, and it is difficult to tell whether the statements are based on scientific analysis or mere speculation. Hinson's book (1977) is a notable exception. Many of her statements are based on her own research experience in dance biomechanics (Hinson, Buckman, Tate, & Sherrill, 1978).

Jensen, Schultz, and Bangerter (1983), using beautiful pictures and Cooper, Adrian, and Glassow (1982) with line drawings, each devote more than a page to discussing the dance leap. But there is no biomechanical explanation of *how* the "illusion of floating" is created. Similarly, Rasch and Burke (1978), after making several references to dance in terms of applied anatomy and sports medicine, almost entirely confine their biomechanical remarks to a picture of dancers of the Ballet Russe de Monte Carlo illustrating the "esthetic appeal of erect posture. . . ." These references tell us little about the actual biomechanics of dance in measurable terms.

Biomechanical Studies in Dance

It was probably Kneeland who first applied the principles and techniques of biomechanics to a study of dance movement (1966). In the late 1950's her film analysis of leading dancers of the Royal Ballet, Bolshoi

Ballet, and New York City Ballet led her to conclude with great surprise that these professionals were often performing "in ways which are different, even contradictory to what is taught in the ballet classroom!" (p 51, May 1966).

Understanding the Movement

Kneeland discussed the movements with physicists and other scientists, applied the principles of biomechanics in the study of dance movement, and after nine years of study began to revolutionize the teaching of dance with her findings. She used just one of the techniques of biomechanics, cinematography, and looked at dance movement in slow motion, applying the laws of Newtonian physics.

Her studies stimulated the growing belief that a better understanding of the human body and of the laws of nature could lead to more graceful and efficient dance movement. In reference to this, Hays (1981) states that, rather than defying those laws, "the most skilled dancer has learned how to work with and to use the laws of nature (physics), whether those ideas were openly introduced into training or an individual dancer intuitively used those laws" (p. 2). But most writers using the word biomechanics were really talking of functional anatomy. It would be another ten years before the laws of physics would again be used in analyzing movement in dance.

Analyzing the Movement

Dance biomechanics took a great leap forward in 1976 when Ryman (1978) did a kinematic analysis of six *grand allegro* jumps at York University. They were performed by one subject, a prima ballerina with the National Ballet of Canada, Vanessa Harwood. The movements studied were *grand jeté en avant, pas de chat jeté, temps levé en avant en arabesque, grand ballonné en avant, grand jeté dessus en tournnant,* and *grand fouetté sauté.* Ryman's three main findings were as follows:

1. The height of the jump is not entirely dependent on the depth of the preceding *plié* as claimed by Karsavina (1962), but rather, is greatest with a moderate *plié* as recommended by Blasis (1944). This is because a very deep prespring crouch causes a mechanical disadvantage at the knee joint which effectively reduces the force of contraction.

2. Suspension during flight is not real but an illusion. The center of gravity rises and falls with respect to the earth in accordance with Newton's laws. It follows a parabolic curve. But the body's center of gravity with respect to the head is lower when the arms are at the side and higher when the arms are raised. So after reaching the height of a jump, if upraised arms are quickly brought down to the sides, the head moves up relative to the center of gravity and thereby creates the illusion that the law of gravity has been defied. As the head has moved up, relative to the center of gravity of the body (which itself is falling), the head and therefore the whole body appears to be suspended in air. Laws, a physicist who also dances, gives an additional reason why the head stays up. Even a ball thrown into the air spends half the time it is in the air within 25% of the peak of its trajectory (1979).

3. Turns are being initiated before the body leaves the ground, not at the height of the jump as is commonly taught. Angular (rotational) momentum created on the push-off is maintained, as stated by the law of conservation of momentum; however, "the velocity (of rotation) . . . may be altered (after leaving the ground) by manipulating the various body segments" (Ryman, 1978, p. 238). This gives the illusion that the turn has just started when in fact it started during push-off. Ryman found that in the *grand jeté en tournant*, for example, the body rotated 90° prior to take-off.

Hinson et al. (1978), in their study of the *tour jeté*, came to similar conclusions, as did Laws (1979a) in his analysis of turns in dance. In two articles Laws (1979a, 1980), elaborated on the rotational mechanics of turns using biomechanical formulas; specifically, (a) the force couple necessary for the initial torque, (b) calculation of angular momentum, and (c) the maintenance of balance in a turn. Law's presentation of this material at the 1979 Dance in Canada Conference (1979b) is expressed more simply and will appeal to the nonphysicist.

Kenneth Laws has expressed the interest of biomechanicians in dance as a "new pas de deux" (Laws, 1979b) with his recent publication of the first-ever book on biomechanics of dance (Laws, 1984). *The Physics of Dance* deals primarily with turns, jumps and partnering. Much of this is based on his own research and experience. The chief advantage of the book lies in the application of the laws of physics to a multitude of dance situations. It is written in language familiar to dancers and presents an approach to dance from the physicist's point of view. This book is already finding a place in university curricula.

The difference between movement in dance and that in athletic performance is worth emphasizing. Gymnasts and divers can and sometimes do initiate turns after leaving the ground. With the athlete's upper limbs outstretched to the side, a continual rotation of the limbs backward will cause the body to rotate forward in a somersault. If the upper limb rotation stops, the forward somersault also stops. But dancers, especially ballet dancers, are aesthetically limited concerning the appearance of the movement and must find more subtle ways to achieve their specific ends. The laws of physics are not broken, but they can be cleverly manipulated to the dancer's advantage.

What Is Learned May Not Be What is Taught

The *grand battement devant* was studied by Ryman and Ranney (1979) in four senior students from the National Ballet School and eight from the Lois Smith School of Dance. They conducted the study using cinematography, force plates, and electromyography of seven muscles of the trunk and thighs. Although this study is still incomplete due to lack of funding for full computer analysis, its preliminary results support Kneeland's (1966) conclusion that the good dancers often perform in ways that contradict the classroom teaching. The following are three specific examples:

1. The buttocks must be kept tight, yet the gluteus maximus has to let go to achieve the highest kick.
2. The pelvis must not move, yet in order to kick high it rotates upward 30°.
3. The foot must be kept turned out, yet it rotates to the straightforward position well before the height of the kick.

If optimization is the goal, then it is essential to know what the body is physically able to do and revise the teaching accordingly (Ranney, 1984).

Implications for Dance Medicine

Lycholat (1982) studied the lifting techniques in English professional dance schools. Filming three male dancers, he used electromyographic activity of the back extensors as an indication of the lifting force exerted on the spine. Although the data he obtained were not quantitative, this project was a very good beginning. Lycholat makes the point well that, in view of the high prevalence of back pain, more attention should be given to the back with regard to strength training and additional research in dance.

In a study of bone-on-bone forces during *relevés en pointe,* Galea and Norman (1985) found the force at the ankle joint to be about 10 times body weight, comparable to that of a runner doing a six-minute mile. In generating the power necessary to perform the dance movement, muscle contraction greatly increased the amount of compression force acting at the joint surface. Unreported data from the same study indicate that the force acting across the joints of the great toe is more than twice body weight (V. Galea, personal communication, 1984). This is a very large force considering the small size of these joints and readily explains both the bone thickening that is characteristic of the dancer's foot and the arthritic changes frequently seen.

Summary

The biomechanics of dance is still in its infancy. Although some inferences have been made from research in athletics, what is true in the world of sports is not necessarily true in dance. Biomechanical studies in dance have been confined to a few movements in classical ballet. Much has been learned about individual differences, particularly the way different dancers move to achieve the same objectives, but much more research needs to be done. Better understanding of body movement and individual differences leads to better instruction and thus better performance. Recent biomechanical studies aid understanding of why some injuries occur and may be useful for injury prevention in the future.

References

Atwater, A.E. (1980). Kinesiology/biomechanics: Perspectives and trends. *Research Quarterly, 51,* 193-218.

Basmajian, J.V. (1973). Recent research in human movement and its implications: Perspectives for electromyography. In J. Boorman & D. Harris (Eds.), *Dance verities, values, visions* (pp. 13-19). Ottawa: CAPHER.

Blasis, C. (1944). *An elementary treatise upon theory and practice of the art of dancing* (M.S. Evans, Trans.). New York: Dover.

Cajori, P. (1946). *Sir Isaac Newton's mathematical principles of natural philosophy and his system of the world, July 5, 1668* (A. Motte, Trans.). Berkeley: University of California.

Contini, R., & Drillis, R. (1966). Biomechanics. In H.N. Abramson (Ed.), *Applied mechanics surveys* (pp. 161-172). New York: Spartan Books.

Cooper, J.M., Adrian, M., & Glassow, M.A. (1982). *Kinesiology.* St. Louis: C.V. Mosby.

Galea, V., & Norman, R.W. (1985). Bone-on-bone forces at the ankle joint during a rapid dynamic movement. In D. Winter (Ed.), *Biomechanics IX A* (pp. 71–76). Champaign, IL: Human Kinetics.

Glassow, R.E. (1966). Modern dance and kinesiology. *Journal of Health, Physical Education and Recreation,* **36**(1), 65–68.

Grieve, D.W., Miller, D., Mitchelson, D.L., Smith, J.P., & Smith, A.J. (1975). *Techniques for the analysis of human movement.* London: Lepus Books.

Hays, J.F. (1979). Back to basics in physical education and dance. *Journal of Physical Education and Recreation,* **50**, 33–35.

Hays, J.P. (1981). *Modern dance: A biomechanical approach to teaching.* St. Louis: C.V. Mosby.

Hinson, M.M. (1977). *Kinesiology.* Dubuque, Iowa: Wm. C. Brown.

Hinson, M., Buckman, S., Tate, J., & Sherrill, C. (1978). The *grand jeté en tournant entrelace (tour jeté):* An analysis through motion photography. *Dance Research Journal,* **10**, 9–13.

Jensen, C.R., Schultz, G.W., & Bangerter, B.L. (1983). *Applied kinesiology and biomechanics.* New York: McGraw-Hill.

Karsavina, T. (1962). *Classical ballet: The flow of movement.* London: Adam and Charles Black.

Kneeland, A. (1966, March–June). The dancer prepares. *Dance Magazine.* (Article continues through four issues. Page numbers, in order, 49-53, 57–59, 65–66, 67–69.)

Laws, K. (1979a). An analysis of turns in dance. *Dance Research Journal,* **11**, 12–19.

Laws, K. (1979b). Physics and ballet: A new *pas de deux.* In D.T. Taplin (Ed.), *New directions in dance* (pp. 137–146). New York: Pergamon.

Laws, K. (1980). Precarious aurora: An example of physics in partnering. *Kinesiology for Dance,* **12**, 2–3.

Laws, K. (1984). *The physics of dance.* New York: Macmillan.

Lycholat, T. (1982). Lifting techniques in dance: A scientific investigation. *Dancing Times,* **73**, 123, 203-204, 287-288, 381, 383.

Merriman, J.S. (1975). Stroboscopic photography as a research instrument. *Research Quarterly,* **46**, 256–261.

Morehouse, L.B., & Rasch, P.J. (1963). *Sports medicine for trainers* (2nd ed.). Philadelphia: W.B. Saunders.

Mott, J.A. (1977). The biomechanics of purposeful movement. In *Conditioning and basic movement concepts* (pp. 4–11). Dubuque, Iowa: Wm. C. Brown.

Nichols, L. (1979). Structure in motion: The influence of morphology, experience, and the ballet *barre* on verticality of alignment in the performance of the *plié*. In D.T. Taplin (Ed.), *New directions in dance* (pp. 147–157). Toronto: Pergamon.

O'Malley, C.D., & Saunders, J.B. (1952). *Leonardo da Vinci on the human body*. New York: Henry Schuman.

Ranney, D.A. (1984, January). *The value of biomechanical research in dance.* ERIC Clearinghouse on Teacher Education. (Microfiche document number SP022 825.)

Rasch, P.J., & Burke, R.R. (1978). *Kinesiology and applied anatomy*. Philadelphia: Lea and Febriger.

Ryman, R.S. (1978). A kinematic analysis of selected *grand allegro* jumps. *CORD Dance Research Annual*, **9**, 231–242.

Ryman, R.S., & Ranney, D.A. (1979). A preliminary investigation of skeletal and muscular action in the *grand battement devant*. *Dance Research Journal*, **11**, 1–2.

Savage, G.J., & Officer, J.M. (1978). CHOREO: An interactive computer model for dance. *International Journal of Man-machine Studies*, **10**, 233–250.

Seireg, A. (1969). Leonardo da Vinci—The biomechanician. In D. Bootzin & H.C. Muffley (Eds.), *Biomechanics* (pp. 69–74). New York: Plenum. Plenum.

Steindler, A. (1935). *Mechanics of normal and pathological locomotion in man*. Springfield: Charles C Thomas.

Sweigard, L.E. (1974). *Human movement potentials: Its ideokinetic facilitation*. New York: Dodd, Mead & Co.

Todd, M.E. (1920a). Principles of posture: First paper. *Boston Medical and Surgical Journal*, **182**, 645–649.

Todd, M.E. (1920b). Principles of posture with special reference to the mechanics of the hip joint. *Boston Medical and Surgical Journal*, **184**, 667–673.

Todd, M.E. (1973). *The thinking body*. New York: Dance Horizons.

Wilson, J. (1977). Kinesiology and the art of centering. *Kinesiology for Dance*, **2**, 5–7.

Winter, D.A. (1982). Camera speeds for normal and pathological gait analyses. *Medical and Biological Engineering and Computing*, **20**, 408–412.

PART III

Medical Aspects of Dance Training

The information presented in Section II dealt with how physiological and biomechanical principls relate to safe, efficient dance training programs. However, the increased technical demands have forced some dancers and some teachers to take shortcuts and make poor training decisions. The end result is usually injury. Although poor training practices may contribute to most of the injuries observed in dancers, even with the most well-designed programs, accidents can occur.

Dancers and teachers should be aware of the types of injury, how to identify them, and what types of treatment are recommended. This is not to say that teachers and dancers should serve as their own physician —certainly not! However, if injuries are recognized promptly, dancers could seek immediate and necessary treatment. Injuries that go untreated are the most dangerous to the body.

Chapters 9 and 10 provide an overview of the injuries seen in dancers. The authors of these chapters are physicians who have associated themselves with dance companies and specialize in the treatment of dancers. They offer advice based upon scientific information as well as their personal experiences. Because of the greater frequency of knee, ankle, and foot injuries, these will be covered in more detail and presented first (chapter 9).

Chapter 11 describes menstrual effects of dance training, and chapter 12 offers information on nutritional habits of dancers. Both chapters pay particular attention to the adolescent dancer. These dancers appear most seriously affected by improper dieting techniques and have a high frequency of diet-related problems such as anorexia and bulimia. The diet restriction and stress (both physiological and psychological) can produce menstrual disorders. These disorders and their treatment are described in chapter 12.

Chapter 9

Dance Injuries: The Knee, Ankle, and Foot

Gordon G. Weiker
Cleveland Clinic

In the past 10 years, a small nucleus of physicians working with dancers has grown to the point where nearly every dance company has access to someone who is making an effort to understand the problems. At the same time, the relationship between physician and dancer has grown considerably. The improved interest, recognition, and cooperation has resulted in an exponential growth in our knowledge of specific medical problems related to dance.

Lest we become complacent, it should be noted that there are still obvious major gaps and weaknesses in the understanding of dance medicine. Although we have reached a point where most entities are well-recognized and many of them can be well-treated, we are still faced with many questions concerning the causes and prevention of these problems.

Recognizing our present level of evolution, I have put this chapter together as an effort to outline and discuss the commonly seen and recognized problems of the dancers' knee, ankle, and foot. The chapter is designed to help in the recognition of problems as well as to point out some of the known causes and generally accepted treatment options. It is not meant to be, and cannot be considered, a comprehensive encyclopedia of all possible injuries and medical problems to these joints.

Each anatomic area is approached according to the general types of problems. The first category deals with acute injuries which result from a specific incident of trauma. These are the problems that are most dramatic in nature, recognized by the media, and discussed among the dancers. Though the acute injuries draw the greatest attention, a far greater percentage of problems are in the second category of chronic problems. The chronic overuse, or misuse, syndromes are the result of wear and tear from repetitive activity done either in excess or in an improper manner. That abuse results in a breakdown of the musculoskeletal system and subsequent disability. In the section on the knee there is also a category dealing with acute problems superimposed on existing deficiencies. The deficiencies may be either anatomic variations that are incompatible with dance or failure to properly manage and rehabilitate previous acute injuries.

In the section on the foot there has been a specific portion dedicated to the problems of the skin and the toenails. Although these problems could also be broken down into the same general categories as the musculoskeletal problems covered earlier, it seems appropriate to separate them into a distinct group.

There is a separate section dealing with the specific problems of aerobic dance. This particular discipline of dance is not one of the performing arts and is a career field only for instructors. Yet, due to the extremely rapid growth of participation in this activity and the unique character of this type of dance, I felt it appropriate to include at least a brief reference to the problems encountered.

Finally, the last section is a brief summarization of treatment principles. Although each dancer and specific medical problem must be treated individually, there are certain guidelines and principles which overlap enough to allow generalization.

Common Dance Injuries of the Knee

Throughout history and across the world the human knee has continued to be a major source of frustration. The knee is the most commonly injured joint in all forms of aggressive physical activity including athletics, industry, and the arts. The human knee is at the disadvantage of having to carry the body's weight at the same time it allows adequate mobility and the mechanical power to propel the body. This desired combination of flexibility, power, speed, and stability has resulted in a functional design that adequately performs but is at great risk of breakdown and failure. Particularly problematic for the dancer is the joint between the kneecap and the front of the thigh which is prone to both acute injuries and to gradual damage by repetitious forces caused by positioning and function in dance.

Anatomy of the Knee

To the casual observer the knee appears to be a simple hinge joint. It is actually a joint that has primarily the flexion-extension hinge motion but also incorporates rotational gliding components. The bony design, with its two major runners (condyles) on the end of the thigh bone (femur) that articulate with very shallow dishes (plateaus) on the top of the tibia, is not inherently stable. The stability is provided by a combination of ligaments and muscle-tendon units that surround the entire structure.

The primary stabilizers for side-to-side motion are the collateral ligaments, medial and lateral (see Figures 9.1a and b). The primary control of front-to-back motion and rotation is by the cruciate ligaments (front or anterior, and back or posterior). These run through the center of the joint between the two condyles of the femur. Incorporating the ligaments around the outside of the knee is a capsular structure that fits like a sleeve and has thickenings in several areas to give additional support. Overlying these static ligament structures is an envelope of tendons that cross the joint and provide dynamic motion as well as additional support.

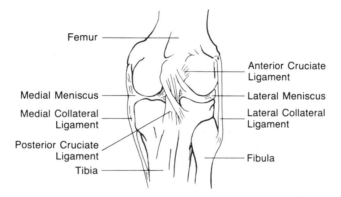

Figure 9.1a Anatomy of the human knee as viewed from the front.

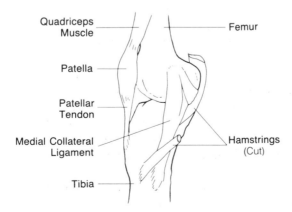

Figure 9.1b Anatomy of the human knee as seen from the side.

The front of the knee is encompassed by the quadriceps mechanism, which includes the main tendon that comes from the bulky muscle on the front of the thigh, incorporates the kneecap (patella), and inserts into the front of the tibia. This muscle is responsible for straightening (or extending) the knee such as in jumping or coming up from a *grand plié*. The hamstring muscles, both medial and lateral, are at the back of the knee and bend (flex) the joint. In addition, the hamstrings help control rotation as they cross the joint, particularly in the flexed position. At the back of the knee, the calf muscle (gastrocnemius) has its origin from the lower end of the femur and therefore crosses the knee to add stability in its course to the heel.

In summary, the inherently unstable knee is controlled and kept in its proper track during motion by a combination of ligaments and muscles. When one looks at the anatomy of the human knee it is not surprising that injuries occur. It is more baffling that anyone can dance or participate in other sports for a lifetime without having significant difficulties.

Acute Trauma

Acute traumas are injuries that result from a specific incident or accident. These injuries include: (a) contusions and abrasions, more commonly referred to as bruises and scrapes, (b) meniscal injuries where the cartilage in the knee is torn or degenerates, (c) patellar, or knee cap, fractures and dislocations, (d) ligamentous injuries to the knee joint, and (e) muscle strains about the knee. These injuries and their treatment will be discussed in the following sections.

Contusions and Abrasions.   The knee is a leading structure in many activities and particularly bears the brunt of landing when a person collides with an object or falls. Therefore, it is common to see bruises (contusions) caused by contact with other dancers, apparatus, walls, or the floor. Scrapes (abrasions) occur in much the same way, and although generally painful, are not considered dangerous.

Both contusions and abrasions are best treated conservatively and usually do not require any prolonged limitation of activity. The contusions should be treated with ice immediately and on a regular basis for 15 to 20 minutes three times a day until they are no longer symptomatic. Range of motion is important. Efforts should be made to maintain as much motion as possible and regain the full motion as soon as possible. If there is significant pain several days after a contusion, or if the range of motion does not return within a few days, a physician should be consulted. At no time should heat be used on the injured knee.

Abrasions do not present a major problem other than the possibility of superimposed infection. They should be washed thoroughly with plain water or with a mild soap and water as soon as they occur and then kept dry and clean afterwards. With both of these injuries, activities should be moderated according to symptoms and the dancer's tolerance.

Meniscal Injury.   The menisci, commonly known as cartilages, are two semi-lunar-shaped structures of particularly resilient cartilage that are interposed between the femur and the tibia. They absorb shock, help control rotation, and assist in lubricating joint surfaces. Although meniscal injury is not common in dancers, it certainly is not a rare finding. Tears are usually caused by entrapment of the meniscus between the two bony ends and subsequent mechanical disruption of the structure.

The menisci are most susceptible to injury in the acutely flexed position (such as the *grand plié*), particularly with associated rotation while bearing weight. The classic schoolchild activity of "duck-walking" (walking or waddling in the deep-knee-bend position) is the ultimate setup for meniscal damage. In addition to the acute meniscal injury, physicians see degeneration of the menisci with multiple degenerative tears in the middle-aged and older persons. Old dancers appear to demonstrate this degenerative problem more often than the general population.

The symptoms of meniscal injury vary to some degree but generally include pain with activity as well as intermittent swelling of the joint (effusion) and mechanical locking. Mechanical locking refers to the joint seeming to catch in a particular position so that the dancer has to work it loose to get it to go the rest of the way. There is usually an associated slight pop or snap sensation as the joint works loose and completes its range of motion. It is possible for a major meniscal fragment to wedge in the joint in a position where it will not work loose; this causes a locked knee and requires surgical release.

With the exception of tears in the extreme periphery, the nature of the meniscus structure does not allow regeneration or healing. Peripheral tears can heal spontaneously or be repaired, but all other tears require surgery to remove the damaged portion. I strongly recommend a trial period of rehabilitation in the knee that is not truly locked, and emphasize weight lifting as the means of regaining strength and function. Dancers are traditionally averse to weight lifting, but a proper program does not interfere with the dancer's abilities and, in reality, seems to increase the height and power of the jumps. When an adequate trial of exercise rehabilitation fails to resolve the symptoms, my present protocol calls for an arthrogram to document and define the injury.[1] If the arthrogram demonstrates meniscal or other soft-tissue pathology, arthroscopic surgical intervention is recommended. This particular form of surgical

---

[1]The arthrogram is an injection of radiocontrast material and air into the knee so that the menisci and other soft-tissue structures are coated. X-ray images (radiographs) can then demonstrate the menisci in profile and confirm or deny the diagnosis in over 90% of the cases.

intervention has greatly improved the possibilities for intervention in dancers.[2] Arthroscopic surgery produces minimal residual scar formation and allows a much faster return to the studio, sometimes as soon as two to three weeks following arthroscopic surgery. It should be clearly understood, though, that the surgery is insufficient without adequate postoperative rehabilitation. The need to lift weights and regain full function of the muscles is even greater after the surgical intervention, including arthroscopic surgery, than during the original rehabilitation trial. The long-term result of surgery on the meniscus is generally excellent and should not prohibit a dancer from returning to full activities.

Patellar Injury. The kneecap (patella) is a bony structure that lies within the quadriceps and serves both as a mechanical assist to the strength of that muscle and a protective barrier at the front of the knee. The "V"-shaped undersurface of the patella is covered by joint surface cartilage. It slides up and down in a matching groove on the front of the femur as the knee is extended and flexed.

The two acute problems encountered in the patellae of dancers are fractures and dislocations. The infrequent fracture is usually caused by dislocation. As the quadriceps tendon unit crosses the knee it angles 10° to 20° toward the outside (lateral) side of the tibia rather than following a straight line. The apex of the lateral angle is the patella. As the knee is straightened, the mechanics of the tendon pull the patella toward the outside, and therefore most dislocations occur toward the lateral side. Generally dislocations occur as a result of losing balance and putting sudden force through the quadriceps tendon at the same time that the leg is being twisted outward. When this happens the patella may shift all the way off the front of the femur (dislocation). This dislocation causes a visible and painful physical deformity which must be manually put back in place (reduced). As the dislocation occurs there is muscle disruption on the inner (medial) border of the kneecap as well as the risk of fracturing the joint surface of the patella. Both subluxation and dislocation require evaluation and treatment by a physician. The initial treatment requires replacement of the dislocated patella, ice, elevation, and compression dressing to control swelling. If radiographs show a fracture, the fragment needs to be removed (usually through the arthroscope).

---

[2]The arthroscope is a fiberoptic light-telescope instrument that has come to the forefront in the past ten years. It allows diagnosis and surgery through small, stab-wound-like incisions. The surgery can be carefully tailored to remove only the tissue that is damaged.

After the early stage of treatment, which may include immobilization for the initial healing, efforts are made to regain range of motion and strength through an exercise protocol. Any of the numerous sleeves and braces on the market may be used to help hold the patella in place during early healing and rehabilitation. If the dislocation episodes become recurrent in spite of full rehabilitation it is necessary to perform a surgical procedure. The nature of the surgery is dependent on the degree of instability and displacement. It may be a simple release of the structures on the lateral side to allow the patella to centralize itself better. In the face of severe pathology it may be necessary to do both a release of the lateral structures and a tightening or reefing of the medial structures. Regardless of the approach taken, injury of this type can be anticipated to prevent the dancer from performing for several weeks to several months.

Ligamentous Injury.   As previously noted, the ligaments about the knee are the major static stabilizers of the joint. They are composed of collagen, which has no inherent flexibility. Therefore, when the joint is forced beyond its normal motion in any plane, the ligament that should have prevented the motion is torn. The collateral ligaments normally prevent sideways bending of the joint. Injury to these ligaments is usually the result of contact with another person or object, and the dancer is acutely aware of the fact that there has been significant damage. All ligament injuries (sprains) are classified in degrees according to the amount of damage that has occurred, and that classification can only be done by someone trained in the examination of the knee. The first degree ligament sprain is defined as having microscopic damage to the collagen fibers but no increased laxity of the ligament. A second-degree sprain is defined as a ligament disrupted enough to be elongated but still in continuity. The joint will demonstrate increased laxity on examination. A third-degree sprain is one in which the ligament has been totally disrupted and there is major instability of the joint.

First-degree collateral ligament sprains are treated purely symptomatically. As with all acute injuries, they are treated with ice and the dancer immediately initiates a range-of-motion and strengthening program. As soon as the joint feels comfortable enough the dancer is free to go back into the studio. Second-degree collateral ligaments are treated somewhat according to their severity. Minor second-degree ligament sprains are treated like first-degree sprains, whereas severe second-degree sprains require some form of protective bracing during the initial stages of the rehabilitation. Once the tenderness is gone and the strength of the muscles is at least 80% of normal, the dancer is allowed a graduated return to the studio. It is important to protect the second-degree sprain during the early stages of rehabilitation to avoid additional injury.

The management of collateral ligament injuries has undergone a major change in recent years. At one time orthopaedists routinely did surgical repairs of collateral ligaments with severe second-degree or third-degree sprains. It is now recognized that the nonoperative treatment of these ligaments can be as successful as the surgical treatment while avoiding the risks of surgery.

The third-degree sprain always requires protective bracing and prolonged rehabilitation. Orthopaedists strongly recommend against casting collateral ligament sprains in the dancer because of the muscle atrophy that occurs during the casting and the subsequent prolonged rehabilitation in order to get back to dancing form. I presently use either a hinged long leg cast or a functional protective brace that allows the dancer to continue working on range-of-motion and rehabilitative strengthening during the protective phase. It is thought that the ligament heals stronger and faster if it is actively worked while at the same time being protected from further damage. With proper protection and rehabilitation the knee should function at or near 100% of its previous capability by 8–12 weeks after a major collateral ligament sprain.

The rupture (sprain) of the cruciate ligaments has become one of the most common disabling injuries in high-velocity activities. Although injury to these ligaments is occasionally seen in dance it is not a common occurrence. Injury to the anterior cruciate is more common and is usually the result of landing on an extended knee while turning. When this occurs, the dancer is most likely to be aware of a popping sensation or sound within the knee and will usually experience major swelling of the knee within the first two to five hours. This particular ligament is within the joint (intraarticular). Therefore the ruptured ends cannot readily oppose themselves and spontaneous healing is essentially unheard of. If no treatment is offered the knee usually begins to feel better at approximately two to three weeks and feels normal by five to six weeks. This initiates the time referred to within the orthopaedic community as the "honeymoon period." During this period of time, which ranges from 6 to 12 months after the injury, the knee seems to function in a normal fashion. That function is dependent on the capsular thickenings or secondary structures. Because these structures have inadequate strength for that function in approximately 80% of people, they gradually begin to stretch. When they stretch to a critical point of laxity the honeymoon comes to an abrupt end, and the knee becomes too unstable to be compatible with dance. Only a qualified physician who routinely deals with knee injuries is able to make the initial diagnosis of cruciate ligament damage.

It is strongly recommended by most sports medicine orthopaedic physicians today that young people who are actively involved in physical activity, including dancers, should have primary surgical care for a ruptured anterior cruciate ligament. The decision is a major commitment on the part of the dancer, since it involves a large surgical procedure and, with today's techniques, a year of recovery and rehabilitation before a return to full activity. The procedure is essentially the same for all active people, but modifications are made to try to assure that the dancer regains full motion. Although the commitment to major surgery and a full year of recovery is a major one by all standards, it appears to be well worth the investment. It appears that the anterior cruciate ligament tear treated without surgery offers the dancer only a 25% to 30% chance of continuing with a full career in dance. The operative approach offers approximately an 85% to 95% probability that the dancer will be able to complete a career. The development of synthetic ligament materials and modified arthroscopic techniques for insertion offers the promise of recovery time somewhere around six months rather than a full year. These materials are not yet proven, and it is uncertain exactly when they will be developed to the point that they can be recommended for routine use.

Muscle Strains.　The most common muscular strains that affect the knee joint are those of the quadriceps mechanism and the hamstrings. By definition, a strained muscle has some torn muscle fibers and internal bleeding. The bleeding initiates an inflammatory response and causes the pain, as in the typical pulled hamstring. Strains, or pulled muscles, are generally the result of inadequate warmup and/or flexibility. Because of the traditional progression of ballet class it is rare for the ballet dancer actually to pull a muscle while dancing in the structured environment. An exception to this is during choreography when dancers may find themselves called upon to dance after standing still and observing for prolonged periods of time. It is important that a dancer continuously work on staying warm and limber during any periods of inactivity.

Ice is the first line of treatment for strains, initially for 30 minutes, and then for 15 to 20 minutes three times a day until totally healed. The second and equally important part of the treatment is to regain the full length of the muscle. This is accomplished by slow, steady stretching until the muscle unit has flexibility to match the opposite side and has no discomfort during the stretching process.

Chronic Problems

Overuse or gradual-onset problems about the knee are far more common than acute injuries. Among the factors causing overuse problems are excessive dancing, anatomic variations that result in excessive loads, dancing on hard surfaces, and poor technique. Regardless of the type of overuse problem that develops, it is critical that the dancer and the physician involved review all of the possible causes and combinations of causes that may be involved. Once the contributing forces are identified they can be dealt with at the same time the primary problem is being treated.

Bursitis.   A bursa is simply a lubricating pocket that allows anatomic structures to slide past each other easily and with minimal friction. A lubricating pocket (bursa) develops every place that a tendon slides over bone, two tendons slide past each other, or any other two moving parts pass. Excessive irritation of any of these bursae can result in inflammation, which is known as bursitis. Inflammation of the bursa that allows the skin to slide across the front of the kneecap (prepatellar bursa) is generally the result of a fall onto the flexed knee and direct contusion of that area (see Figure 9.2). The pes anserinous bursa is a lubricating pocket on the front medial side just below the knee where the inner (medial) hamstrings wrap around the front of the tibia to their insertion. This is particularly painful when the dancer attempts a *demi plié* or *grand plié* because these muscles tighten to stabilize the knee in that position. The iliotibial band is a long tendinous structure that runs down the outer aspect of the thigh and crosses the knee. The bursa where the iliotibial band passes the knee can also be inflamed on the lateral side of the knee. Finally, there is a bursa beneath the portion of the quadriceps that run from the kneecap to the tibia (patellar tendon). That bursa can also become inflamed and actually bulge out on one or both sides of the patellar tendon in the front of the knee.

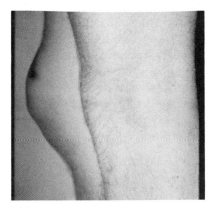

Figure 9.2   Lateral view of the knees showing major swelling of the prepatellar bursa on the right knee (prepatellar bursitis).

Bursitis is not dangerous but may be painful enough to be temporarily disabling. The treatment is modification of the activity as necessary along with ice and anti-inflammatory medication. Anti-inflammatory medications by mouth (oral) are generally effective, but on rare occasions injection of a cortisone preparation is necessary.

Tendonitis.   Although there are many tendons that pass the human knee, most of them do not present a problem as far as inflammatory change. As with the other overuse problems, tendonitis is the result of excessive stress. Overstressing the muscle-tendon unit causes irritation and, in most cases, some individual segmental damage to the tendon itself; this results in a reactive inflammatory response and therefore tendonitis.

In the dancer, the main forces across the knee and the most frequent tendonitis problems involve the quadriceps mechanism. The tendon-bone junctions at both ends of the patella are vulnerable to inflammatory change and represent the most common sites of tendonitis in the dancer's knee. At the lower (inferior) end of the patella a form of tendonitis may develop that is commonly known in sports medicine as *jumper's knee*. This term was coined because the entity was first described and is most often seen in people doing jumping activities. The repetitive stress causes an area of the tendon to lose its blood supply and die. The dead tissue causes an inflammatory response and tenderness. The symptoms may range from a dull aching sensation after activities to disabling pain that prevents participation. The diagnosis is made by a combination of history and the finding of pinpoint tenderness at the tip of the patella.

Although the symptoms may be disabling, the dancer can take comfort in the fact that this is not a dangerous situation and does not offer significant risk of tendon rupture or long-term disability. Untreated jumper's knee will eventually resolve spontaneously, although it may take as long as three to five years for resolution. A comparable area of tenderness at the upper end of the patella where the quadriceps tendon inserts is a little less frequently seen but follows the same course as jumper's knee.

There is a small muscle known as the popliteus that wraps around the lateral side of the knee, and this frequently becomes troublesome and inflamed in certain types of dance. It is generally not a problem in classical ballet but is frequently seen in flamenco dance and other forms of dancing that require very rapid aggressive activities. Because this is easily confused with problems of the lateral meniscus or the lateral collateral ligament, a physician used to dealing with the dancer's knee should evaluate the problem.

Management of tendonitis is much the same as for bursitis. Ice is utilized to help control the inflammatory response and oral nonsteroidal anti-inflammatory medications are taken to try to break the inflammatory cycle. The dancer also needs to review activities to see if a change in training or non-dance-related activities may have precipitated the situation. Injection of steroids is never recommended in tendonitis because of the deleterious effect that steroids have on collagen structure and the possibility of precipitating a tendon rupture. If that were to occur in the quadriceps mechanism, repair would be possible, but the likelihood of regaining full functional return to professional dance participation is not great.

Patellofemoral Syndrome.   Inflammation between the patella and the front of the femur has been known for many years as chondromalacia patellae and more recently as patellofemoral syndrome. This represents any of several underlying causes for pain between the kneecap and the front of the femur. One of these problems is truly chondromalacia patellae, degeneration of the articular cartilage surface of the patella. Anything that causes the patella to track abnormally in its groove on the femur can result in undue wear and tear on this joint and subsequent patellofemoral disease.

This entity is most commonly seen in students who are reaching the point where they are seriously considering the possibility of a professional career. At that point, the young dancer thinks it is most important to impress instructors and starts to cheat more and more on the turnout mechanism. Although everyone recognizes that the turnout should come from the hips and not from the knees, it is still very tempting for students, and on occasion professionals, to make a habit of screwing the knee home and cheating the turnout. This is done by quickly flexing the knee, which relaxes the ligaments and allows excessive external rotation. The feet are then planted on the floor and the knees forced straight, which gives the feet dramatic turnout at the expense of abnormally positioning the knee and the patella.

Other causes of patellofemoral syndrome include poor rehabilitation of muscle tone following injury or surgery of the leg, anatomic malalignment, and general technique. In addition to all of the previously mentioned factors that can lead to patellofemoral syndrome, young females are most prone to this problem in the population at large.

The vast majority of patellofemoral syndrome problems can be managed by conservative means. After identifying and correcting flaws in the dancer's training program a specific weight training program is initiated. Weight lifting done in the traditional method is detrimental to patellofemoral syndrome since the routine quadriceps extension exercises place a large compressive force across the patellofemoral joint. The exercises are therefore modified so that the individual lifts with the quadriceps from 30° of flexion out to a straight knee position. It is also beneficial to limit the amount of work done in the *grand plié* position of deep knee flexion during the acute stages of the problem. As with all rehabilitation programs the quadriceps lifting needs to be counter-balanced by hamstring strengthening at the same time.

If the dancer who achieves a level of 30 to 35 lb on the quadriceps lift through the limited range of motion for three sets of ten repetitions still does not have satisfactory relief of symptoms, surgical intervention is indicated. An arthrogram and arthroscopy should be performed to be certain there are no other underlying mechanical abnormalities in the joint. After completing the evaluation, the tissues down the lateral side of the patella are released (lateral retinacular release) to allow the patella to shift more toward the midline and decrease the abnormal stresses. When this procedure is followed by proper rehabilitation, 90% to 95% of dancers should regain satisfactory level of function in 6 to 10 weeks to return to dance without significant discomfort.

Osgood-Schlatter's Disease.   The point at which the quadriceps mechanism (patellar tendon) inserts into the front of the tibia is an area that is subjected to large stresses in dance. During the active years of development, the growth plate at the upper end of the tibia includes the prominence where the tendon inserts (tibial tubercle). This area is prone to inflammation and when that occurs a visible bump develops, which is exquisitely tender. This entity has been recognized for many years and has not been found to be a harbinger of any long-term major disabilities. There is no evidence that Osgood-Schlatter's disease predisposes an individual to tendon rupture, premature arthritis, or any other permanent disabilities.

Management of Osgood-Schlatter's disease is strictly symptomatic. Ice treatment will decrease the inflammatory response, and soft padding as necessary will protect the tender bump from bruising and acute flares of pain. There appears to be some benefit in increasing the flexibility of the quadriceps mechanism and strengthening the hamstring muscles, although there is no absolute proof that this changes the natural course of the disease. Most importantly, it should be noted that Osgood-Schlatter's disease is not a valid reason to tell an athlete in any sport to discontinue activity and certainly is not an indication to apply a cast. A prolonged period of time in a cast will result in the symptoms abating and the knee feeling better; however, there will be associated muscle atrophy and the likelihood of more severe symptoms upon attempted return to dancing. The dance instructor should be sympathetic with the symptoms caused by this problem and should recognize that the pain may reach a point that rest is required in order to reduce it. The vast majority of dancers will find that the symptoms totally resolve upon completion of growth, even though the bump will be permanent. In the rare instance that the symptoms fail to resolve with maturation, surgical intervention might be considered in order to relieve the dancer of the discomfort. The surgery involved is a very simple excision of little bony fragments that are embedded within the tendon and are causing the chronic irritation.

Arthritis.   Although arthritis is generally pictured as occurring in the elderly, and most people think in terms of rheumatoid arthritis, which is a crippling and deforming disease, wear and tear (degenerative) arthritis is the most common form. Dancers are more prone to degenerative arthritis of the knees and hips than is the general public. In some cases degenerative arthritis is thought to occur as a direct result of inadequate treatment and/or rehabilitation of previous injuries, but the majority of cases do not fall into that category. It appears that there is a direct correlation between the stresses placed across the joints and the relatively early onset of wear-and-tear changes. When this occurs during the dancer's active career there is no major intervention that can be offered to relieve the problem. Physicians must rely on anti-inflammatory medications and nonnarcotic pain medicines to prolong the dancer's career as much as possible. When the problem becomes very severe, either after a dancer's career or while still actively teaching, it is possible to operate and do things to alleviate the symptoms to a reasonable degree.

Acute Problems Superimposed on the Chronic Situation

Sometimes existing deficiencies lead to an unstable situation in which an acute injury can occur. These deficiencies may be either anatomical variations that are incompatible with dance training, or they may represent a failure to properly rehabilitate a previous injury. Two particular conditions will be described in this section, plica/shelf and osteochondritis dissecans.

Plica/Shelf.   Approximately 20% to 30% of people are born with a thin membrane of joint lining (synovium) that partially divides the open pouch that is around and above the kneecap. These curtains (plicae) that divide the knee space are named according to their anatomic position, and the one that is known as a horizontal shelf has the potential to cause problems. That particular plica comes from the upper medial corner of the patella down the medial or inner side of the knee and ends in the notch between the two halves of the joint. In early years it is filmy and soft and causes no problem, so the dancer is unaware of its presence. With repetitious activity, possibly exacerbated by blunt trauma to the area or twisting injuries, the plica begins to scar, becoming thicker and tighter. Eventually this tight heavy band of scar tissue that spans the knee begins to catch and irritate the joint with activity. The symptomatic plica can mimic a torn meniscus or patellofemoral syndrome and is therefore difficult to diagnose.

When conservative (exercise) programs fail to resolve knee symptoms and the arthrogram is negative, arthroscopy is the next step of evaluation. A physician who routinely treats dancers should be aware of the plica syndrome and make a specific effort to look at that area through the arthroscope. When the fibrotic shelf is discovered at the time of arthroscopy it can be transected and removed through the arthroscope, generally with improvement in symptoms and a quick return to full activity. This is probably the most satisfying diagnosis to make at the time of arthroscopy because the structure being removed is not a normal part of the knee and its removal results in a normal joint.

Osteochondritis Dissecans. Osteochondritis dissecans is a disease in which the blood supply is lost to a segment of bone underlying the joint surface; it most commonly occurs in the knees of adolescents. When the blood supply to a segment of bone is lost, the natural progression of events is for the body to invade that segment with new blood vessels, remove the dead bone, and replace it with new bone. During the time that this process is taking place the architectural support under the joint surface cartilage is weakened in the area that is undergoing the revitalization process. Because the dancer is asymptomatic and unaware of any problem in the knee during that phase, the level of activity is not interrupted. The stresses through a joint with altered architectural support can result in the cracking of the joint surface (articular cartilage). If that happens, joint fluid can penetrate the crack and prevent adequate healing. The fragment of dead bone with the attached joint surface cartilage may work loose and either become a free body floating within the joint or remain attached at one edge only and flip in and out of place, much like a trap door. Either event results in mechanical symptoms of catching and locking in the joint that are incompatible with activity.

The diagnosis is made by clinical suspicion of the condition, leading to radiographs which will frequently show the area of defect. Arthrography and arthroscopy document the exact degree of injury. The fragment may be removed from the joint or reattached to its bed depending on the amount of bone that is attached to the articular cartilage and the size of the defect. Either approach is likely to result in excellent recovery and return to dancing.

Loose bodies are occasionally encountered in the joint without evidence of their source. These are thought to be either from an osteochondritis dissecans lesion that broke loose and the defect subsequently healed over, or from a small fracture of the joint surface. In any event these loose bodies may be removed through the arthroscope with the anticipation of the return to full activity.

In the patient with true chondromalacia patellae, found on arthroscopy, the treatment is the same as that described under patellofemoral syndrome, but the prognosis or future likelihood of return to activity is lessened. In the early stages of chondromalacia, the lateral release, as previously described, and the conservative exercise program are the treatment of choice. Aspirin has been shown to have a beneficial anti-inflammatory effect when it is taken on a regular basis, and there is some evidence that it inhibits an enzyme that is chemically involved in the overall process of chondromalacia. Therefore, some physicians routinely recommend one or two aspirin tablets four times a day depending on the size of the individual and tolerance for the drug.

In the more advanced stages of chondromalacia it is necessary to trim the degenerative joint surface cartilage off and often to be more aggressive in the surgical efforts to improve the tracking mechanism. In the most advanced stages of the disease, which are basically incompatible with dance, it is often necessary to drill or debride the underlying bone in an effort to get it to generate a new surface. If that fails and the individual is totally incapacitated, it is occasionally necessary actually to remove the patella, a procedure that is absolutely incompatible with dance activity.

Common Dance Injuries of the Ankle

As the foot grips the floor and the lower extremity propels the human body, the ankle serves as the crucial point of contact between the stable and the moving extremity. The anatomy of the ankle, which will be discussed, is a feat of engineering that nearly defies belief. Despite the fact that the ankle carries the full weight of the body and is prone to multiple small injuries, the inherent design mechanics result in a joint that very rarely has any arthritic problems even in later age. After discussing the basic anatomy and the function of the ankle this chapter will go on into the multiple types of injuries that can occur and the methods to deal with these.

Anatomy of the Ankle

The human ankle is classified as a mortise and tenon joint, which is inherently stable in its configuration. The ankle bone (talus) is a dome-shaped structure when viewed from the side and flat-topped when viewed from the front or back. It slides back and forth in a mortise or fitted groove that is made up of the end of the tibia, the inner shin bone (medial malleolus), which is a projection of the tibia on the inner side of the ankle, and the lateral shin bone (lateral malleolus), which is the extension of the fibula and overlaps the talus on the outer side. Because of this configuration, the ankle has no inherent lateral tilting built into it (see Figures 9.3a,b,c). The lateral positioning of the foot, such as standing sideways on the incline, is accommodated by joints of the foot.

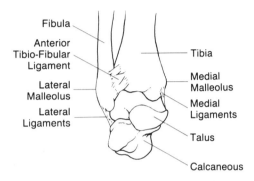

Figure 9.3a Anatomy of the human ankle as seen from the front.

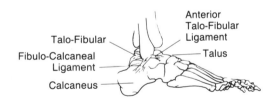

Figure 9.3b Anatomy of the human ankle as seen from the lateral (outer) side.

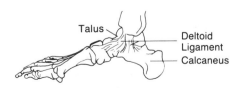

Figure 9.3c Human ankle as seen from the medial (inner) side.

The primary function of the ankle is dorsiflexion (the position of the *grand plié*) and plantar flexion (the position *en pointe*). The stability of the ankle is dependent primarily on the static bony configuration and the ligaments that cross both the medial and lateral sides of the joint. The tendons are too close to the center of rotation and at such a mechanical disadvantage that they offer little functional stability. The inherent bony stability is limited in that the talar dome is not uniform in its width. The mortise is designed to accommodate the widest portion of the talus, which is the very front of it or the portion that is in the joint when the dancer is in the *grand plié*. The back of the talar dome, which is in position *en pointe*, is narrower and therefore offers less stability until full *pointe* is reached and the ankle locks into position.

Acute Trauma

The most common acute injury to the ankle is ligament sprain. Interesting generalizations concerning ankle sprain include intrinsic or environmental factors such as the type of choreography, the background of the dancer, the amount of work being done, and the floor surface used. All of these factors have a direct correlation with the number of sprains that a given company will sustain. In addition, it has been well-recognized that sprains most often occur during rehearsals and are probably related to fatigue and efforts to learn and perfect new steps. The left ankle, which is most often the working foot, is more frequently injured than the right, and the most common cause is landing wrong from a jump. Dancers with high arches are more prone to ankle sprain than those with normal or lower than normal arches. Finally, there is a strong correlation showing that a dancer who has once had a significant sprain is very prone to recurrent additional sprains if a full rehabilitation program is not accomplished.

Lateral Sprain. The most common ankle sprain in all sports is that of the lateral side. These ligaments are primarily responsible for keeping the ankle from twisting in under the leg and preventing the talus from slipping forward out from underneath the mortise. The position of sprain is generally with the foot plantar flexed near the *pointe* position and twisted inward. There is often a sensation of a popping in the ankle and immediate severe pain. Within the first two to three hours swelling occurs over the area of the ligament damage, and frequently the individual is unable to walk in a normal fashion. After several hours there is limitation of motion and discoloration, which may extend down as far as the toes. Lateral ankle sprains are not only the most frequent but are also generally the most severe.

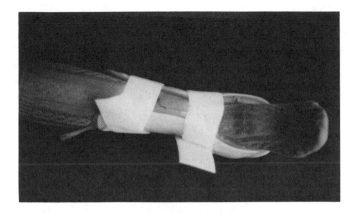

Figure 9.4   Air cast in place on an injured ankle.

The treatment for first- and second-degree sprains is conservative, whereas treatment of the complete third-degree tear of the ligament is thought by some to warrant surgical intervention (Frye, 1983). Acute dislocation of the peroneal tendons, in which the tendon tears loose from its tethering sheath and pops up and over the lateral shin bone, can mimic lateral ankle sprains and may be very difficult for the dancer or the uninitiated physician to identify. The telltale part of the history is that dislocation of the peroneal tendons is usually related to a mechanism of the foot turning in and being jammed up in dorsiflexion rather than down in plantar flexion.

First- and second-degree sprains are treated nonoperatively and yet aggressively. Inadequate treatment results in a chronically unstable ankle which can easily lead to recurrent episodes of ankle sprain with minimal force. The ankle is initially elevated, iced, and placed in a compression dressing. After the initial swelling is under control, protective splinting may or may not be utilized depending on the preference of the physician. The majority of sports medicine doctors today use a device known as an air cast (see Figure 9.4). This is an air-filled bladder system with a hard plastic shell that allows normal plantar and dorsiflexion while it prevents the turning in and out that results in ankle sprain. The pneumatic bladders put pressure where it is most effective to control the swelling and the amount of bleeding. The dancer is treated with anti-inflammatory medications and ice baths and started immediately on a controlled range of motion program. As rapidly as the swelling and discomfort abate, the range of motion program is increased and an exercise program is started both to return to full motion and to start strengthening the muscles around the ankle.

In addition, a balance board routine is initiated as a means of regaining position sense (proprioception). This concept is based on evidence that a severe ankle sprain causes disruption of fine nerves about the ankle and leaves the dancer unable to subconsciously appreciate the position of the foot and the ankle in space during a jump. Without that automatic positioning ability the dancer may land with the foot already in the sprain position and sustain a sprain before the muscles have time to react and correct the position. Among the different methods of trying to retrain proprioception is the use of an 18-inch circle of 5/8-inch plywood with 1/2 of a croquet ball mounted in the center of the bottom (see Figure 9. 5). The dancer learns to balance on the board for one minute without letting the edges touch, with eyes open and holding onto a bar. Once that is accomplished the bar is released and the balancing retraining is done standing free on the board. When that is accomplished, it is done with the eyes closed. Once the dancer is able to balance for a full minute with the eyes closed and not touching anything, the same process is repeated utilizing one foot at a time. Although there is no scientific proof of the value of proprioceptive retraining, there is definite clinical evidence that this form of training does decrease the rate of second and third sprains.

Ballet dancers need to add an exercise to rehabilitate the peroneal muscle function in *pointe* position. This is best done by lying on a couch with the injured leg up and the heel resting on the arm of the couch. A weighted purse is hung from the forefoot in *pointe* position and lifted repeatedly.

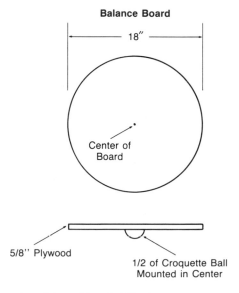

Balance Board

18"

Center of
Board

5/8" Plywood

1/2 of Croquette Ball
Mounted in Center

Figure 9.5 Balance board for ankle rehabilitation.

In the third-degree sprain the surgeon and the dancer must decide whether to use surgical repair or attempt the same program as with the second-degree sprain, realizing that it will take a longer period of time to heal. I see little value in the surgical approach to this problem because the time of recovery is essentially equal with or without surgery and my long-term results have been as good without surgical intervention. There are those in the orthopaedic community who feel strongly that their results are better with surgical repair, and to date there is no absolute proof as to which is the more valid approach. The most important thing to keep in mind is that an ankle sprain is a serious injury and requires aggressive treatment, whether surgical or nonsurgical. In the rare case that has persistent instability, delayed reconstruction of the ligaments is generally very successful.

The peroneal tendon dislocation is treated in much the same manner as the lateral ankle sprain, except that specific effort is made to limit dorsiflexion during the early stages of healing. A "J"-shaped piece of felt is placed around the back and end of the lateral malleolus to hold the tendons in place while the sheath has a chance to heal.

The rate of recovery from ankle sprain is extremely variable and very unpredictable, ranging from 10 days to 5 months. The major handicap is the difficulty in obtaining full *pointe* position following a significant ankle sprain. The rate of recovery needs to be monitored on a regular basis by the physician involved, and the anticipated date of return to dancing adjusted week-by-week as the progress is observed. Ankle sprains lend themselves very well to the pool routine. The dancer stands in chest deep water and exercises the ankle, then progresses to the bar routine, and finally the floor routine, aided by the bouyancy of the water.

Medial Sprain.   Injuries to the inner ligament (deltoid ligament) of the ankle are much less frequent than those of the lateral sides. The complete disruption or third-degree sprain of the medial ligament is extremely rare but when it does occur it is possible for tendons in that area to become dislocated into the joint and require surgical intervention. The majority of medial ligament sprains are first- or mild second-degree and are treated conservatively, much in the manner of a lateral sprain but with the anticipation of a more rapid recovery.

Mixed Sprain.   It is possible to have a whiplash-type effect where the ankle sprains one way and then in reaction snaps back too far the other way. The dancer has pain both medially and laterally. These are also treated in a conservative manner, with initial protection from further injury and recovery of motion and strength as rapidly as tolerated.

The final thing to note about ankle sprains is damage to the ligament that holds the two bones of the leg together at the ankle. As previously noted, the ankle is inherently stable because of the mortise effect of the two bones surrounding the dome of the talus, but it is possible to disrupt the ligaments that hold them together. This is an extremely rare injury in the dancer's ankle, but when it does occur it is also the slowest of all ankle sprains to heal. The treatment is the same as for lateral and medial sprains.

Fractures.   Minor variations in foot position and the amount of compressive load on the ankle at the time of injury can protect the ligaments and cause fractures of the bony structure instead. Much as the lateral ligaments of the ankle are most likely to be sprained, the lateral malleolus is most likely to fracture. When this happens it occurs generally just above the level of the joint line and may or may not be associated with deltoid ligament injury. The safest and most conservative method of treating the lateral malleolar fracture is an initial period of casting followed by protective splinting with an air cast, graduated rehabilitation, and return to activity.

More rapid healing and return to dancing can generally be accomplished by operative treatment in which a plate with small screws is used to fix the lateral malleolus in place. Either method of treatment is usually successful in the long run and it is a matter of personal decision to trade off the risks of surgery in order to gain two to four weeks of time on the recovery.

The medial malleolus or medial shin bone also may be broken. As with the ligament, this is much less frequently seen than on the lateral side and should be responsive to conservative treatment, although it does require surgery with internal fixation on occasion.

Talar Dome Fractures.   As the ankle sprains, the talus is tilted and wedged in the mortise. That mechanism of wedging may cause a fragment of the joint surface cartilage and the underlying bone to break loose. The dancer is generally unaware of this problem because the primary pain and awareness is directed toward the sprain. Routine radiographs should be taken of every significantly sprained ankle to rule out fracture, but even those may miss this avulsion-type fracture. If rehabilitation for an ankle sprain does not progress at an acceptable rate, fracture of the dome of the talus should be considered as a possible explanation.

The definitive diagnosis of a talar dome fracture requires a special radiographic technique known as tomoarthrography. In that technique the ankle is filled with dye and air, and tomographic Xray images are taken. For tomography the Xray is focused at various depths through the ankle to give a clear image at the different depths. When an osteochondral fracture of the talar dome is identified, surgery is the only treatment that is likely to be successful. This procedure is frequently done through the arthroscope, but, on occasion, it does require a formal incision and surgical removal of the fragment. It is fully anticipated that the dancer will return to full activity within six to ten weeks of that operation.

Problems of the Os Trigonum.   At the back (posterior edge) of the joint surface of the talus there is a projection called the posterior process. The size of this process is extremely variable among people and occasionally is large enough to be obvious on radiographs and prone to injury. In some people the posterior process is actually a separate bone, which is known as the os trigonum (see Figure 9.6). This structure sits just behind the talus and is located where it can be trapped between the body of the talus and the back of the tibia in the full *pointe* position.

The os trigonum may offer several difficulties to the dancer. When it is trapped and locked between the back of the ankle and the back of the tibia it will limit plantar flexion enough to prevent assumption of acceptable *pointe* position. Repetitive efforts to force *pointe* may eventually crush the os trigonum and result in fragmentation that causes chronic irritation and pain. More dramatically, on occasion the os trigonum can be trapped and pop out the back of the ankle, much as one would shoot a watermelon seed by pinching it between the thumb and finger. When this happens, the dancer has an abrupt severe pain in the posterior aspect of the ankle and then finds improved *pointe* ability after the pain subsides a few days later.

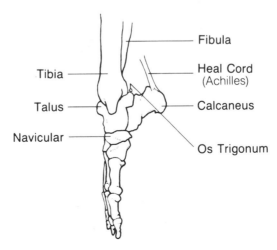

Figure 9.6 Lateral view of the foot and ankles showing os trigonum with foot *en pointe*.

Permanent entrapment or crushing of the os trigonum may cause impaired performance because of pain or lack of *pointe*. There is no reasonable nonoperative approach for this problem, so the recommendation is to have the os trigonum excised. This is a relatively simple surgical procedure and should allow return to full activity within four to six weeks.

Chronic Problems

There are several conditions that dancers suffer with for a relatively long period of time and which seem to reoccur with variable frequency. Common problems in dance are bursitis, tendonitis, stress fractures about the ankle, anterior tibio-talar spurs, and arthritis. The following sections will describe each condition and its treatment.

Bursitis.   As previously noted in the section on the knee, the body forms lubricating pockets or bursae wherever they are needed to allow free motion without friction. Several bursae about the ankle may cause problems for the dancer, but only two of these occur frequently.

There are bursae superficial to (between skin and tendon) and deep within (between tendon and bone) the Achilles tendon near its insertion into the heel bone (calcaneus). These bursae can become inflamed due to work or rubbing by the edge of the ballet shoe, which rides on the bursa. An excessively tight Achilles tendon can also predispose an individual to inflammation of the deep bursa (retrocalcaneal bursa).

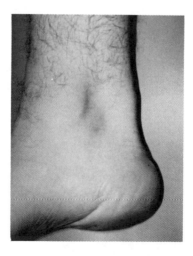

Figure 9.7   Ankle with nodular prominence overlying the Achilles tendon which represents an area of chronic Achilles tendinitis.

Inflammation of these bursae is treated in the standard, conservative fashion. If this problem fails to respond to a reasonable trial of ice and oral anti-inflammatory medication, injection with steroids will usually give complete and rapid relief. Although injection of the bursa is not dangerous, care must be taken to avoid injecting any steroid directly into the Achilles tendon, because that could lead to tendon rupture. In the rare instance that bursitis fails to respond to this treatment, surgical excision of the sac is possible. During surgery it is occasionally necessary to trim off a prominence on the calcaneous that causes chronic irritation. Recovery should be complete three to four weeks after the operation.

Tendinitis.   The main tendon of support for the great toe is called the flexor hallucis longus. It runs down the back of the leg, passes behind the ankle, under the medial malleolus, and along the undersurface of the foot to insert into the big toe. The flexor hallucis longus and Achilles tendons are the most frequent sites of tendinitis about the ankle. The tendon passes through a tunnel at the back of the ankle immediately adjacent to the os trigonum or posterior process of the talus. That position and a tendency for the muscle belly to extend abnormally low on the tendon lead to the problems. The distance the tendon must travel to accommodate positioning *en pointe* (tightened maximally) to *grand plié* (maximally stretched) can be two to three inches. The extreme excursion of this tendon allows a muscle belly with a slightly lower than normal extension to be pulled into and trapped in the tendon sheath when attempting *grand plié.* The excursion of the tendon is limited as the muscle belly is pulled like a cork into a bottle neck and wedges.

In addition to that mechanical aberration, chronic overuse irritation and inflammation can occur, occasionally leading to partial tendon death (necrosis) and even rupture. Examine the great toe with the foot in a relaxed partial *pointe* position and see how far back it can be bent. Then bring the foot into maximum dorsiflexion and retest the motion. If the toe has normal motion in the *pointe* position but has dramatically limited motion in the dorsiflexed position, the flexor hallucis longus tendon is tethered either mechanically or by inflammation.

The posterior tibial tendon is adjacent to the flexor hallucis longus; it helps position the foot in *pointe,* and is prone to inflammatory disease (tendinitis). Tendinitis of the posterior tibial tendon usually occurs at the point where it turns sharply around the medial malleolus to enter the foot. The peroneus longus and brevis tendons, on the lateral aspect of the ankle, are prone to tendinitis, as is the heel cord (Achilles tendon). The Achilles tendon is the combination of two tendons coming from the gastrocnemius and soleus muscles in the back of the calf. It attaches to the back of the calcaneus and supplies the main force for *pointe* and leaps (see Figure 9.7). Chronic inflammation and irritation of the Achilles tendon is an extremely common entity in all sports that require aggressive activity with the legs. Achilles tendinitis can generally be localized by palpation (feeling) for an area of tenderness. This hourglass-shaped tendon is thinnest, and most vulnerable, approximately 3 1/2 to 4 1/2 cm from its insertion. Because Achilles tendinitis frequently includes a segment of central tissue death (necrosis), untreated or unsuccessfully treated tendinitis carries significant risk of rupture. Of the many tendons that cross the front of the ankle, the anterior tibial and peroneus tertius tendons are the most frequently inflamed in dance.

In all tendinitis about the ankle the treatment principles are essentially the same. An initial period of treatment with ice and relative rest is required, along with anti-inflammatory medication. Under no conditions should any tendon be injected with cortisone. If the tendon responds to the rest and medication, an initial period of stretching to regain full, pain-free motion is followed by a gradual strengthening program and graduated return to dance.

When conservative methods fail to clear the symptoms or if they return every time dancing is attempted, surgical intervention is recommended. For inflammation of the flexor hallucis longus the tendon is surgically explored, the os trigonum is excised, and occasionally part of the muscle belly is removed or the tendon sheath is released. The Achilles tendon should be surgically explored if it fails to respond to conservative treatment over six months. The exploration should include splitting the tendon lengthwise to look for areas of necrosis within its substance, and those areas should be removed (excised). On occasion the lining around the Achilles tendon is the primary offender, and excision of that lining is sufficient to relieve the symptoms. The other tendons around the ankle seldom require surgical intervention but, when it is necessary, the tendons should be explored for areas of necrosis.

It is important to keep in mind with all tendinitis that the results of early surgical intervention are dramatically better than are the results of repairing a ruptured tendon.

Stress Fractures About the Ankle.   Although the stress fractures do not occur specifically in the ankle, it seems appropriate to treat them in this part of the chapter. A stress fracture occurs due to the body's failure to tolerate repetitive forces being placed through a bone. As forces on the skeleton are increased or changed, the body attempts to modify the internal architecture to accommodate the new stresses. As with urban renewal, our ability to tear down the old is greater than our ability to build the new. That imbalance can result in a temporarily weakened bone that develops a crack. A stress fracture is not grossly unstable but, if inadequately treated, it can lead to a full break (fracture).

The most common site of stress fracture is the small bone down the outer side of the leg (fibula). This usually occurs approximately three to four inches above the ankle where, not by coincidence, the satin ribbons for *pointe* shoes are tied. There is a strong suspicion that a tightly tied ribbon causes an area of stress concentration that leads to the stress fracture. The main bone of the leg (tibia) is also prone to stress fracture, and some dancers may have as many as four or five stress fractures in this bone at once (see Figure 9.8). The neck of the ankle bone (talus) is also prone to stress fracture, which is extremely difficult to diagnose. There is a distinct correlation between the occurrence of stress fractures and the dancer's level of work, conditioning, and available floor surface. Excessive work by a poorly conditioned dancer on a nonresilient floor is a set-up for stress fractures.

If pain around the ankle or leg does not respond to standard conservative treatment, an underlying stress fracture should be suspected. If there is a suspicion of stress fracture and plain X-ray radiographs are normal, it is wise to perform radionucleotide scanning. The study is basically a method of putting a tracer element in the system that is picked up in areas of increased bony activity and can be demonstrated on a recording device. Areas of inflammatory change, including stress fracture, will be demonstrated by increased uptake.

Regrettably, the treatment for stress fracture is limited to the one thing that dancers like least, and that is *rest*. The rest program can be modified to allow reasonable maintenance of conditioning and technique without interfering in the healing process.

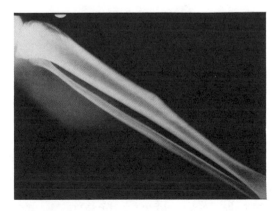

Figure 9.8   Stress fracture midshaft of the tibia as seen from the side on X ray.

Anterior Tibio-Talar Spurs. The problems with the os trigonum and impingement in back of the ankle are the result of plantar flexion (pointe), but the maximum dorsiflexion position can also cause front (anterior) ankle impingement. Anterior impingement causes a dull, chronic aching sensation in front of the ankle joint that is sensitive to work in the dorsiflexed position. X-ray radiographs of that area will show bony spurs (exostoses) where the front of the talus makes contact with the front of the tibia. If the exostoses continue to enlarge and remain inflamed, dorsiflexion (the reverse of *pointe*) will be limited, and this will interfere with performance.

Initial treatment is directed toward conservative care with ice and anti-inflammatory medications. If those fail the only recourse is surgical removal of the exostoses in the effort to regain full painfree motion. The operation is usually successful but requires six to eight weeks for complete recovery.

Arthritis. Arthritis of the human ankle is an extremely rare occurrence and particularly rare in dancers. Most ankles that become arthritic do so because of mechanical abnormality, due either to chronic instability or irregular joint surfaces from previous trauma. If arthritis does occur in the ankle it will present itself as the chronic aching and stiffness as seen in other arthritic joints. There are currently no surgical procedures available to deal with true arthritis of the ankle that still leave a dancer fit to perform, so treatment is restricted to the usual conservative measures.

Common Dance Injuries of the Foot

The foot is again an accomplishment of surprising engineering with approximately twenty-six bones and between thirty and fifty joints depending on the method of counting. With this complexity, including all the necessary ligaments and muscle tendon units to drive the foot, there are still surprisingly few major problems. All sports do cause some problems and injuries to the feet but nowhere is the foot abused as much as it is by being forced into the *pointe* shoe. This section will cover the acute injuries that occur as well as the chronic overuse problems and will offer some suggestions regarding prevention and treatment.

Problems with the dancer's feet occur in all forms of dance but are particularly related to the use of the *pointe* shoes. When the Italian ballerina, Marie Taglioni, introduced the use of *pointe* shoes in 1832, she revolutionized ballet but also set the stage for the devastation of many feet. The ballet shoe has remained essentially unchanged for the last one hundred years; the foot is crushed into the shoe rather than having the shoe designed to fit the foot. The *pointe* position tightly locks the foot into the shoe and transmits forces through the toes, the mid-foot, and into the leg (Figures 9.9 and 9.10). The ideal foot for *pointe* work is relatively short and sturdy with an average arch, a broad forefoot, and the first three toes nearly equal in length. Regrettably, few dancers have the perfect foot for *pointe* shoes, and therein lies the source of many problems.

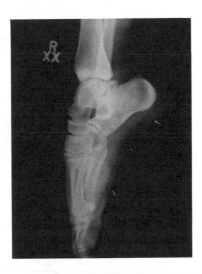

Figure 9.9   X ray of a dancer's foot *en pointe* in *pointe* shoes.

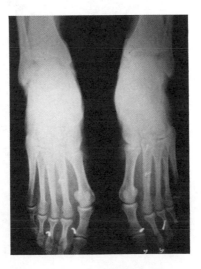

Figure 9.10   X ray of a dancer's foot *en pointe* position demonstrating good foot alignment as well as nonsymptomatic os trigonum with the foot in the *pointe* shoe.

The most common question asked of physicians dealing with ballet is "When should my daughter go *en pointe?*" There is no simple and clear answer to this question but a general rule of thumb has evolved. The student should have a minimum of two to four years of ballet experience and be technically ready to dance *en pointe*. She must have satisfactory strength and coordination to avoid the errors of sickling, knuckling down, (see Figure 9.11) and doing many other things that can go wrong in the *pointe* position. General experience has shown that this usually occurs around the ages of eleven to thirteen, but each young dancer should be evaluated by a qualified instructor, and the decision should be based on the individual's level of readiness.

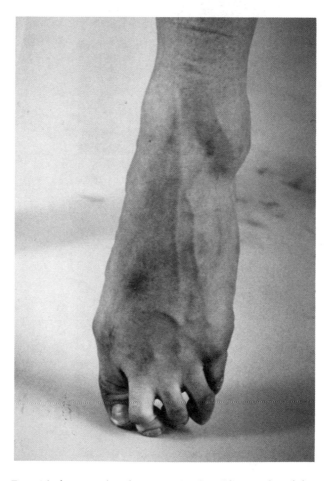

Figure 9.11 Dancer's foot *en pointe* demonstrating knuckling under of the second toe.

Acute Trauma

Acute injuries to the foot are few in number compared with the chronic overuse problems.

Fractures and Dislocations.   Fractures and dislocations about the foot do occur in significant numbers and generally result in six to ten weeks of disability. Fracture of the base of the fifth metatarsal where the peroneus brevis tendon inserts is usually caused by a mechanism similar to that of the lateral ankle sprain. Other metatarsals (the long bones in the mid-portion of the foot, see Figure 9.12) may be fractured at any point along the course. I recently treated a young male dancer who misjudged a jump and landed in the *pointe* position without the proper footwear (or preparation to be *en pointe*). He sheared the joint surface (head) of the metatarsal off and displaced it up the foot. That injury required reduction of the fragment to give him a functioning foot for future dance. Fractures and dislocations of the small bones (phalanges) of the toes do occur on regular occasions. Fracture and dislocation of the sesamoid bones[3] do occur, but infrequently, in dancers.

Fractures and dislocations of the foot are treated with an initial period of protective immobilization, ice, and elevation as necessary to control swelling and inflammation. A graduated return to activity, with the use of pool exercises and physical therapy, is necessary to return the foot to full function. Most fractures and dislocations of the foot will require six to ten weeks of recovery and rehabilitation before returning to dance.

Strains and Sprains.   The foot, including the toes, has over thirty joints. Each of them is held together by multiple ligaments and controlled by the tendons that cross them. Any of these multiple ligaments may be sprained, and any of the muscle-tendon units may be strained. Most acute midfoot sprains occur when the dancer goes up *en pointe,* loses balance, and falls across the foot. Sprains of the toes may be related to either hyperextension or hyperflexion and, in young dancers, are often related to knuckling under when they attempt *pointe* before they are physiologically and technically ready.

The treatment of the foot strains and sprains is strictly symptomatic, with the return to dance decided on a day-to-day basis. The initial treatment is again ice, elevation, compression, and rest. After the initial pain subsides, the dancer progresses through graduated exercise, pool routine,

---

[3]The sesamoids are two small bones that are embedded within the flexor hallucis longus tendon under the base of the large toe.

and return to dance as the symptoms subside and the range of motion returns to normal.

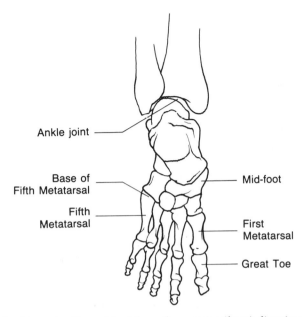

Figure 9.12 Human ankle and foot from the anterior (front) direction.

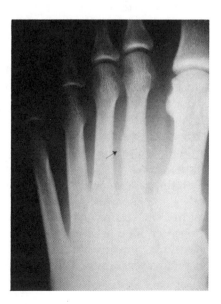

Figure 9.13 X ray of a dancer's foot demonstrating a stress fracture in the shaft of the second metatarsal.

Chronic Problems

Chronic tendinitis does occur in the foot, although it is not nearly as frequent as in the ankle. There is an overlap between ankle and foot tendinitis in that the peroneus tersius on the front outer (anterolateral) aspect of the ankle courses into the top (dorsum) of the foot. It may be inflamed anywhere along its course. The same can be said of the anterior tibial tendon and the flexor tendons of the toes. They pass into the foot, and the inflammation may be either at the level of the ankle or in the foot. Tendinitis within the foot generally does not require surgical intervention and usually is rapidly responsive to ice and anti-inflammatory medications. In the rare occasion that tendinitis of the foot fails to respond to conservative measures, it may be necessary to do a surgical exploration and trim the area of primary inflammation.

Stress Fractures.   Stress fracture, as previously noted in the section on the ankle, is the result of excessive stress that causes remodeling of bone at a rate more rapid than the body can tolerate. This leads to a relative weakness during the remodeling that can subsequently cause an actual structural crack through the bone. The onset of symptoms from stress fracture is gradual and insidious without specific association to a date, time, or injury. The most common site of stress fracture in the dancer's foot is the metatarsals (see Figure 9.13). The second metatarsal seems to be most prone to stress fracture, followed by the third metatarsal, and then the first metatarsal. Unlike most activities, such as marching, running, or basketball, the stress fractures of dancers frequently occur at the upper end (base) of the metatarsal rather than in the midshaft. The physician dealing with the dancer's foot should be aware of this, because it is much more difficult to make the diagnosis in that area. Clinical suspicion along with normal, plain, X-ray radiography should be considered reason enough to perform a bone scan. Dancer's stress fracture also occurs in the neck of the main ankle bone (talus), where the weight-bearing portion articulating with the ankle and the portion that forms a joint with the midfoot are joined. The bone that articulates with the talus in the midfoot is known as the tarsal navicular (tarsal scaphoid) and is also prone to stress fractures in dancers. This is extremely difficult to evaluate, so suspicion of a stress fracture, along with normal, plain radiographs should lead to tomography and/or bone scanning for evaluation (see Figure 9.14). Finally, any of the other foot (tarsal) bones may develop stress fractures although none of them are frequently involved.

Stress fractures are managed in a manner most disconcerting for the dancer, because the only effective treatment is rest. This may be relative rest, as discussed in the latter part of this chapter, but some form of rest is necessary which is long enough to allow both resolution of symptoms and radiographic evidence of healing. Once the fracture is healed it is important that the dancer make a gradual progressive return to activity to avoid reinjury. Sesamoid stress fractures are highly resistant to healing because the bone rests within a tendon and is constantly under tension; it is often necessary to remove these bones surgically in order to relieve the symptoms. Finally, any stress fracture may be refractory to primary healing with rest only, and it may be necessary to use more dramatic means of treatment, such as electrical stimulation and/or surgery to effect primary healing.

Osteochondroses.   Osteochondroses are a group of diseases in actively growing children in which the blood supply to a segment of the bone is disrupted (see the paragraphs on osteochondritis dissecans in the section on the knee). There are three primary osteochondroses that occur in the foot, and all of them are seen with regularity in young dancers.

- *Freiberg's infraction:* There is a specific tendency for the end of the second metatarsal that articulates with the toe (the head of the metatarsal) to lose its blood supply and subsequently fragment and collapse. If this occurs and goes unrecognized until there is deformity, it will cause significant disability and, in all probability, will preclude any possibility of a professional career in dancing. This seems to happen more frequently in dancers with the Morton's foot configuration, in which the second metatarsal is excessively longer than the first metatarsal. It also appears to be more frequent in young women who are placed on *en pointe* too early.
- *Köhlers disease:* The comparable loss of blood supply to the tarsal navicular can cause a loss of structural integrity in that bone and subsequent collapse and fragmentation.
- *Sever's disease:* The growth plate at the very back of the heel (calcaneus) in the area where the Achilles tendon attaches is stressed by landing on the heel and constant pulling of the Achilles tendon. Loss of blood supply to this area (Sever's disease) causes fragmentation of the bone, pain, and tenderness.

The management of these problems is again relegated to rest. Ice and anti-inflammatory medication will decrease the initial symptoms but only time and the body's natural mechanism of rejuvenation will resolve the underlying problem. It is critical that the young dancer rest these areas until they are healed, because continued pressure during the active stages will result in deformity that is permanent and all too often disabling.

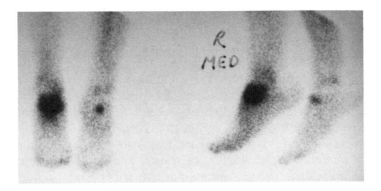

Figure 9.14 Bone scan of a dancer's lower leg, foot, and ankle demonstrating an area of increased uptake (increased density) in the neck of the talus (ankle) bone.

Plantar Fasciitis.   There is a heavy band of fibrous (tendon-like) tissue, the plantar fascia, that runs from the base of the calcaneus out into the ball of the foot. This structure helps support and give the springiness to the arch rather than being a rigid structural member. All forms of dance and activity put stress across the plantar fascia, and in any level of dancing it can become inflamed and irritated. Plantar fasciitis is most often seen in the older dancers, but it has been seen in dancers as young as twelve and thirteen years. Both choreography that requires a great deal of jumping and dancing on hard surfaces increase the likelihood of developing this problem.

The treatment is a combination of ice and anti-inflammatory medication, along with stretching of the Achilles tendon and the plantar fascia. Additional benefit can be gained from an exercise program that is designed specifically to strengthen the muscles that reside within the sole of the foot and help support the plantar fascia. Soft arch-supports in the dancer's everyday shoes can be of benefit in taking some of the load off this fascia while it is healing.

There is no specific timeframe for return to activity with this problem, because it is not perceived as dangerous and the day-to-day level of activity must be related to the symptoms. There have been reported cases of rupture of the plantar fascia, which causes extreme but short-lived pain and disability (1 1/2 to 2 1/2 weeks). The practice of routinely removing so-called "heel spurs," which are actually a traction outgrowth of bone in the plantar fascia is not recommended. They are normal in the active person and should be operated on only if the spur is fractured. The injection of steroids into the plantar fascia is also not recommended because it increases the likelihood and possibility of rupture of that structure.

Hallux Rigidus.   The inability to put the great toe through a full range of motion is known as hallux rigidus. This may be either a functional hallux rigidus or an actual fixed arthritic change. Functional limitation is similar to that described in the earlier section involving the flexor hallucis longus tendon. In that particular form, the great toe has full and normal range of motion when the foot is in its *semipointe* position but has very limited hyperextension when the ankle is up in the dorsiflexed position. This is due to tethering of the tendon rather than actual pathology in the joint.

True hallux rigidus is a form of arthritis within the joint, and the limitation of motion is a combination of muscle spasm, arthritic spurs that impinge, and tightening of the capsular structures. There is no satisfactory treatment presently available for hallux rigidus in the dancer, and the only recommendation we can make is that he or she continue to dance as long as it is tolerable. The time can be extended by the usual conservative measures of ice treatment, taping, and anti-inflammatory medications. When and if a disease becomes totally intolerable, surgery can be done either to place a plastic spacer in the joint or to remove one side of the joint. Both of these procedures work well for the relief of the pain in the sedentary individual but are not compatible with a continued career in dance.

Sesamoiditis.   The sesamoid bones of the foot, as previously described, are floating bones within the major flexor tendons of the great toe. They have an actual joint that articulates with the undersurface of the first metatarsal and that can become inflamed and irritated (sesamoiditis).

In running and many other activities the symptoms can be satisfactorily controlled by using a felt pad, which takes the load off the sesamoid joints. In the dancer this is extremely difficult because the bulk of the discomfort and problem is related to the hyperextension of the great toe, which is necessary in all forms of dance. The usual modalities of ice treatment, anti-inflammatory medications, and relative rest are all that physicians have to offer the dancer unless the duration and severity of the symptoms require surgical intervention to remove the sesamoid. This is not uniformly successful but, in the majority of cases, allows resumption of full activity.

Bunions and Bunionettes.   Largely due to the shape of the *pointe* shoe, the vast majority of serious ballet dancers have major bunion deformities. They also do occur in the general population and in dancers of all types. A bunion deformity basically is a deviation of the great toe towards the lateral or outer side of the foot with a prominent medial bump at the base of the toe (see Figure 9.15). This bump is chronically irritated by the shoe and develops a callus on the surface, an underlying bony exostosis, and a bursa between the callus and the bone. It is the bursa that eventually becomes painful to the point that it is a handicap for the dancer.

A bunionette is a comparable problem of medial deviation of the little toe and a callus and bursa on the outer aspect of the foot.

As long as people continue to wear shoes that are not designed to fit the foot, and especially the *pointe* shoe, we will continue to see bunions. The treatment for the bunion or bunionette in the dancer is strictly conservative, with good management of the callus and conservative ice treatment and anti-inflammatory medication. There are excellent surgical procedures available for the correction of bunion deformities but the likelihood of a full return to dancing after surgery is not good. Bunions and bunionettes should be treated conservatively and symptomatically until the dancer is ready to retire from professional dance. At that time a surgical procedure can be performed and the foot realigned to a reasonable degree if the ex-dancer desires.

Clawtoes.   When the tips or the middle joints of the toes go into a fixed position of flexion and the base joint (metatarsal phalangeal joint) goes into hyperextension, it is referred to as clawing of the toes. This is not common in dancers, and when it does occur is best treated conservatively with padding and protection. Like bunions, there are good surgical procedures available for releasing clawed toes but the rate of return to dance is not high enough to warrant surgery in the active dancer.

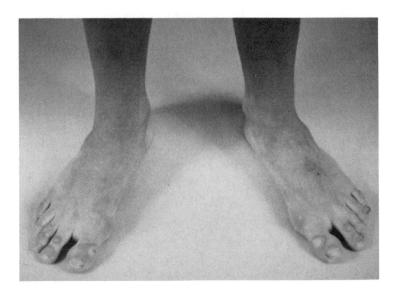

Figure 9.15 Dancer's feet with early bunion deformities and typical multiple calluses.

Ganglia.   On occasion a dancer will notice a painful nodule on the front of the ankle or anywhere along the many joints of the foot. These frequently change in character from week to week. They may be hard and prominent at one time and then soft and indistinct at another time. This nodule (ganglion) is a small outpouching of the joint lining. The lining still has the capability to produce joint fluid, so if the ganglion twists enough to pinch off its drainage into the joint, the fluid being produced causes a pressure buildup, much like a water-filled balloon.

Although ganglia may be tender, they usually do not require any form of intervention. If they do become intolerable, injection with steroids can be attempted to try to resolve the symptoms. If that fails it is possible to perform a relatively minor operative procedure to remove the ganglion and open a window in the joint lining at that point. The procedure can be done at the dancer's discretion during the off-season so that the one to two weeks of time necessary for skin healing are available before returning to dance.

Morton's Neuroma.   The skin nerves go through the foot in a pattern that brings one large main trunk nerve down between each pair of metatarsals. They divide near the end of the metatarsals and go to the adjacent sides of two adjoining toes. Where the nerves lie between the metatarsals, they are vulnerable to impingment and pinching. If this occurs chronically a small benign tumor of the nerve's lining cells can occur (Morton's neuroma). The symptom is a sharp pain with a cramping sensation at the level of the ball of the foot; this is more evident when wearing tight shoes and less evident when barefooted.

Conservative measures, such as wearing wider shoes and taking anti-inflammatory medications, may offer some relief; steroid injection is also safe in this area. If no treatment is done, the Morton's neuroma will generally clear after several years. If the discomfort becomes unacceptable for the dancer, it is possible to perform a relatively minor operative procedure in the off-season. The procedure involves cutting the nerve above and below the level of the neuroma; this leaves the adjacent sides of the two involved toes without sensation. This is not particularly disconcerting and should in no way interfere with the dancer's ability.

Skin and Nail Problems

If one fact can be made clear to dancers in general, it should be the extreme importance of using meticulous hygiene to prevent skin problems and complications. The majority of problems related to the skin and nails are directly or indirectly related to poor habit patterns. The dance shoes accumulate moisture and salt from perspiration during dancing, while the skin becomes somewhat soft and macerated. Every dancer should remove the dance shoes between rehearsal sessions, wash the feet, and thoroughly dry them before going back into the next session. Every dancer should know how to trim toenails properly and to pare calluses down if necessary. Simple measures of that nature which the dancer can learn from a podiatrist will prevent the vast majority of the problems about to be discussed.

Calluses and Corns.   Calluses are accumulations of skin surface layer (epidermis) in direct response to rubbing and friction on the surface. As any laborer can attest, the hands develop calluses on the palms and the fingers as a response to heavy manual labor. In the dancer, the feet are being used for the labor, and calluses develop over the dorsum or top of the toes, over the ball of the foot, around the heel, over bunion and bunionette deformities, and at any other point at which a particular type of shoe or style of dance causes friction and rubbing. The calluses are not dangerous in themselves, but with improper care they may become painful or infected.

To care for calluses a dancer must keep them clean and dry, pare them down or sand them off as they thicken, and use donut-shaped padding and taping for protection. A single layer of micropore tape with donut-shaped padding for calluses on the top of the toes (corns) will help protect them and prevent breakdown. In addition, dancers should keep in mind that if they are out of the studio for a few weeks, calluses will weaken and soften. The key to safe return to dance, as for all of the problems we have discussed, is a graduated logical return to dance rather than an abrupt transition from minimal activity into a full schedule.

Soft Corn.   When a pressure spot develops in an area that stays constantly moist, the epithelial build-up is a soft corn (clavus) (see Figure 9.16). This is basically identical to a callus except that the tissue does not get the hard, dry feeling because of the constant moisture in an area such as the space between the toes. Treatment in this area is to put a small sponge-rubber, felt, or rayon pad between the toes to relieve the pressure. If padding fails to resolve the symptoms, a small surgical procedure may be done during the off-season to trim the underlying bump of bone and get rid of pressure. Soft corns tend to be far more painful than hard corns and prevent the dancer from wearing the *pointe* shoe. Other skin problems that occur on the foot include fissuring and fungal infections of the toenails (onycholysis).

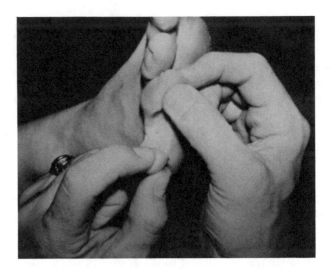

Figure 9.16   Clavus (soft corn) between the fourth and fifth toes of the dancer's right foot.

Ingrown Toenails.   There is a tendency for the nail of the great toe to become wedged in the soft tissue adjacent to it. This causes chronic irritation and inflammation, and sets up the possibility of infection. The dancer should see a health care specialist who is qualified in the care of nails and learn the proper way to trim the nails as well as a method of packing under the nail edge to help it grow in the direct and correct course. If the nail bed does become infected, it is important that medical help be sought immediately and, on rare occasion, to have part of the nail removed.

Blisters.   Blisters are a common hazard of all active people. A blister is the result of excessive friction causing the layers of the skin to separate. Fluid accumulates in the area of separation, and a bubble or blister forms. The best way to manage blisters is to prevent their occurrence in the first place. The gradual return to activity after a period of layoff and careful selection of footwear decrease the likelihood of blister formation. In sensitive areas use a single layer of micropore tape to decrease the friction and the likelihood of blister formation. Also, the use of dry shoes when possible and proper hygiene between rehearsals both have a significant benefit, but nothing will totally prevent blisters.

Avoid having the blister rupture as long as possible, because intact skin prevents the invasion of bacteria. Once the skin is broken that barrier is gone, and care must be taken to avoid infection. If the blister is prominent and painful enough to preclude dancing, it should be evacuated under sterile conditions. Ideally this should be done by a physician, who can prepare, and evacuate the skin with a needle rather than making a large opening or peeling the surface skin off.

Abscesses.   All of the problems relating to the skin and nails of the foot offer a potential source of invasion of bacteria. When the bacteria do invade the system in a level excessive for the body's ability to fight them off, then an infection is started; once it becomes an enclosed infection it is known as an abscess. Abscesses are common in feet, again due to the problem of hygiene and the temptation to try to get rid of lesions by picking at them or trying to cut them off. In the event that routine personal hygiene fails to prevent infection, it is again critical that the dancer seek the help of a health care specialist who can offer proper drainage and antibiotic therapy before significant damage is done.

Aerobic Dance Injuries

The bulk of this chapter is related directly to ballet, although it is applicable, in most cases, to other forms of dance. It seems appropriate to include a specific section on aerobic dance because of its present popularity as a form of physical conditioning for the average lay person. The term was coined around 1969 and, as of 1983, there were over 150,000 aerobics participants in this country. The concept of aerobic dance hinges around continuous motion with resultant weight loss, increased cardiorespiratory fitness, and increased musculoskeletal strength. The side-effect is the overall sense of well-being and accomplishment that goes with good health.

Most of the problems related to aerobic dance injuries concern overuse. This is partially due to an early concept of aerobic dance that landing flat-footed could jar fat off the body. Experience has proven that the human is not designed for flat-footed landing, and we are well aware that jarring does not selectively remove fat tissue. Instead, jarring causes a dramatic acceleration of the musculoskeletal system's remodeling efforts, as previously discussed under overuse syndromes. Since this intentional jarring is most frequently done on concrete/tile floors by people who are overweight and out of shape, it is easy to understand the high rate of overuse syndrome problems.

As in most activities the instructors are the key to resolving the problems with aerobic dance. It is important that they understand the value of landing on the ball of the foot and cushioning onto the heel rather than landing flatfooted. It is also important that they understand the value of having some form of a resilient floor or, if that is not available, to be certain that the dancers wear shoes with satisfactory cushioning built in.

Finally, instructors must be able to observe a new class and recognize the levels of fitness, then bring the class along at a rate gradual enough to encourage conditioning rather than destruction.

Aerobic dance, jazzercise, dancersize, and other forms of dance exercise can be very beneficial in improving the overall physiological and psychological well-being of the general public. It is important that those who are involved in dance be aware of the difference in levels of commitment between the serious dancer and the average person who takes a dance class for fun and fitness.

General Principles and Philosophy

After having covered an extensive amount of material in the initial portion of this chapter it seems appropriate to summarize the whole area and give some general recommendations.

Causes of Lower Extremity Problems

To some extent injuries are inherent to the activities of dance. We must accept the fact that not all people are anatomically correct for a career in the field of dancing. Pierre Beauchamp (choreographer for King Louis XIV) formalized the five classic positions of the feet in ballet, based on original fencing positions. The day that these positions became accepted as the ideal for ballet, a certain type of dancer was predetermined. People with limited anatomic turnout and those with abnormal shape or alignment of the knee were automatically placed at high risk. The young dancers' desire to satisfy themselves and their instructors by attaining a maximum turnout has led to the process of cheating. The cheating or screwing home of the knee leads to patellofemoral problems, and there seems to be a significant risk of causing tears of the meniscus by leaping from the cheated position. The development of *pointe* places the person with an excessively long second metatarsal or with a high arched foot at risk of developing foot and toe problems.

The controllable things that have a definite effect on injury occurrence include choreography, fatigue, and the type of surface used for practices and performances. Fatigue seems to be one of the most important controllable items; not only should the dancers be aware of their own stamina, but instructors, choreographers, and company directors need to be aware of the inherent danger in overwork.

Despite every effort to select, train, supervise, and protect the dancers there will continue to be injuries and medical problems.

Acute Injuries

In the face of an acute injury such as a sprain, strain, fracture, dislocation, or contusion, it is important that those involved in the dance program be aware of initial emergency care. The most important thing in the initial treatment of an injury is to prevent additional damage. Ideally, injured extremities should be splinted as is and the dancer transferred for proper medical care. When no one is qualified to splint adequately and transport, accept the limitation and call an emergency response facility for professional help. A dancer with an injury that prevents weight bearing, causes severe pain for over five minutes, involves visible deformity, or causes loss of sensation or pulses in an extremity should be treated as an emergency case and transported to a proper medical facility.

The best time to select a person to give medical care is before an injury occurs. A relationship should be established with a physician in the local community who is both medically qualified and either already knowledgeable in dance or willing to be taught. Under those conditions dancers can anticipate care that is most likely to return them to the studio safely and as rapidly as possible.

Chronic Problems

Recognizing chronic (overuse) problems requires understanding and concern. All dancers, from the beginning student to the company member, should be confident that recognition of a medical problem will not jeopardize their future or their position. Even though most overuse syndromes respond well to rest, anti-inflammatory medication, and appropriate rehabilitation protocols, the rate of response is dramatically affected by the timing of the initial recognition and treatment. An acceptable rule of thumb is that any problem that is severe enough to limit the dancer's participation or fails to resolve spontaneously within ten days requires evaluation by a qualified physician. Ideally, the involved physician should be available on a weekly basis to deal with the nagging, chronic, low-grade problems that any of the dancers are experiencing. This availability encourages the dancer to be examined early in the development of a problem. Early treatment offers quicker and easier resolution than does treatment delayed until the dancer is disabled.

Companies or schools with an inordinate number of cases of over-use syndrome should carefully review the previously noted controllable factors. Specifically, what is the floor surface upon which the dancers are training? What is the pattern of work and rest? Are the dancers being properly conditioned and prepared for the level of work they are performing? Is the choreography becoming too aggressive and athletic for the type of company member involved?

Treatment and Rehabilitation

It is difficult for a lay person to evaluate the quality of medical care that is received in any circumstance. Within dance it is even more difficult to evaluate because of the superstition and mythology that has surrounded the medical care of dancers for many generations. This chapter will conclude with some general guidelines for the dancer and the dance instructor to use in selecting and evaluating their medical care.

1. A very small percentage of the problems encountered in dancers should require any form of surgical intervention. A physician who repetitively recommends surgery for the vast majority of problems seen should be suspect of questionable judgment. Although there are some specific entities that require surgical intervention, this should be limited to major injuries and refractory overuse problems that do not respond to a full conservative treatment program.

2. There is a place for the use of massage, manipulative mechano-therapists, chiropractic manipulation, podiatric treatment, and other forms of treatment. The problem with utilizing these modalities initially is that the individuals offering the treatments are frequently not fully qualified to evaluate and recognize problems that require a different approach. All problems should be evaluated by a qualified, interested physician before referral to one of the other individuals noted.

3. Although rest is frequently referred to in the treatment protocols for dancers, it would be far more accurate to think in terms of relative rest. Most problems can be managed by specifically altering class and dance activity to avoid stress on that particular area. That may range from only allowing bar work chest deep in a pool for the buoyancy effect and massaging action of the water, through the opposite extreme of allowing everything except leaps. On occasion, limiting only the *grand plié* position to avoid the deep knee bend may be appropriate while allowing all other forms of work. The physician who understands both the physical and the psychological aspects of dance will very seldom ask the dancer to undertake

total rest. There are many ways of altering a program to allow maintenance of physical fitness, flexibility, and skill level at the same time that the injured part is rested.

4. The physician should be willing to refer patients to the other health deliverers previously noted and to utilize physical therapy modalities such as ultrasound, transcutaneous neuromuscular stimulation, cryotherapy, and protective functional bracing. The company or school should be associated with a physician who is willing to use a variable approach to problems and listen to the wisdom that has been handed down through the ages of experience within the dance community.

The final point that should be made absolutely clear is that there is very little place for the use of heat in extremity injuries. When dealing with the thigh, knee, leg, ankle, or foot remember, when in doubt, use ice. Useful mnemonic phrases are, "Ice is nice" and, for the injured dancer, "Have a NICE day" which is synonymous with "Have an ICE day."

Addendum. The author apologizes to those readers who are primarily interested in forms of dance other than ballet. The literature and the experience available are strongly weighted toward the area of ballet. It is the organized form of dance, that we, as physicians, have had the greatest chance to explore and experience. The information on injury problems and specific characteristics of other dancers is gradually becoming available but there is not yet enough to warrant drawing major conclusions or making major recommendations specific to those areas.

References

Bergfeld, J.A. (1982). The dancer disabled. The dancer's knee. *Emergency Medicine, 14,* 32–41.

Bergfeld, J.A., Micheli, L.J., Hamilton, W.G., Clippinger, K., Weiker, G.G., Hudacek, L.A., Sammarco, G.J., Molnar, M., & Calabrese, L.H. (1982). Medical problems in ballet: A roundtable discussion. *The Physician and Sportsmedicine, 10*(3), 98–114.

Brodelius, A. (1961). Osteoarthrosis of the talar joints in the footballers and ballet dancers. *Osteoarthritis of the Talar Joints,* 309–314.

Calabrese, L.H. (1981, May). *Dietary problems of dancers.* Paper presented at the annual meeting of the American College of Sports Medicine, Miami, FL.

Calabrese, L.H. (1982). The dancer disabled: Other miseries of the dance. *Emergency Medicine, 14,* 57–64.

Fry, R.M. (1983). Dance and orthopaedics: Each type has its special medical problems. *Orthopaedic Review, 12*(11), 49–56.

Grahame, R., & Jenkins, J.M. (1972). Joint hypermobility: Asset or liability? A study of joint mobility in ballet dancers. *Annals of Rheumatic Disease, 31*, 109–111.

Hamilton, W.G. (1982a). Sprained ankles in ballet dancers. *Foot and Ankle, 3*(2), 99–102.

Hamilton, W.G. (1982b). The dancer disabled. The dancer's ankle. *Emergency Medicine, 14*, 42–49.

Horosko, M. (1982, May). The personal you. Feet: Avoiding painful pitfalls. *Dancemagazine,* p. 24.

Liderbach, M. (1983). Sports medicine in action: A primer on aerobic dance. *Muscle and Bone, 3*(4), 3–11.

Lovell, W.W., & Winter, R.D. (Eds.). (1978). *Pediatric Orthopaedics* (Vol. 2). Philadelphia: J.B. Lippincott Co.

Miller, E.H., Callander, J.N., Lawhon, S.M., & Sammarco, G.J. (1984). Orthopaedics and the classical ballet dancer. *Contemporary Orthopedics, 8*, 72–97.

Miller, E.H., Schneider, H.J., Bronson, J.L., & McLain, D. (1975). A new consideration in athletic injuries: The classical ballet dancer. *Clinical Orthopaedics and Related Research, 3*, 181–191.

Sammarco, G.J. (1982). The dancer disabled: The dancer's forefoot. *Emergency Medicine, 14*, 49–59.

Sammarco, G.J. (1984). Treating dancers. *Contemporary Orthopedics, 8*, 15–27.

Thomasen, E. (1982). *Diseases and injuries of ballet dancers.* Aarhuus Stiftsbogtrykkerie.

Trucco, T. (1982, March). To the pointe. *Dance Magazine,* pp. 20–24.

Weiker, G.G. (1982). The dancer disabled: The dancer's spine. *Emergency Medicine, 14*, pp. 28–32.

Weiker, G.G. (1983, September). *Injury to the professional dancer.* Paper presented at a dance medicine symposium, sponsored by Children's Hospital Medical Center, Boston, MA.

Chapter 10

Dance Injuries: The Back, Hip, and Pelvis

Lyle J. Micheli
Children's Hospital Medical Center

My experience in treating injured dancers for a number of years has led me to make some tentative conclusions regarding injuries to the back, hip, and pelvis. First, although other parts of the body are injured in dance with greater frequency, such as the knee or foot, injuries to the hip and back are often more serious and difficult to treat. A back or hip injury may end a promising career for a young dancer or be the final chapter in the career of a mature dancer.

A second conclusion is that many of these injuries are preventable if proper attention is directed to early recognition and preventive exercise and technique (Micheli, 1982b). This awareness must begin early in a dancer's career, regardless of whether it concerns classical ballet, modern, or jazz dancers. Whereas certain injuries, which will be discussed, appear to result primarily from ballet technique, they may be encountered in any dancer, because most dancers, despite primary allegiance to other idioms, still take ballet technique.

Types and Mechanisms of Injury

Injuries to dancers fall into two general classes, based on the mechanism in which the injury occurs: acute injuries, resulting from a single impact or deforming force, such as a fall or a twist; and overuse injuries resulting from repetitive microtrauma, such as repetitive *pliés* at the knee or repetitive hyperextension movements (*arabesque*) of the back (Micheli, 1982a).

The prevention of acute injuries is analogous to accident prevention of any type. However, the prevention of overuse injuries can be dramatically enhanced by careful analysis of host and environmental risk factors which may increase the chance of tissue injury. In dance, these risk factors include:

- too rapid a change in the rate, duration, or intensity of training
- dance technique which places improper demands on the body
- muscle imbalance of strength, endurance, or flexibility
- anatomic malalignments of the dancer, such as internally rotated hips (femoral anteversion), bowed legs, or flat feet
- hardness of dance surface
- shoewear, including improperly fitting or designed ballet or jazz shoes and other associated conditions such as differences of leg lengths; and
- the presence of conditions such as scoliosis of the spine

In the young dancer, the onset of the adolescent growth spurt must be considered an additional risk factor insofar as dramatic imbalances and tightnesses of the muscle groups may develop quite rapidly.

The occurrence of a given injury in a given dancer is usually not the result of a solitary risk factor. Usually, two or even three of these factors may be present in the occurrence of injury. As an example, a young dancer beginning a summer dance program may develop knee pain as a result of the sudden increase in the number of hours danced per week. Additionally, she may change her technique as she begins to force turnout by "screwing out" the lower legs. A third, coexistent risk factor might be onset of a growth spurt, which results in a relative tightening of the thigh muscles and further pressure upon the knee.

Back Injuries

Back injuries are encountered among dancers of all ages and at all levels (see Figure 10.1). We have found that, unlike in other types of dance injuries, such as those of the lower extremities, the length of dancing experience is not a factor in back injury patterns. Male and female dancers both incur back injuries; however, there may be more occurrences among males, due to their lifting activities. Back injuries occur frequently among dancers, rating as the fourth most common site of dance injury in a recent survey of dance injuries in our Sports Medicine Division. Back injuries are often more severe than other types of injuries and require long periods of time-off from dancing to be corrected (Micheli, 1983).

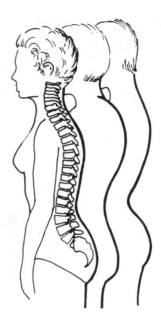

Figure 10.1 The spine consists of 7 cervical vertebrae, 12 thoracic vertebrae, and 5 lumbar vertebrae, with the sacrum at the base. There is a normal cervical lordosis (forward curve), thoracic kyphosis (posterior curve), and lumber lordosis.

Back injuries may be of the single macrotrauma type, resulting from a single twist or fall, or more commonly, of the repetitive microtrauma type. In either case, it is important not only to examine the dancer's back but to evaluate the relative strength, flexibility, and range of motion of their entire body, including the upper and lower extremities. Assessment of the dancer's technique and style is necessary to understand the mechanism of injury and to successfully work towards preventing reinjury. Such an evaluation is necessary to determine which risk factors may be contributing to the occurrence of the injury in question.

There are four categories of back problems encountered most commonly in dancers. These are (a) mechanical low back pain, (b) back pain due to disc disease, (c) spondylolysis, and (d) upper back strain. All four of these very different etiologies of back pain may begin with only pain and stiffness. Back pain due to a ruptured or bulging disc may be associated with pain, numbness, or tingling radiating down the leg to the calf or foot (sciatica). Pain due to a spondylolysis is often increased by extending the back as in an *arabesque*.

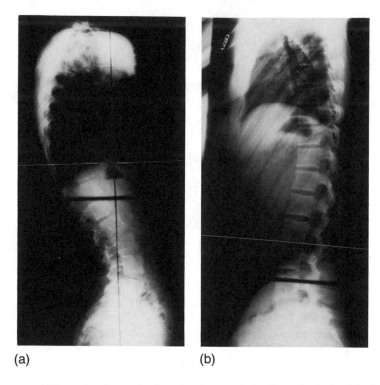

(a)   (b)

Figure 10.2   (a) Lateral radiograph of a spine demonstrating hyperlordosis of the lumbar spine. Contrast this with the lateral radiograph of a more normally contoured spine (b).

Mechanical Low Back Pain

Mechanical low back pain is the back disorder most frequently encountered in young dancers. This problem is usually associated with hyperlordotic posturing of the low back, or sway back (see Figure 10.2). Hyperlordosis in a dancer is almost always an acquired posture, which is observable during *barre* or floor work. This posture is usually due to a combination muscle imbalance with relatively weak abdominals and relatively tight lumbodorsal fascia. This posture may also be the result of poor technique, as the dancer attempts to increase his or her turnout at the hip by swaying the back. This trick of increasing turnout should be corrected as soon as it is observed; besides being aesthetically displeasing, it increases the chance of back injury to the dancer.

Thus moving, lifting, and turning with hyperlordotic posture often leads to mechanical low back pain. The diagnosis should be made only after more specific entities have been eliminated such as discogenic back pain (due to a rupture or bulge of the disc—"cushion"), spondylolysis, tumors or infections of the spine, and all other diseases of the young (Micheli, 1979). Management of this condition usually consists of a directed exercise program to strengthen the abdominal muscles; in addition, the dance teacher is advised to emphasize the avoidance of hyperlordosis while dancing. In mechanical back pain with lumbar lordosis that does not respond to exercises alone, we have used an antilordotic brace in addition to the exercise program (Micheli, Hall, & Miller, 1980) (see Figure 10.3). Treatment usually lasts four to six months, with the dancer wearing the brace full-time, except during dance activities.

Discogenic Back Pain

Another type of low back pain encountered in the dancer is discogenic back pain, with or without associated sciatica. This problem is usually encountered in the male dancer, and again, is associated with hyperlordosis during either free dancing or lifting. Every attempt is made to treat this nonoperatively. Initial treatment may be that of relative rest, permitting the dancer to continue dancing on a limited basis, while discontinuing lifting and avoiding all painful moves. A directed exercise program including abdominal strengthening, lower extremity stretching exercises, and swimming is also prescribed. Anti-inflammatory and muscle relaxant medications may be helpful. At times, we will prescribe a brace to help support the back while the body heals the injury.

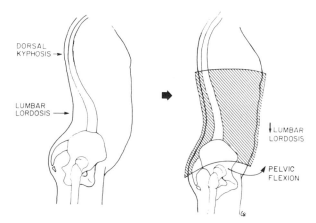

Figure 10.3 Antilordotic bracing for hyperlordotic back pain, decreasing lumbar lordosis and helping to forward flex the pelvis.

A dancer with a serious disc herniation, involving disabling pain and progressive neurologic loss, requires a more drastic treatment program of complete bed rest, local heat, analgesics, and muscle relaxants. In certain cases, a Chymopapain injection (chymopapain is an enzyme made from papaya juice, which can dissolve bulging disc material) may be considered as an additional treatment. This measure may be an effective alternative to surgery in certain cases. If a surgical discectomy is absolutely necessary, the dancer must be informed that he or she will be unable to perform fully for twelve months, that an extensive rehabilitation program will be required, and that the possibility of further professional dancing will depend totally on the extent of recovery (Micheli, 1985b).

Spondylolysis

The third category of back injury in the dancer is spondylolysis. The incidence of spondylolysis among dancers perhaps equals that of gymnasts, which is greater than that of the general population (Micheli, 1985a). Dance and gymnastics both require repetitive flexion and extension of the spine, which may result in a stress fracture through the pars interarticularis portion of the lumbar spine. Spondylolysis should be strongly suspected in dancers with persistent low back pain, who do not respond to the treatment outlined earlier for mechanical low back pain. Pain during hyperextension of the back while standing on one foot, as in the *arabesque*, is often the first sign of a spondylolytic stress fracture. Physical examination usually reveals a limited movement in the lumbar spine on forward bending and pain with hyperextension of the back. These findings are frequently accompanied by tight hamstrings, but, except for rare occasions of associated sciatica, the neurological examination of the lower extremities is usually unremarkable.

Oblique radiographs of the lumbosacral spine often are needed to diagnose a pars fracture. If the radiograph does not reveal a fractured pars, however, a bone scan is done, because radiographic change may not be evident at the site of a stress fracture until a significant period of time after injury (Rosen, Micheli, & Treves, 1982) (see Figure 10.4). Spondylolysis in a young dancer, associated with pain of less than six months in duration, should be treated as a fracture, and an antilordotic brace should be used to achieve reduction and immobilization. In addition, we recommend an antilordotic exercise program. Dance training may be continued through the bracing period, as long as there is no pain.

Spondylolytic lesions which do not heal do not necessarily have to end a dancer's career. Often, a directed antilordotic and abdominal strengthening program, coupled with the avoidance of painful technique and jumping activities, eliminates pain and allows for dance participation. This type of spondylolysis is a stable condition and usually does not result in further forward slipping, or spondylolisthesis. The dancer has a stable back and, although they may not be able to dance comfortably, they may dance safely.

A dancer with spondylolysis, unresponsive to treatment, may be relieved of pain through fusion of the unstable segment (Micheli, 1985b). Dancing may be resumed after solid fusion is attained, which usually takes 12 months.

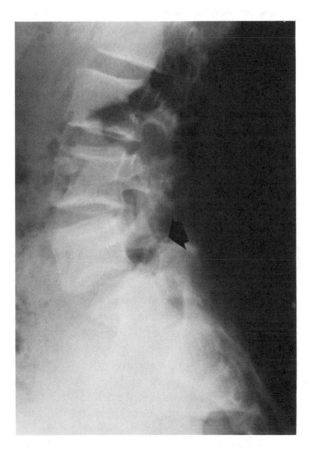

Figure 10.4 Lateral radiograph of the lumbar spine demonstrating a spondylolytic fracture through the Pars Interarticularis of the fifth lumbar vertebrae.

Upper Back Strain

The fourth type of back injury encountered in dancers is upper back strain. Injuries to the soft tissue of the upper back and periscapular musculature occur in both male and female dancers. Female dancers usually injure this area while performing movements requiring elevation and rotation of the upper arm. The male dancer is prone to acute muscle-tendon strains from lifting, especially if a lift is attempted while the dancer is off-balance.

The management of both types of strain is similar. A cold spray or ice massage will provide immediate symptomatic relief, permitting completion of a performance. Immediate mechanical massage may reduce limitation of motion and associated muscle spasms. Use of mild nonsteroidal anti-inflammatory medications may help to speed recovery and relieve muscle stiffness. Ice massage before rehearsal helps eliminate pain, and heat and massage after class appear to limit the extent of stiffness. Simple strengthening exercises, using a dumbbell or hand resistance, have been useful in speeding recovery and preventing recurrence in both male and female dancers.

Injury Prevention

The prevention of back injuries among dancers begins with the dance training of the young boy or girl dancer. The instructor should check for lordotic posturing at the *barre* and during floor exercises and correct it promptly, stressing that the dancer should pull up into the torso. Specific exercises to strengthen the abdominals and increase the flexibility of the lumbodorsal fascia will also help to counteract hyperlordotic tendencies. An adolescent dancer should be watched closely during periods of rapid growth to prevent development of this incorrect posture.

The older dancers must also pay strict attention to their technique and possibly use supplementary exercises to avoid a hyperlordotic posture. The male dancer should always use proper lifting technique, using strong quads and gluteii, while avoiding a lordotic sway in their back. Weight training of the entire body is a helpful step towards protecting the back, and if done properly, does not interfere with dance technique.

Finally, it is important to remember that a 20 to 30 minute period of slow progressive stretching should always be done before a class or performance. While most dancers and dance teachers realize the role a proper warm-up plays in the prevention of injuries, this should be frequently emphasized to the young dancer.

Injuries to The Hip and Pelvis

Dance related injuries to the hip and pelvis include avulsions of tendons seen in young dancers, muscle strains or contusions, hip sprains, stress fractures, "snapping hip," and arthritis.

Avulsion Injuries

Avulsion injuries about the hip and pelvis are acute macrotrauma injuries in which the site of insertion of a tendon into bone is pulled away (Rosen, Micheli, & Treves, 1982). These injuries are only encountered in young dancers who are still growing and in whom the site of insertion (the apophysis) is relatively weaker than both the tendon and the bone, because it consists of growth cartilage. These avulsions may occur wherever major muscle groups insert out of the bones of the pelvis. These injuries include avulsions of the iliac crest, the site of insertion of the lateral abdominal muscles; the anterior superior spine of the pelvis, the site of sarterious muscle insertions; the anterior inferior iliac spine, or origin of the rectus femorous; ischeal tuberosity, common origin of the hamstring muscles; and the lesser trochanter of the hip, the site of insertion of the powerful iliopsoas muscle (see Figure 10.5).

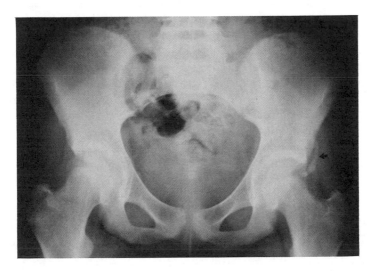

Figure 10.5 Avulsion of the apophyseal site of insertion of the rectus femoris muscle from the front of the hip.

These injuries can be extremely painful, initially. Diagnosis is made by careful examination to determine the site of maximal tenderness and by radiographic assessment. Special X-ray views may be required to show the fracture. Oblique views of the pelvis as well as inlet and outlet views should be considered if plain radiographs do not clearly show an avulsion.

Treatment usually consists of icing, rest, slow resumption of activity, and strength exercises as the injury heals. Follow-up radiographs should be obtained to determine satisfactory union, which almost always occurs. Very rarely, persistent pain at the site of avulsion, usually due to bony overgrowth at the site of healing, may require surgical excision of the hypertrophic bone. This appears to happen most frequently at the sites of major ischial avulsions in the buttock.

Stress Fractures

As at other sites in the body, stress fractures about the hip and pelvis are often diagnosed late, frequently being confused with tendinitis or fasciitis. Persistent pain, unresponsive to the usual conservative management of tendinitis, combined with localized tenderness over the bone in question should raise the suspicion of stress fracture. Stress fractures may occur in the pelvis itself (in the pubic or ischial rami) or in the hip (usually at the base of the neck or femur). Stress fractures at these sites often may be difficult to visualize by plain radiographs, and bone scan may be necessary to confirm the diagnosis (Rosen, Micheli, & Treves, 1982). Suspicion of this relatively rare injury should arise in the observance of any unusual, persistent pain at this site, particularly if the onset of pain has followed a relative increase of rate, intensity, or duration of training.

Once diagnosed, treatment is that of relative rest. Stress fractures of the femur usually require crutch support. If pain persists despite crutch support, spica cast immobilization may be required. We have never had to perform pin fixation in a dancer or athlete in order to obtain healing in stress fractures of the hip, although some reports in the medical literature recommend this (Hajeck & Noble, 1982).

Usually the dancer can be successfully treated with six weeks of crutch gait, while being maintained on a swimming and exercise cycle program to support fitness. Training is then resumed in a progressive fashion, proceeding from floor *barre* to full *barre*. Jumping can usually be resumed after 12 weeks of treatment.

Musculotendinous Injuries

Muscle strains and contusions, as well as hip sprains, are occasionally encountered as acute injuries in the dancer. These are both managed initially, as with any acute injury in the athlete or dancer, according to the acronym RICE: relative rest, icing, compression, and elevation.

Icing is often best attained using ice massage. This is conveniently done by freezing water in a styrofoam cup, then removing the top edge, and while holding the butt edge, massaging the injured area for a maximum of 12 to 15 minutes. Therapeutic exercises, to restore the strength and range of motion of the hip, are begun as soon as possible. Dance technique is then advanced as rapidly as possible without causing recurrence of pain, swelling, or tenderness. These injuries may be fully resolved within 3 weeks, although a bad hip sprain may require as much as 12 weeks to heal.

Snapping Hip

A relatively frequent complaint encountered in dancers is that of "snapping hip." In actuality, snapping about the hip appears to have two distinct anatomic sites: on the lateral (outer) surface of the hip overlying the trochanter, and antermedial (near the groin), deep to the great vessels (Jacobs & Young, 1978; Lindenberg, Pinshaw, & Noakes, 1984). Snapping may exist at both of these sites without associated pain. However, it has been our experience that, if snapping is allowed to persist, both sites will usually become painful and will limit dancing.

The lateral snapping hip, iliotibial band friction syndrome, is easily diagnosed and treated (Lindenberg et al., 1984). Examination reveals the site of maximum tenderness to be immediately over the prominence of the greater trochanter. A particular examination and maneuver, the Ober test, is useful in confirming this diagnosis. The dancer is asked to lie on his or her side with the painful side uppermost. The contralateral, lower leg is flexed to 90 degrees at the hip and knee. The examiner then stands behind the dancer and places one hand above the hip and one hand beneath the knee, in effect cradling the weight of the entire leg. This leg is then also flexed to 90 degrees at the hip and knee and is then abducted and extended at the hip, while keeping the knee flexed. The leg is then allowed to adduct toward the examining table. This will reproduce the snap and the pain as the iliotibial band, which is usually tight and tender, impinges on the greater trochanter of the hip. This condition is usually satisfactorily treated by anti-inflammatory medications, therapeutic exercises to stretch the ileotibial band, and icing. Occasionally a corticosteroid injection into the trochanter bursa beneath the ileotibial band may be required if inflammation persists in the bursa, despite progressive stretching of the ileotibial band.

The inner, or medial snapping hip has been a source of much more controversy (Sammarco, 1983). Some physicians have suggested that the snap is due to a subluxation (partial dislocation) of the hip out of its socket. Recent observations, however, have suggested that its snap is due to the iliopsoas tendon sliding over the neck of the femur (Schaberg, Harper, & Allen, 1985).

Usually, the dancer complains of a painful snap while performing a *ronds de jambe* (circumduction of lower limb) or *developpé en l'air*. Often, the snap occurs as the leg is returned to the floor. On examination, the dancer can reproduce the painful snap while standing. We have usually not been able to reproduce the snap with the dancer supine. Supine examination, however, will elicit pain when hip flexion is resisted from the neutral or frog position. Often, tenderness can be elicited by palpation of the lesser trochanter with the hip postured in the frog position, flexed and externally rotated.

We believe that this mechanical irritation of the iliopsoas tendon is due, at least in part, to the development of an abduction, external rotation contracture about the hip, particularly in ballet dancers. Poor postural alignment and poor technique, by which the dancer tends to posture and work with excessive pelvic extension (i.e., hanging on the front of the hip), may also be contributing factors.

Proper management consists of correcting the muscle imbalance about the hip and working carefully with the dancer's technique and posture to take the strain off the iliopsoas tendon and prevent the impingement on the femoral neck. These therapeutic exercises consist of stretching and flexibility exercises to the hip external rotators, and strengthening of the hip extensors, adductors, and internal rotators. Anti-inflammatory medication and therapeutic modalities, such as deep heat and ultrasound, may also be helpful in the early stages of management. This approach has been quite successful in our clinic for managing this condition. In three cases that were unresponsive to this treatment, with persistent pain and snapping despite prolonged conservative management, it was necessary to surgically release the iliopsoas sheath. This was successfully performed in all three cases using the medial, transadducter approach.

Arthritis of the Hip

Occasionally, complaints of persistent hip pain after dancing may be the first sign of degenerative arthritis of the hip. Clues to this diagnosis may be subtle loss of hip rotation and abduction and pain elicited by internal rotation of the hip after it has been flexed to 90 degrees. Anteroposterior and lateral radiographs will usually confirm this diagnosis. Mild hip arthritis in the dancer may be successfully managed for years with anti-inflammatory medication and gentle exercise to maintain the range of motion and strength about the hip. In our experience, the majority of dancers who have developed degenerative arthritis of the hip have been males. Interestingly, this usually affects the left hip, at least initially; a possible explanation for this affinity for the left hip may be the fact that landings from jumps occur with greater frequency on the left leg. Although many dancers with early arthritis may continue to dance effectively for a number of years after the initial diagnosis with proper management, loss of motion and pain may ultimately prevent continued performance. Despite this, the dancer may continue successful teaching for many years.

If the hip arthritis and pain becomes severe, reconstructive surgery of the hip, including hip replacement, may be necessary. A number of well-known dancers, including Edward Villella, have undergone successful hip replacement and continued functioning and teaching.

Summary

The back is the fourth most common site of dance injuries. There are four types of commonly occurring back injuries: mechanical low back pain, back pain due to disc disease, spondylolysis, and upper back strain. Mechanical low back pain is frequently found in young dancers and is usually associated with hyperlordotic posturing of the low back. Strength and flexibility exercises for muscle imbalances can help to correct this problem. Pain due to disc disease is usually encountered in male dancers and is also associated with hyperlordosis of the lower back. In milder cases, strengthening and flexibility exercises are a successful treatment; in more severe cases, where there is disc herniation, more drastic treatment of complete rest and muscle relaxants is recommended.

Spondylolysis is the third category of back injury and is basically a stress fracture in the lumbar spine. This condition is oftentimes treated with a brace and/or an abdominal strengthening program. Upper back strain, the fourth type of back injury, is a result of acute muscle-tendon strains from lifting a partner in the case of male dancers, and from movements requiring elevation and rotation of the upper arm in the case of female dancers. Ice massage and sometimes nonsteroidal, anti-inflammatory medications are used as treatments.

Injuries to the hip and pelvis include avulsion of the tendons, muscle strains or contusions, hip sprains, stress fractures, and arthritis. Avulsion injuries about the hip and pelvis are acute microtrauma in which the tendon is pulled away from the bone. These occur most frequently in growing dancers. In mild forms, the treatment consists of icing, rest, and slow resumption of normal movement. Stress fractures are diagnosed and treated in much the same way as described for the back.

Musculotendinous injuries, including strains, contusions and hip sprains, are encountered as acute injuries and are treated by rest, ice, compression, and elevation. Arthritis of the hip is diagnosed as a persistent pain with subtle loss of rotation and abduction. In the mild form, anti-inflammatory medication may allow the dancer to successfully manage a career for years. In a more severe form, the pain and loss of motion may ultimately prevent continued performance.

This chapter has provided a description of the types of injuries and their diagnosis and treatment that occur in the back, hip, and pelvis of dancers.

References

Hajek, M.R., & Noble, H.B. (1982). Stress fractures of the femoral neck in runners. *American Journal of Sports Medicine, 10*, 112-116.

Jacobs, M., & Young, R. (1978). Snapping hip phenomenon among dancers. *American Corrective Therapy Journal, 32*(3), 92-98.

Lindenberg, G., Pinshaw, R., & Noakes, T.D. (1984). Ileotibial band friction syndrome in runners. *Physician and Sportsmedicine, 12*(5), 118-130.

Micheli, L.J. (1979). Low back pain in the adolescent: Differential diagnosis. *American Journal of Sports Medicine, 7*(6), 362-364.

Micheli, L.J. (1982a). Lower extremity injuries. In R.C. Cantu (Ed.), *Sports medicine in primary care* (pp. 195-216). Lexington, MA: Collamore.

Micheli, L.J. (1982b). Prevention of dance injuries. In R.C. Cantu & W.J. Gillespie (Eds.), *Sports medicine, sports science: Bridging the gap* (pp. 137-141). Lexington, MA: Collamore.

Micheli, L.J. (1983). Back injuries in dancers. *Clinics in Sports Medicine,* **2**(3), 473-484.

Micheli, L.J. (1985a). Back injuries in gymnastics. *Clinics in Sports Medicine,* **4**(1), 85-93.

Micheli, L.J. (1985b). Sports following spine surgery in the young athlete. *Clinical Orthopaedic and Related Research,* **188**, 152-157.

Micheli, L.J., Hall, J.E., & Miller, M.E. (1980). Use of the modified Boston brace for back injuries in athletes. *American Journal of Sports Medicine,* **8**, 351-356.

Papanicolaou, N., Wilkinson, R.H., Emans, J.B., Treves, S., & Micheli, L.J. (in press). Bone scintography and radiology in young athletes with low back pain. *American Journal of Roentgenology.*

Rosen, P.R., Micheli, L.J., & Treves, S. (1982). Early scintographic diagsis of bone stress and fracture in adolescent athletes. *Pediatrics,* **70**(1), 11-15.

Sammarco, G.J. (1983). The dancer's hip. *Clinics in Sports Medicine,* **2**(3), 485.

Schaberg, J., Harper, M.C., & Allen, W. (1984). Snapping hip syndrome. *American Journal of Sports Medicine,* **12**, 361-365.

Chapter 11

Menstrual Effects of Dance Training

Michelle P. Warren
St. Luke's–Roosevelt Hospital – Roosevelt Site

Dancers, like gymnasts, figure skaters, and certain athletes rely to a great degree on the maintenance of an ideal body form to project their art. In dance, the ideal form is generally thin, ranging from 10 to 20% below ideal weight (Brooks-Gunn, Warren, & Hamilton, in press). Along with strength, coordination, and talent, this highly desirable physique is more easily attainable in certain individuals than in others.

In sports, where low body weight is desirable for aesthetic or performance reasons, female athletes may engage in moderate to severe dieting (Hamilton, Brooks-Gunn, & Warren, 1985; Warren, 1985b). The extensive physical training that accompanies dieting to maintain an ideal thin body form is associated with a number of physiological changes and medical problems including delayed pubertal and delayed menarche (age of first period). Some of these problems appear to be compounded by the extensive training in adolescence which occurs in dance, particularly ballet. The problems which emerge are further enhanced by the fact that certain forms of dance, particularly ballet, attract primarily middle- to upper-class, adolescent white females. In this group, eating disorders are much more common, and these may also contribute to delayed puberty. The somatotype associated with a condition such as delayed puberty also favors a superior athletic performance. This is particularly true in certain disciplines (Wakat, Sweeney, & Rogol, 1982; Expenschade, 1940; Sinning & Lindberg, 1972; Wilmore, Brown, & Davis, 1977; Malina, 1978), especially in ballet.

Although some researchers believe that training and diet affect the onset of puberty, another theory proposes that children who have a delay in pubertal development may be socialized into competitive athletics or ballet (Malina, 1983). Thus there are compelling reasons to suggest that the problems which emerge in the dance setting are a result of inherited, physical, and metabolic or social forces, or a most likely combination of all the factors. In addition, these observations may apply to girls but not to boys, as the immature somatotype which favors performance in girls may not be important for performance in boys. In fact, one study showed that the more mature somatotype with the more advanced bone age favors athletic performance in boys (Cumming, Garand, & Borysyk, 1972).

Whatever the dynamic factors are which influence the emergence of these medical problems, certain conditions are now well-known: Classical ballet is a discipline where training starts before puberty, and both the physical and artistic pursuits involved do not demand the high-energy expenditure of many other athletic endeavors (Kirkendall & Calabrese, 1983; Schantz & Astrand, 1984; Seliger, Glucksmann, Pachlopnik, & Pachlopnik, 1970). Because dance is basically nonaerobic, weight control and thinness are primarily achieved through dietary restriction, rather than from endurance training (Calabrese & Kirkendall, 1983; Cohen, Potosnak, Frank, & Baker, 1985). The incidence of anorexia nervosa from psychiatric case studies is fairly low (0.3/100,000) (Kendell, Hall, Harley, & Babigan, 1973). Among adolescent girls in private schools in the U.S. and abroad, the incidence runs somewhere between 1 in 100, and 1 in 200, respectively (Crisp, Palmer, & Kalucy, 1976). In specialized groups, the incidence of this condition rises dramatically. A professional dance company reports an incidence of 1 in 20 (Garner & Garfinkel, 1978). Recent data indicate that the incidence of this problem in dancers is really much higher than 1 in 20 and may be in fact as high as 1 in 5 (Hamilton, Brooks-Gunn, & Warren, 1985). Thus the high incidence of anorexia nervosa among ballet dancers is a possible reflection of environmental influences such as dieting.

In order to understand menstrual problems which occur in dancers, it is important to understand the mechanisms which initiate normal pubertal development and menstrual cycles in females and to examine their relationship to weight, dieting, and stress. The problems associated with alterations in menstrual cycles as they are seen in dancers will also be explored.

Reproductive Development in the Female Ballet Dancer

With the onset of reproductive maturity at the age of 9 or 10, adolescent females start to secrete estrogen. One of the first physiological indications of this hormonal secretion is the accumulation of body fat (Warren, 1983). This is a normal event with the development of reproductive maturity and occurs both in women and in men. Women have a large increase in body fat, representing as much as 11 kg over a two to three year period. Unfortunately, this rapid increase in body fat is unacceptable to certain athletic disciplines and, as a result, young dancers will start to diet. At every age studied, dancers are significantly lower in weight than their peers. Most likely as a result of this dieting, ballet dancers have a delay in pubertal development and in menarche when compared with other groups (Malina, 1983).

On average, 15- to 16-year-old boys in the United States are expected to have 14 to 16% of their body weight as fat. Girls will have considerably more (Bray, 1976). Champion high school wrestlers, male gymnasts, and distance runners however, will only have 5 to 7% of their body weight estimated to be fat. High school girls who are not particularly athletic have between 20 and 27% body fat (Tcheng & Tipton, 1973) (see Figure 11.1). Female dancers are often urged to reduce their body fat to less than 10% of their body weight. This dieting behavior will arrest or delay normal pubertal development which is associated with fat accumulation (Warren, 1983).

Delayed Menarche

Delayed menarche in dancers has been well-documented (Warren, 1980; Frisch, Wyshak, & Vincent, 1980). It seems likely that dieting and nutrition are the main causes of pubertal delay in dancers. One study (Brooks-Gunn & Warren, in press) showed that dancer's menarcheal age was most influenced by leanness, rather than the mother's menarcheal age. Generally mother and daughter menarcheal age is closely related, reflecting genetic influences. Recent evidence suggests also that the large energy drain associated with training in adolescents may affect pubertal development. In fact, one study of athletes has suggested that the delay in menarche is directly related to the amount of training in early adolescence, with a four-month delay occurring for each year of training prior to menarche (Frisch et al., 1981).

Warren (1980) followed dancers in a professional ballet school for three to five years. The advancement of pubertal stages occurred during times of rest revealing evidence of a training and activity effect. The training and activity effect was all the more impressive because of the rapidity of development during the nontraining times. Normal girls may take an average of 1.9 $\pm$ 0.95 years (mean $\pm$ SD) to progress from a Tanner breast stage two to stage four, whereas in some dancers, during nontraining, an extraordinary progression was noted in as little as four months (Warren, 1980). Thus, in some dancers, rest leads to a striking catch-up in puberty. These effects are more notable in women of lower body weight or body fat. However, it is important to note that these individuals who are training heavily and eating marginally do not generally appear malnourished.

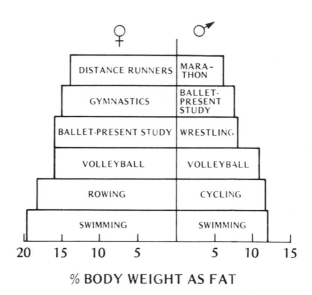

Figure 11.1   Percentage body fat in various sports. From *Physiological Aspects of Dance* by D.T. Kirkendall and L.H. Calabrese, 1983, p. 529. Reprinted by permission.

Another observation is that reproductive abnormalities are more common in those who are more stressed while exercising. Stress is a very difficult variable to control because it is extremely subjective. The Warren (1980) study revealed, however, that young musicians who trained and performed professionally did not show the same delay in puberty as was seen in the young dancers. This suggests that other variables besides stress are operative in the dancers (see Figure 11.2.).

Reproductive abnormalities also appear in those who lose significant amounts of weight. According to Frisch, the onset of menarche in normal girls is correlated to not only weight but a calculated amount of body fat (approx. 16 kg). This represents a percentage of total weight between 22% and 24% (Frisch & McArthur, 1974; Malina, Spirduso, Tate, & Baylor, 1978; Frisch, Revelle, & Cooks, 1973; Frisch, 1976).

Warren's study (1980) of ballet dancers revealed another interesting abnormality. A remarkable dichotomy is noted in the order of pubertal development: Pubarche, or the development of body hair, is reached at a nearly normal age, but breast development and other estrogen related factors are suppressed. The large individual variation among normal girls suggest that there may be independent central mechanisms for triggering these two aspects of pubertal development. The fairly normal pubarche and the remarkable delay in thelarche (breast development) in dancers suggest that the mechanism for pubic hair development was either not affected or, possibly was enhanced by the large caloric demands, whereas the mechanism affecting both breast development and menarche is definitely suppressed (Warren, 1983).

Bone age among dancers is delayed, and growth has been noted as late as 18 and 19 years old. Long-term effects of a delay in puberty on growth and development are not known. Skeletal measurements in our dancers suggest that the delay in menarche may influence long bone growth. The dancers were observed to have a decreased upper to lower body ratio and a significantly increased arm span compared to the female members of the family (Warren, 1980). Final heights (two years post menarche), however, did not differ. The prolonged hypogonadism (lack of sex hormone secretion) may favor long bone growth, leading to eunuchoidal (long extremities) proportions such as are seen in similar syndromes which are congenital (e.g., sexual immaturity due to lack of pituitary gonadotropic function). Nutritional deprivation (Dreizen, Spirakis, & Stone, 1967) may delay epiphyseal closure in the growth centers of the bones as seen in ballet dancers, although a change in skeletal proportions has not been reported on the basis of nutritional factors alone. This should not rule out the possibility, however, that the ballet may be attracting girls with these physical characteristics; consequently, these children may represent a select group.

Other authors have suggested that the physical characteristics associated with later maturation in females are more suitable for successful athletic performance (Wakat et al., 1982; Expenschade, 1940; Sinning & Lindberg, 1972; Wilmore et al., 1977; Malina, 1978). Another study found that the group of women with later menarche were more successful runners (Feicht, Johnson, Martin, Sparkes, & Wagner, 1978). Other studies indicate that gymnasts, runners, and other athletes may have characteristic physiques, suggesting a selective phenomenon (Sinning & Lindberg, 1972; Wilmore et al., 1977; Malina, 1978); this may apply to ballet dancers as well.

The effects of prolonged estrogen deficiency in the adolescent are not known. Recent studies suggest that hypoestrogenism (or lack of the hormone, estrogen) in young athletic women may decrease bone density and, because of this, the specter of premature osteoporosis and delayed bone maturation is a very real concern (Cann, Martin, Genant, & Jaffe, 1984; Drinkwater, Nilson, Chestnut, Bremner, Shainholtz, & Southworth, 1984; Rigotti, Nussbaum, Herzog, & Neer, 1984; Lindberg et al., 1984). This problem may be compounded by the poor diets women follow; ballet dancers have diets which are deficient in vitamin D and calcium (Calabrese & Kirkendall, 1983; Cohen et al., 1985).

Recent studies have also suggested that dieting due to fear of obesity in children may permanently stunt growth (Pugliese, Lifshitz, Grad, Fort, & Marks-Katz, 1983). Although stunted growth has not been reported in dancers, dieting behavior in this group is extremely common, and this problem has not been systematically examined. With respect to dietary behavior, a study on 98 female ballet students (Brooks-Gunn & Warren, in press), ages 11–18, found that weights fell in the lower 50th percentile for age and height. The great majority of the dancers were unsatisfied with their weights and wanted to be thinner. This was definitely unrealistic as many of this group reported a desired weight in the lower tenth percentile. Twenty percent of the entire sample have restrained eating scores (indicative of dietary behavior), reflecting significant dieting behavior ranging from 10% in the 11- to 14-year-olds to over 36% in the 15- to 18-year-olds. The high incidence of anorexia nervosa which emerges in this setting (5–10%) (Hamilton, Brooks-Gunn, & Warren, 1985; Crisp, Palmer, & Kalucy, 1976) and the severe medical problems associated with this disease are of concern to both medical and dance communities. It is important to remember that anorexia nervosa is always accompanied by absence of menses, and menstrual problems may be the first indication that the dancer needs to be brought to the attention of a physician.

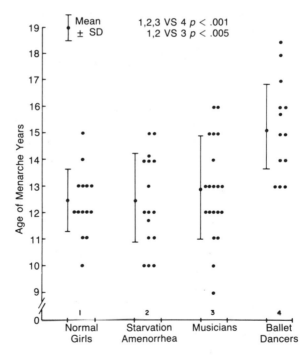

Figure 11.2 Age of menarche in dancers compared to three other groups. From ''The Effects of Exercise on Pubertal Progression and Reproductive Function in Girls,'' by M.P. Warren, 1980, *Journal of Clinical Endocrinology and Metabolism*, **51**(5), p. 1151. Reprinted by permission.

Secondary Amenorrhea and Other Menstrual Disorders

Young ballet dancers who are far more physically active than most of their nondancing contemporaries also experience irregular or absent menstrual periods. Amenorrhea and abnormal cycling, with a shortened luteal phase, have been observed increasingly in women who exercise very heavily, particularly runners, and may be as high as 30% (Shangold, Freeman, Thysen, & Gatz, 1979; Dale, Gerlach, & Wilhite, 1979; Schwartz et al., 1981; Speroff & Redwine, 1980). It is likely that the same phenomenon occurs in dancers. Again, problems are more frequent in dancers with lower body weights and in those who are most active. Their incidence of problems (see Figure 11.3) is directly influenced by these two variables: Increased activity and low body weight are associated with a higher incidence of secondary amenorrhea. These conditions can all be reversed by reducing the amount of exercise. For example, injuries preventing exercise in amenorrheic dancers may precipitate menarche or resumption of menses (Warren, 1980).

Temporal Relationships to Exercise, Stress, and Weight

The impressive temporal relationships between activity, weight delay in menarche, and amenorrhea are exemplified in Figure 11.4. The first dancer had her first menses near her 17th birthday during a vacation interval. There was little change in weight or percent body fat. She developed secondary amenorrhea but menses recurred on two occasions associated with rest.

A second patient showed the same pattern, with menarche occurring during an interval of forced rest due to an injury at age 15. No change in body weight or calculated percent of body fat occurred. With resumption of dancing, however, amenorrhea recurred. Each dancer appears to have her own threshold, and this would tie in with the observation that some subjects lose more weight than others to uncover abnormalities.

A follow-up study of 16 formerly amenorrheic dancers found that resumption of menstruation was associated with a small increase in weight (Warren, 1985a). It has also been reported that the percent of total calories taken as dietary protein was significantly lower in amenorrheic runners than in both runners with normal cycles and nonrunners (Drinkwater et al., 1984). Thus the composition of the diet also may be of importance. A further finding was that leanness alone, without activity, does not necessarily produce amenorrhea, nor does weight gain correct it.

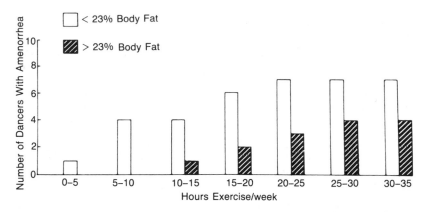

Figure 11.3 Relationship of exercise to amenorrhea in ballet dancers. From ''The Effects of Exercise on Pubertal Progression and Reproductive Function in Girls,'' by M.P. Warren, 1980, *Journal of Clinical Endocrinology Metabolism*, **51**(5), p. 1153. Reprinted by permission.

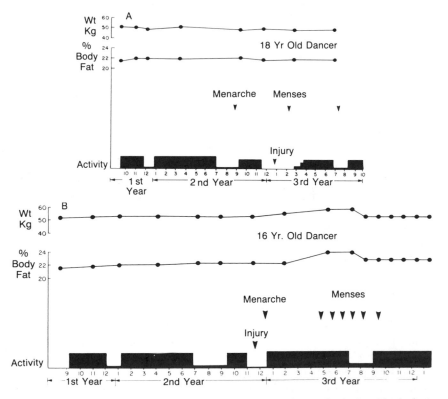

Figure 11.4 Relationships between menses, exercise, weights, and calculated body fat in a young ballet dancer. From ''The Effects of Exercise on Pubertal Progression and Reproductive Function in Girls,'' by M.P. Warren, 1980, *Journal of Clinical Endocrinology Metabolism*, **51**(5), p. 1153. Reprinted by permission.

Although the precise mechanisms involved are unclear, exercise, like weight loss, appears to promote amenorrhea by inhibiting normal release of gonadotropins from the pituitary gland (Warren, 1985b). The continuous, low luteinizing hormone (LH) and low estrogen levels seen in these dancers suggest an abnormality in the part of the brain called the hypothalamus. This organ releases the hormone which stimulates the pituitary hormones LH and follicle stimulating hormone (FSH). LH secretion decreases in subjects with amenorrhea, and the episodic character of secretion is lost. Exercise may interfere with pathways in the arcuate nucleus, an area in the hypothalamus. This would affect neuronal systems known to influence pulsatile release of gonadotropin releasing hormone (GnRH). This hormone determines LH and FSH release from the anterior pituitary. Prolactin is another hormone secreted by the anterior pituitary which can have an important effect on menstrual cycles. Prolactin elevations also have been reported with exercise, although they are generally thought to be unimportant in causing amenorrhea.

Other menstrual problems that may arise include vaginal bleeding of an irregular or heavy nature due to lack of ovulation (anovulation). Anovulation may lead to a heavy period with severe blood loss, anemia, and fainting. Fortunately, this is rare; the more common symptom is very irregular bleeding or rare periods. Lack of adequate hormones, in particular progesterone, after ovulation may cause inadequate luteal phases. The second half of the cycle is shortened due to this hormone imbalance, and periods appear more frequently. More commonly, however, the first part of the menstrual cycle prior to ovulation is prolonged, and cycles may be longer. It is often difficult to differentiate this problem from anovulatory cycles.

Treatment

If all these menstrual effects are reversible, what are the long-term dangers of menstrual irregularities in the dancer? Again, recent evidence suggests that intervals of hypoestrogenism, even in the young women, may lead to premature bone loss. This increases the risk of osteoporosis and the risk of injury in a profession where injuries are common. Thus these menstrual effects, when accompanied by hypoestrogenism, may play an important role in shortening the professional life of a talented performer. One study showed that the bone density of young amenorrheic runners was similar to women in their early fifties (Drinkwater et al., 1984). Although bone densities have not been studied in ballet dancers, similar mechanisms are operative.

Infertility during times of menstrual irregularity or absence of periods is a common event. Because these problems are usually reversible (in severe cases by treatment), they are not usually of great concern to the professional dancer. The menstrual problems can be treated or controlled by hormones with a relatively simple regimen.

Current therapy for amenorrhea involves removing nutritional insults, promoting weight gain, or decreasing exercise. However, pumps which inject GnRH to simulate normal functioning will soon be available to stimulate normal pulsatile secretion and induce puberty, folliculogenesis, ovulation, and menses (Hurley, 1984; Loucopoulus et al., 1984). Exercise-related amenorrheas should respond particularly well to this new form of therapy.

In patients with anovulatory periods, therapy usually is limited to the administration of a progesterone compound such as Provera for 5 to 10 days a month to prevent build-up of the endometrium and hemorrhage. This therapy is also known to prevent the development of precancerous changes that can develop with very prolonged anovulation and estrogen stimulation of the uterus.

The crucial questions concern the necessity for estrogen replacement if the dancer is deficient in this hormone. If a dancer is not producing estrogen, she will probably need estrogen to protect her bones. A tiny dose such as Premarin 0.625 mg or its equivalent is sufficient to protect against osteoporosis in older women and is probably sufficient for young women, too. Provera 10 mg for ten days is usually added to a 21-day cycle of permarin to prevent overgrowth of the uterine lining and rare precancerous changes. The long-term effects of delayed puberty, menstrual irregularity, and amenorrhea in dancers bear further investigation.

Dance, in particular, classical ballet, may have a significant effect on pubertal development and the menstrual cycle. Most of these affects appear to be mediated via hypothalamic mechanisms, involving pathways in the brain which influence Gonadotropin Relaxing Hormone (GWRH). Weight, nutrition, and exercise appear to affect these pathways by mechanisms that are not completely understood. Long-term effects of these abnormalities have yet to be explored, although provocative evidence suggests that the skeleton of young dancers may be adversely influenced by prolonged intervals of amenorrhea. These observations merit further research.

References

Bray, G.A. (1976). Changing body composition from gestation through adult life. In L.H. Smith, Jr. (Ed.), *The obese patient. Major problems in internal medicine* (Vol. 9, pp. 23–33). Philadelphia: W.B. Saunders.

Brooks-Gunn, J., & Warren, M.P. (in press). Effects of delayed menarche as a function of social context. *Journal of Youth and Adolescence.*

Brooks-Gunn, J., & Warren, M.P. (1987). *Delayed menarche in adolescent athletes: Genetic and environment influences.* Manuscript submitted for publication.

Brooks-Gunn, J., Warren, M.P., & Hamilton, L.H. (1987). The relationship of eating disorders to amenorrhea in ballet dancers. *Medicine and Science in Sports and Exercise,* **19**, 41-44.

Calabrese, L.H., & Kirkendall, D.T. (1983). Nutritional and medical considerations in dancers. *Clinics in Sports Medicine,* **2**(3), 539-548.

Cann, E.E., Martin, M.C., Genant, H.K., & Jaffe, R.B. (1984). Decreased spinal mineral content in amenorrheic women. *Journal of the American Medical Association,* **251**, 626-629.

Cohen, J.L., Potosnak, L., Frank, O., & Baker, H. (1985). A nutritional and hematologic assessment of elite ballet dancers. *The Physician and Sportsmedicine,* **13**(50), 43-54.

Crisp, A.H., Palmer, R.L., & Kalucy, R.S. (1976). How common is anorexia nervosa? A prevalence study. *British Journal of Psychiatry,* **128**, 549.

Cumming, G.R., Garand, T., & Borysyk, L. (1972). Correlation of performance in track and field events with bone age. *Journal of Pediatrics,* **80**, 970-973.

Dale, E., Gerlach, D.H., & Wilhite, A.L. (1979). Menstrual dysfunction in distance runners. *Obstetrics and Gynecology,* **54**, 47.

Dreizen, S., Spirakis, C.N., & Stone, R.E. (1967). A comparison of skeletal growth and maturation in undernourished and well-nourished girls before and after menarche. *Journal of Pediatrics,* **70**, 256.

Drinkwater, B.L., Nilson, K., Chestnut, C.H., Bremner, W.J., Shainholtz, S., & Southworth, M.B. (1984). Bone mineral content of amenorrheic and eumenorrheic athletes. *New England Journal of Medicine,* **311**, 277-281.

Expenschade, A. (1940). Motor performance in adolescence. *Monograph Society for Research in Child Development,* **5**, 1-125.

Feicht, C.B., Johnson, T.S., Martin, B.J., Sparkes, K.E., & Wagner, W.W., Jr. (1978). Secondary amenorrhea in athletes. *Lancet,* **2**, 1145.

Frisch, R.E. (1976). Fatness of girls from menarche to age 18 years with a nomogram. *Human Biology,* **48**, 353-359.

Frisch, R.E., Gotz-Welbergen von, A., McArthur, J.W., Albrite, T., Witschi, J., Bullen, S., & Bernko, J. (1981). Delayed menarche and amenorrhea of college athletes in relation to age of onset of training. *Journal of the American Medical Association,* **246**, 1559-1590.

Frisch, R.E., & McArthur, J.W. (1974). Menstrual cycles: Fatness as a determinant of minimum weight and height necessary for their maintenance or onset. *Science,* **185**, 949-951.

Frisch, R.E., Revelle, R., & Cooke, R. (1973). Components of weight at menarche and the initiation of the adolescent growth spurt in girls: Estimated total water, lean body weight and fat. *Human Biology, 45,* 469-483.

Frisch, R.E., Wyshak, G., & Vincent, L. (1980). Delayed menarche and amenorrhea in ballet dancers. *New England Journal of Medicine, 303,* 17-19.

Garner, D.M., & Garfinkel, P.E. (1978). Sociocultural factors in anorexia nervosa. *Lancet, 2,* 674.

Hamilton, L.H., Brooks-Gunn, J., & Warren, M.P. (1985). Sociocultural influences on eating disorders in professional female ballet dancers. *International Journal of Eating Disorders, 4*(4), 465-477.

Hurley, D., Brian, R., Quich, K., Stockdale, J., Fry, A., Hackman, C., Clarke, E., & Berger, H.G. (1984). Induction of ovulation and fertility in amenorrheic women by pulsatile low-dose gonadotrophin releasing hormone. *New England Journal of Medicine, 310,* 1068.

Kendell, R.E., Hall, D.J., Harley, A., & Babigan, H.M. (1973). The epidemiology and anorexia nervosa. *Psychological Medicine, 2,* 200-203.

Kirkendall, D.T., & Calabrese, L.H. (1983). Physiologic aspects of dance. *Clinics in Sports Medicine, 2,* 525.

Lindberg, J.S., Fears, W.B., Hunt, M.M., Powell, M.R., Boll, D., & Wade, C.E. (1984). Exercise-induced amenorrhea and bone density. *Annals of Internal Medicine, 101,* 647-648.

Loucopoulos, A., Ferin, M., VandeWiele, R.L., Dyrenfurth, I., Linkie, D., Yeh, M., & Jewelewicz, R. (1984). Pulsatile administration of gonadotrophin releasing hormone for induction of ovulation. *American Journal of Obstetrics and Gynecology, 148,* 895.

Malina, M. (1978). Physical growth and maturity characteristics of young athletes. In R.A. Magil, H.S. Ash, & F.L. Small (Eds.), *Children in sport: A contemporary anthology* (pp. 79-101). Champaign, IL: Human Kinetics.

Malina, R.M. (1983). Menarche in athletes: A synthesis and hypothesis. *Annals of Human Biology, 10,* 1-24.

Malina, R.M., Spirduso, W.W., Tate, C., & Baylor, A.M. (1978). Age at menarche and selected menstrual charcteristics in athletes at different competitive levels and in different sports. *Medicine and Science in Sports and Exercise, 10,* 218-222.

Pugliese, M.T., Lifshitz, F., Grad, G., Fort, F., & Marks-Katz, M. (1983). Fear of obesity: A cause of short statute and delayed puberty. *New England Journal of Medicine, 309,* 513-518.

Rigotti, N.A., Nussbaum, S.R., Herzog, D.B., & Neer, R.M. (1984). Osteoporosis in women with anorexia nervosa. *New England Journal of Medicine, 311,* 1601-1606.

Schantz, P.G., & Astrand, P. (1984). Physiological characteristics of classical ballet. *Medicine and Science in Sports and Exercise,* **16**(5), 472–476.

Schwartz, B., Cumming, D.C., Riordan, E., Selye, M., Yen, S.S.C., & Rebar, R.W. (1981). Exercise associated amenorrhea: A distinct entity? *American Journal of Obstetrics and Gynecology,* **141**, 662.

Seliger, V., Glucksmann, J., Pachlopnik, J., & Pachlopnik, I. (1970). Evaluation of stage artist's activities on the basis of telemetrical measurements of heart rates. *International Review of Physiology,* **228**, 86–104.

Shangold, M., Freeman, R., Thysen, B., & Gatz, M. (1979). The relationship between long distance running, plasma progesterone, and luteal phase length. *Fertility and Sterility,* **31**, 130.

Sinning, W.E., & Lindberg, G.D. (1972). Physical characteristics of college age women gymnasts. *Research Quarterly,* **43**, 226–234.

Speroff, L., & Redwine, D. (1980). Exercise and menstrual function. *The Physician and Sportsmedicine,* **8**, 42.

Tcheng, T.K., & Tipton, C.M. (1973). Iowa wrestling study: Anthropometric measurements and the predictions of a "minimal" body weight for high school wrestlers. *Medicine and Science in Sports,* **5**, 1–10.

Wakat, D.K., Sweeney, K.A., & Rogol, A.D. (1982). Reproductive system function in women cross-country runners. *Medicine and Science in Sports and Exercise,* **14**, 263–269.

Warren, M.P. (1980). The effects of exercise on pubertal progression and reproductive function in girls. *Journal of Clinical Endocrinological Metabolism,* **51**, 1150–1157.

Warren, M.P. (1983). Physical and biological aspects of puberty. In J. Brooks-Gunn & A. Petersen (Eds.), *Girls in puberty: Biological and psychological perspectives* (pp. 3-28). New York: Plenum.

Warren, M.P. (1985a). Effects of exercise and physical training on menarche. *Seminars in Reproductive Endocrinology,* **3**, 17–26.

Warren, M.P. (1985b). When weight loss accompanies amenorrhea. *Contemporary Obstetrics and Gynecology,* **25**(4), 183–190.

Wilmore, J.H., Brown, C.N., & Davis, J.A. (1977). Body physique and composition of the female distance runner. *Annals of the New York Academy of Science,* **301**, 764-776.

Chapter 12

Nutritional Considerations For Ballet Dancers

Joan E. Benson
Donna M. Gillien
Kathy Bourdet
Alvin R. Loosli
Center for Sports Medicine
Saint Francis Memorial Hospital

In the past few years ballet dancers and their medical problems have received more than perfunctory interest. Investigations into the cardiovascular status of dancers have shown that ballet activity produces VO_2 max values in the range of nonendurance athletes. Calorie expenditure of ballet has been quantified. Recent reports have documented eating disorders, menstrual dysfunction, and increased risk of injury in female ballet dancers of low body weight. Fundamental to all of these issues are the nutrient intake and eating behaviors of dancers.

Prolonged hours of dance training, optimal performance, and excellent health require sufficient calories to maintain body protein and glycogen stores. Sufficient vitamins and minerals are needed to support the metabolic processes of exercise as well as basal functions. In addition, good nutrition practices are particularly important for the adolescent ballet dancer, because pubertal growth and development increase the dietary needs for calories, protein, and micronutrients.

This chapter has two main focuses: the nutritional behaviors of adolescent female ballet dancers and the broader nutritional concerns of adult dancers, including modern dancers. Meal planning, energy needs, and fluid replacement are emphasized.

Inadequate Nutrition and Chronic Calorie Restriction Among Adolescent Ballet Dancers

The medical consequences of inadequate nutrition and chronic calorie restriction in high-performance athletes such as ballet dancers, ice skaters, and gymnasts have received wide recognition and public attention. Increased risk of disturbance in growth and development (Warren, 1983), amenorrhea (Drinkwater, Shangold, Loucks, Wilmore, & Foreman, 1981), decreased bone density (Drinkwater et al., 1984), and anemia (Peterson, 1982) is thought to be prevalent in the chronically dieting population of dancers. In addition, the postulation that the inadequacy of bone nutrients is somehow correlated with the multiple, difficult-to-heal stress fractures in ballet dancers is of interest (Calabrese & Kirkendall, 1983). Although few studies have documented the nutrition status of ballet dancers, Calabrese and others (Calabrese et al., 1983) demonstrated that adult professional female ballet dancers frequently consume a diet of low energy and density. To perform on a professional level, ballet dancers must maintain a sylphlike body, which has been an aesthetic requirement of the art for more than 150 years. Also, like all athletes, they must maintain a high standard of technical proficiency.

In a recent survey (Druss, 1979), ballet dancers listed weight and diet as their chief concerns and admitted to an average daily intake of only 1,000 calories, despite the fact that they exercise six hours a day, six days a week. Ballet is a discipline, however, in which training and technique do not require high-energy expenditure as do other endurance sports. This poses an additional dilemma; dancers can't rely on their training alone to maintain their weight. The incidence of anorexia nervosa in a group of professional ballet dancers was 1 in 20—100 times that of the general population (Garner & Garfinkel, 1978). The ballet population appears to be more susceptible to bizarre eating patterns. Intentional dehydration, laxative abuse, self-induced vomiting, and fasting are all common methods of weight control (Maloney, 1983).

In a recent study we examined the nutritional characteristics of 92 female ballet students ranging in age from 12 to 17 years. Table 12.1 shows mean intake plus or minus SD and the percentage of dancers who consumed less than two-thirds of the RDA for each vitamin or mineral. Of special concern was the percentage of dancers below two-thirds of the RDA in B_6, folacin, calcium, iron, and zinc.

Table 12.1 Vitamin/Mineral Intake of Ballet Dancers

Vitamin/Mineral	Mean Intake	SD	No. Consuming < 2/3 of RDA (%)
Vitamin E (mg a-TE)	9.4	11.4	38.0
Vitamin A (μgRE)	1,410.0	1,067.7	9.7
Vitamin C (mg)	148.3	108.9	7.6
Thiamine (mg)	1.65	1.90	11.9
Riboflavin (mg)	1.95	.99	2.1
Niacin (mgNE)	20.2	10.5	7.6
Vitamin B_6 (mg)	1.56	1.04	42.3
Vitamin B_{12} (μg)	5.13	5.6	16.3
Folacin (μg)	266.0	179.3	58.6
Calcium (mg)	932.8	458.9	40.2
Phosphorus (mg)	1,214.2	415.4	17.3
Magnesium (mg)	227.6	89.1	43.4
Iron (mg)	13.4	7.6	48.9
Zinc (mg)	7.65	3.4	75.0

The RDA as a standard is open to criticism because the RDAs do not represent individual requirements. They are merely recommendations for population groups and can only estimate needs. However, when the proportion of individuals with low intake is as extensive as we found for several nutrients, the risk of deficiency in the study group is high.

Table 12.2 lists means (plus or minus SD) for diet composition, indicating the percentage of calories derived from fats, protein, carbohydrates, and alcohol, and Figure 12.1 shows total calories consumed per day.

Calorie Intake and Diet Composition

Each rehearsal period of choreographed dance requires only a few minutes with a high-energy demand. However, during basic training classes the energy yield is low (Schantz & Astrand, 1984). This creates a dilemma for the adolescent ballerina who aspires to dance professionally in a discipline that demands an extremely lean body but does not require massive calorie expenditure. The nutrition requirements of adolescence reflect the needs of a growing, rapidly changing, active body. Approximately 15% of adult height and 48% of skeletal mass are attained during adolescence. Therefore, these dancers must follow a low-calorie, high-nutrient diet.

The average daily calorie intake of our subjects was 1,890.2 kcal (Figure 12.1). However, 48.1% consumed less than 1,800 kcal per day, 28.9% consumed less than 1,500 kcal per day, and an alarming 10.8% consumed less than 1,200 kcal per day. The energy requirement for 11- to 14-year-old girls is approximately 14.0 kcal/cm. For the dancers we studied (mean age 14.6 years, mean height 160.2 cm) the recommended calorie intake is therefore 2,243 kcal per day. Our subjects consumed an average of 350 kcal less each day than is recommended by the National Research Council to support normal growth. Pugliese, Lifshitz, Grad, Fort, and Marks-Katz (1983) described disturbances in growth and failure to achieve optimal height in a group of adolescents who chronically restricted calorie intake to avoid gaining weight.

A high proportion of kcal/day in the dancers' diet (see Table 12.2) came from fats (mean 34.6%), whereas an average of 49.8% was derived from carbohydrates and 15.6% from protein. This is misleading when one observes that 25% of the dancers derived more than 40% of kcal from fat, 56.6% derived more than 15% of kcal from protein, and less than 10.8% of the dancers derived more than 60% of their kcal from carbohydrates. With diets so low in calories, it is not surprising to find a low nutrition intake (see Table 12.1) as well. Similar findings of diets low in calories and nutrition density among professional ballet dancers have been reported (Calabrese et al., 1983).

Ballet dancers frequently engage in fad diets, fasting, and abuse of laxatives or diuretics to maintain lean bodies and low percent body fat. In

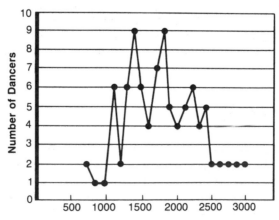

Figure 12.1 Daily caloric intake of dancers.

Table 12.2   Nutrient Intake of Ballet Dancers

Nutrient	Mean Intake	SD	Kcal/day (%)
Protein (kcal)	72.3	24.0	15.6
Fat (kcal)	75.3	36.7	34.6
Carbohydrate (kcal)	235.6	100.7	49.8
Sodium (mg)	2,075.6	871.8	—
Potassium (mg)	2,619.6	993.1	—
Cholesterol (mg)	271.7	159.4	—

Note.   From "Inadequate Nutrition and Chronic Calorie Restriction in Adolescent Ballerinas" by J. Benson et al., *The Physician and Sportsmedicine*, **13**(10), p. 77-90.

addition, diets that severely restrict calorie intake have serious physiological ramifications such as hypoglycemia; ketonuria; decreased urinary output; loss of electrolytes, minerals, and lean tissue; glycogen depletion; weakness; and fainting. Furthermore, dancers may suffer from fatigue and lack of energy because of poor nutrition habits and many hours of training. Thus the dancer is at high risk for musculo-skeletal injuries.

Protein.   The usual RDA for protein is 0.8 gm/kg of body weight; 1.0 to 1.5 gm/kg of body weight seems to be adequate for people who exercise. In contrast to the finding of Calabrese et al. (1983), of a borderline protein intake (mean 47.4 gm/53.1 kg body weight) among professional ballet dancers, with a mean protein intake of 72.3 gm and a mean weight of 46.8 kg (103.2 lb), all 92 dancers were well above the RDA. As reported in other nutrition studies (Short & Short, 1983), some athletes consume excess protein at the expense of fat and carbohydrates. In the group of dancers we surveyed, 56.6% derived more than 20% of their kcal from protein sources.

Fat.   We found a mean fat intake of 75.3 gm and a polyunsaturated to saturated ratio of two to three in the dancers. The mean cholesterol intake of 271.1 mg falls within the range of the general U.S. population (200 to 1,500 mg) (Hegsted, 1979). It is common to see young dancers consuming candy bars, pastry, and sodas between classes because of time restrictions and misconceptions about the differences between fats and carbohydrates as energy sources. It is easy to understand why 25% of the dancers derived more than 40% of their calorie intake from fat.

misconceptions about the differences between fats and carbohydrates as energy sources. It is easy to understand why 25% of the dancers derived more than 40% of their calorie intake from fat.

Carbohydrates.   Ballet dancers believe that carbohydrates are high-calorie foods. Although the mean intake of carbohydrates in the dancers studied was 49.8% of the total kcal consumed, these were sources of simple rather than complex carbohydrates. When analyzing the dancers' diets we found few sources of complex carbohydrates in the form of fruits, vegetables, pasta, potatoes, and whole grains.

Vitamins and Minerals.   Bone requires an adequate supply of calcium, phosphorus, and vitamin D. Forty-eight percent of skeletal mass is attained during adolescence. Therefore, it is significant that the dancers we studied have a mean calcium intake 932.8 mg and that 40.2% of them consume less than two-thirds of the RDA. Although none of the dancers was low in vitamin D, a mean intake of 1,214.2 mg was reported for phosphorus, and 17.3% consumed less than two-thirds of the RDA of 1,200 mg. Thus there is still a need for concern.

It is tempting to postulate that the high frequency of multiple, difficult-to-heal stress fractures seen in the lower extremities of dancers may be caused by the inadequate intake of these bone nutrients. Female dancers have been reported (Calabrese et al., 1983; Schantz & Astrand, 1984) to have a high incidence of menstrual abnormalities such as secondary amenorrhea, irregular cycles, and anovulatory cycles. Fifty-eight percent of the dancers we studied reported irregular menses. Amenorrheic women have decreased levels of estrogen (Dale, Gerlach, Martin, & Alexander, 1979), and amenorrheic runners have been found to have osteopenia (Drinkwater et al., 1984) when compared with women with regular menses. Female dancers may have the additional factor of hypoestrogenemia, which contributes to subclinical osteopenia and results in an increased incidence of stress fractures.

Iron.   Of the dancers in our study, 48.9% consumed less than two-thirds of the RDA of iron. Iron is an essential component of hemoglobin, the oxygen transporting pigment of muscle. Iron is also an essential component of cytochromes (the body's energy transport system) and of various enzymes. Vigorous physical activity causes an increased requirement for iron (Frederickson, Puhl, & Runyan, 1983), which, in addition to menstrual losses, places the exercising woman at risk for iron deficiency. Some studies (Frederickson et al., 1983) have documented the prevalence of both clinical and subclinical iron deficiency in female athletes. Whereas iron deficiency anemia is known to significantly affect endurance and physical performance, the effects of subclinical iron deficiency on performance are disputed. In general, subjects with low iron stores but no anemia have normal exercise capacity. Schoene et al. (1983) found that women with iron deficiency and minimally decreased hemoglobin levels showed increased lactate production at physical exhaustion. This increase was reversed with iron therapy. Nilson, Schone, and Robertson (1981) also reported postexercise hyperlactacidemia in iron-depleted athletes with normal hemoglobin concentrations. With such bizarre diet habits and many of the dancers consuming less than two-thirds of the RDA for iron, it would be interesting to examine hemoglobin and hematocrit levels in this group.

Vitamin B₆. Of our subjects, 42.3% consumed less than two-thirds of the RDA for vitamin B_6. One can speculate about the consequence of inadequate intake on energy utilization and protein synthesis for growth. Laurence (1974) studied competitive swimmers to see if supplementation with 5 mg of vitamin B_6 over a six-month period would affect endurance. No improvement was noted, although the group taking supplements displayed more saturated B_6 status than did the control group. Dietary inadequacy of B_6 was not evident in either group.

Folacin, Magnesium, Zinc. Of our subjects, 58.6% were at risk for folate hypovitaminosis. The main metabolic consequence of folic acid deficiency is altered DNA metabolism, especially in rapidly dividing cells such as red blood cells. Regarding the dancers' magnesium and zinc intake, 43.4% and 75%, respectively, were below two-thirds of the RDA. Little research has been done concerning the effect of magnesium deficiency on physical performance. The consequences of marginal zinc deficiency in this injury-plagued population may include prolonged or poor healing as well as disruption in the growth process.

It is interesting to compare these findings with results obtained by various nutrient intake surveys of the teenage population as a whole. Greger et al. (1978) analyzed the diet of a group of adolescent girls in Indiana and found that they consumed less than two-thirds of the RDA for calcium (35%), iron (58%), and zinc (37%). Schorr, Sanjur, and Erickson (1972) reported on three-day diet records of girls in 7th through 12th grades. The percentages of girls consuming less than two-thirds of the RDA for calcium and iron were 56% and 91%, respectively. Little research has been done on zinc, folate, vitamin E, or vitamin B_6 intake patterns in adolescents.

Vitamin/Mineral Supplementation

We found that 60% of our subjects routinely took vitamin or mineral supplements but rarely consumed the proper types or amounts to cover nutrition inadequacies. Only 7% of the dancers who took supplements improved in nutrition intake enough to raise their intake of at least one nutrient to more than two-thirds of the RDA. In addition, many dancers took large doses (more than 200% of the RDA) of B vitamins, vitamin C, and vitamin A when no deficiency was evident.

The hazards associated with excess dosing of the fat-soluble vitamins and vitamin B_6 are well documented (Wason, 1982). One dancer took a combination of supplements that resulted in a daily vitamin A intake of 50,000 IU. Hypervitaminosis A has been observed in children taking 25,000 IU per day for a period of time. Simonsen (1974) and Keren and Epstein (1980) studied high-dose B complex and vitamin C supplementation on work performance, and stated that high-dose supplementation of these nutrients seems to have no beneficial effect on aerobic or anaerobic performance.

Counseling the Ballet Dancer

Two considerations are important when counseling the ballet dancer: The dancer must maintain a body weight well below the standard for height to compete realistically in the dance world, and the schedule of the ballet dancer makes it difficult to eat regular meals.

It is futile for the nutrition counselor to insist that the dancer comply with weight/height and calorie standards designated as desirable by the Metropolitan Life Insurance Company or the National Research Council. The ballerina would simply dismiss the counselor as an outsider who doesn't understand the needs of dancers. Indeed, the pursuit of the willowy dance body may compromise optimal health, but this look won't change soon. The challenge to the nutrition counselor is to help dancers achieve the thin body as safely as possible. Although there are no standard weight tables for dancers, the ballet concept of ideal weight is approximately 10 lb lighter than the normal population of 12- to 17-year-olds. The general weight standards allow for 87 to 90 lb for the first 5 feet of height and 4 lb for every inch thereafter.

Recommendations for energy needs are 30 kcal/lb of ideal dance weight during growth spurt, and 15 kcal/lb of ideal weight thereafter. A 15-year-old dancer who is 5 ft 4 in. tall and weighs approximately 106 lb would require 1,650 kcal/day to cover her energy expenditure.

The nutritionist must work with the dancer to structure time throughout the day to allow for at least three or four small meals and perhaps one snack. Class and rehearsal schedules as well as food preferences must be considered. Oddly enough, dancers may refuse low calorie items such as salad and fresh fruit before going to practice at the bar, because these high fiber foods will cause their stomachs to stick out. However, juices do not make the dancer's stomach stick out, and she is satisfied with her image in the mirror. Dancers do not resist nutrition information. They understand that a healthy, well-nourished body is essential to a successful career. However, they have no formal education in nutrition; they get most of their instruction from dance teachers and other students. Therefore, a nutrition class should be included in dance education programs so that dancers may achieve the desired look as safely as possible.

The clinical criteria for diagnosing these eating disorders have been well described (Maloney, 1983). It is difficult to diagnose anorexia nervosa accurately in a ballerina who is obliged to be thin and is therefore preoccupied with her weight. Garner, Olmsted, Poling, and Garfinkel (1984) have shown that many women who are highly preoccupied with weight display psychopathy similar to anorexia nervosa but do not meet the rigorous diagnostic standard. More research into the eating behavior of ballet dancers is warranted.

Conclusions

The need for a ballet dancer to maintain a sylphlike image is a product of the mid-19th century romantic period of dance. The relatively low energy expenditure in addition to observing oneself in the mirror day after day creates a predicament for the adolescent ballerina aspiring to professional status.

Although the data presented here are descriptive, it is interesting to postulate the role of inadequate nutrition and chronic dieting in many of the difficulties seen in ballet dancers. Of major concern is the possible correlation between the role of the low weight-to-height ratio in amenorrhea seen in this population. Further study on bone mineral density among ballet dancers is needed. Furthermore, one might hypothesize that if amenorrheic dancers have lower bone density than women in control groups, the problems of multiple, difficult-to-heal stress fractures would only be compounded by inadequate bone nutrients resulting from poor nutrition habits.

At such a critical time of growth—when skeletal mass and height are of major concern—the dietary habits of dancers warrant attention. Although some of the dancers supplement their diets, most of them do so incorrectly. Proper education on dietary intake and supplementation needs to be incorporated into the dance school curriculum.

Nutritional Considerations for Adult Dancers

Although the consequences of poor nutrition in a growing population are of concern, it is apparent that faulty eating practices among adult dancers may precipitate nutritionally related health problems, as well as hinder dance performance. Calabrese et al. (1983) investigated the nutrition practices of adult professional ballet dancers. Twenty-five female dancers recorded their food intake for three days in food diaries which were then analyzed for nutrient and calorie content. It was found that these dancers were consuming less than optimal amounts of calories when compared to age-, height-, and weight-matched controls. In addition, whereas the use of nutritional supplements was common (40%), the supplements were usually narrow ranged so that their net effects on the corrections of dietary deficiencies during the study period were minimal. Of the 24 dancers found to have diets that were low (< 75% RDA) in folate, only 4 dancers were able to correct this deficiency with supplementation. In addition, 24 dancers were found to be low with respect to dietary zinc intake, and none improved this inadequacy with supplements. Similar findings were reported with respect to iron and calcium. Cohen, Potosnak, Frank, and Baker (1985) performed a nutritional and hematological assessment of 10 male and 12 female elite adult professional ballet dancers. Each dancer completed a six-day food diary, which was then analyzed for nutrient content.

Again, a suboptimal intake of iron, folate, biotin, and calories was observed among the female dancers, even after supplementation. The male dancers in the study consumed adequate calories, but over 30% were still low with respect to dietary folate and biotin even after supplementation was considered. Although blood vitamin levels were within normal limits for all of the dancers, low ferritin levels in eight women and three men confirmed low iron stores. In addition, the authors found that the carbohydrate consumption of both the men (38% of calories) and the women (50% of calories) was not consistent with optimal dietary practices for performance and strenuous exercise. In addition, the female dancers consumed an average of 400–600 less calories than their predicted requirements. It is suggested that the calorie deficit may be a factor in producing amenorrhea. A preliminary analysis of data collected by a research team in Arizona indicates that dancers who have abnormal menstrual patterns, low body fat levels, and a low daily calorie intake also have a low bone-mineral mass (Armann & Wells, 1985).

Other nutritional studies have been performed among high-level male dancers. Calorie consumption was generally sufficient, and the gross nutritional inadequacies seen in their female counterparts were not observed. Male dancers are more concerned with gaining upper body strength, leg power, and flexibility than with weight control, and therefore rarely have nutritional problems.

Information about the dietary habits of other dance idioms, such as modern dance, is scarce. However, a comparison of anthropometric and body composition data has shown that successful ballet dancers are taller and have a lower body weight than modern dancers (Dolgener, Spasoff, and St. John, 1980). Modern dancers may not be at similar risk for nutritional deficits, because body size requirements appear to be less strict than for ballet. Nevertheless, any dancer, like any athlete, can benefit from sound nutrition practices.

Planning the Diet

A fundamental objective for dancers should be to adjust their diet to meet the energy requirement of training and performance activities. Research has shown that the calorie expenditure for ballet exercise is 0.09 calories/kg/min for men, and 0.08 calories/kg/min for women for *barre* work, and 0.13 calories/kg/min for men and 0.10 calories/kg/min for women for center floor dancing (Cohen et al., 1985). Average energy expenditures for one hour of ballet class are 300 calories for men and 200 calories for women. Daily calorie needs have been estimated to be 2000 to 2200 calories per day for women, and 2900 to 3100 calories for men. Sixty percent of these calories should be from carbohydrates, especially complex carbohydrates found in breads, grains, fruits, and vegetables. Protein should constitute 12–15% of the total energy, or 1–1.5 grams of protein per kg body weight. Fat should be limited to less than 25% of the total energy.

Nutritional adequacy is achieved by including the following foods in the daily diet:

Low-Fat Milk Group. Two servings for adults, 4 for adolescents. One serving equals 8 oz. skim milk, 8 oz. non-fat yogurt, 1 1/2 oz. low-fat cheese (light cheese or mozzarella), 1/2 cup cottage cheese. These foods provide protein, calcium, and riboflavin.

Low-Fat Meat Group. Two servings. One serving is equal to 2 oz. of cooked lean beef, poultry, pork, or fish, or 1 cup of cooked beans or 1/2 cup of tofu. These foods are sources of iron, zinc, B vitamins, and high quality protein.

Fruits and Vegetables.   Four servings. One cup raw or 1/2 cup cooked vegetables, or 1/2 cup juice, or one piece of fresh fruit is one serving. Dark, leafy, green, or orange vegetables are high in vitamin A and are recommended 3 or 4 times a week. Citrus fruits are rich in vitamin C and are recommended daily. All of these foods are good sources of carbohydrates and fiber.

Grain Group.   Four servings. One slice of bread, 1 cup of dry cereal or 1/2 cup of cooked cereal, cooked pasta, rice, or corn equals, one serving. Whole grain foods are preferable. All are sources of complex carbohydrates, B vitamins, and fiber.

The above recommendations provide approximately 1200 calories a day, and represent a minimum intake for weight loss. Increasing the servings of grains, fruits, vegetables, and to a lesser extent lean meats will provide more calories if needed, without greatly increasing fat intake. When and in what form the above foods are consumed are issues decided upon by the dancer and her nutritionist. A supplement providing 100% of the RDA for vitamins and minerals, particularly iron, may be advisable, if an erratic eating schedule or a weight loss diet interferes with proper eating.

Special attention should be given to water intake. During prolonged exercise, especially in hot weather, the need for fluids increases greatly. Dehydration can lead to muscle cramping, exhaustion, nausea, and injury due to fatigue. Dancers should be alert to situations in which dehydration will occur: heavy costume, high temperatures, high humidity, air travel, and prolonged practice or performance. By weighing oneself before and after dance activity, water loss can be determined. Replacing lost fluids with juices or water is preferable. There is no advantage to using electrolyte containing sports drinks. Hydrating well before, and sipping water throughout, dance activity is recommended.

Summary

Leanness is an aesthetic and physical necessity that makes constant dieting a way of life for both adolescent and adult dancers. Good nutrition is often sacrificed in the pursuit of that slender look. Methods of incorporating information obtained from studies of dancers into dance curriculum should be developed.

Part one of this paper is based on the article "Inadequate Nutrition and Chronic Calorie Restriction in Adolescent Ballerinas," 1985, which first appeared in *The Physician and Sportsmedicine:* **13**(10), pp. 79–90. Reprinted by permission.

References

Armann, S.A., & Wells, C.L. (1985). A study of bone loss in ballerinas: A report of unpublished data. *Nutrition News, 48*(12), 16–17.

Calabrese, L.H., & Kirkendall, D.T. (1983). Nutritional and medical considerations in dancers. *Clinics in Sports Medicine, 2*(3), 539–548.

Calabrese, L.H., Kirkendall, D.T., Floyd, M., Rapoport, S., Williams, G.W., Weiker, G.G., & Bergfeld, J.A. (1983). Menstrual abnormalities, nutritional patterns and body composition in female classical ballet dancers. *The Physician and Sportsmedicine, 11*(2), 86–98.

Cohen, J.L., Potosnak, L., Frank, O., & Baker, H. (1985). A nutritional and hematologic assessment of elite ballet dancers. *The Physician and Sportsmedicine, 13*(5), 43–54.

Dale, E., Gerlach, D.H., Martin, D.E., & Alexander, C.R. (1979). Physical fitness profiles and reproductive physiology of the female distance runner. *The Physician and Sportsmedicine, 7*(1), 83–98.

Dolgener, F.A., Spasoff, T.E., & St. John, W.E. (1980). Body build and body composition of high ability female dancers. *Research Quarterly Exercise and Sport, 51,* 599–607.

Drinkwater, B.L., Nilson, K.L., Chesnut, C.S., III, Bremner, W.J., Shainholte, S., & Southworth, M.B. (1984). Bone mineral content of amenorrheic and eumenorrheic athletes. *New England Journal of Medicine, 311,* 277–281.

Drinkwater, B.L., Shangold, M.M., Loucks, A., Wilmore, J.H., & Foreman, K.E. (1981). Menstrual changes in athletes. *The Physician and Sportsmedicine, 9*(11), 98–112.

Druss, R.G. (1979). Body image and perfection of ballerinas: Comparison and contrast with anorexia nervosa. *General Hospital Psychiatry, 2,* 115–121.

Frederickson, S.A., Puhl, J.L., & Runyan, W.S. (1983). Effects of training on indices of iron states of young female cross-country runners. *Medicine and Science in Sports and Exercise, 14*(4), 271–276.

Garner, D.M., & Garfinkel, P.E. (1978). Sociocultural factors in anorexia nervosa. *Lancet, 2,* 674.

Garner, D.M., Olmsted, M.P., Poling, M., & Garfinkel, P.E. (1984). Comparison between weight preoccupied women and anorexia nervosa. *Psychosomatic Medicine, 46,* 255–266.

Greger, J.L., Higgins, M.M., Abernathy, R.R., Kirksey, A., DeCorso, M.B., & Baligar, P. (1978). Nutritional status of adolescent girls in regard to zinc, copper and iron. *American Journal of Clinical Nutrition, 31*(2), 269–274.

Hegsted, D.M. (1979). *What Americans are eating now: Preliminary results of US RDA Food Consumption Survey.* Paper presented at conference on nutritional guidelines: Toward a nutritional strategy, Washington, D.C.

Keren, G., & Epstein, Y. (1980). The effect of high dosage vitamin C intake on aerobic and anaerobic capacity. *Journal of Sports Medicine and Physical Fitness, 20*(6), 145–148.

Laurence, G. (1974). The effect of alpha tocopheral and pyridoxine on the swimming endurance of trained swimmers. *Journal of the American College Health Association, 23,* 219–222.

Maloney, M.J. (1983). Anorexia nervosa and bulimia in dancers. *Clinics in Sports Medicine, 2*(11), 549–555.

Nilson, K., Schone, R., & Robertson, H. (1981). The effect of iron repletion on exercise-induced lactate produced in minimally iron-depleted subjects. *Medicine and Science in Sports and Exercise, 13,* 92.

Peterson, M.S. (1982). Nutritional concerns for the dancer. *The Physician and Sportsmedicine, 10*(3), 137–143.

Pugliese, M.T., Lifshitz, F., Grad, G., Fort, F., & Marks-Katz, M. (1983). Fear of obesity: A cause of short stature and delayed puberty. *New England Journal of Medicine, 309,* 513–518.

Schantz, P.G., & Astrand, P. (1984). Physiological characteristics of classical ballet. *Medicine and Science in Sports and Exercise, 16*(5), 472–476.

Schoene, R.N., Escourron, P., Robertson, H.T., Nilson, K.L., Parsons, J.R., & Smith, N.J. (1983). Iron repletion decreases maximal exercise lactate concentrations in female athletes with minimal iron deficiency anemia. *Journal of Laboratory and Clinical Medicine, 102*(8), 306–312.

Schorr, B.C., Sanjur, D., & Erickson, E.C. (1972). Teenage food habits: A multidimensional analysis. *Journal of the American Dietetic Association, 61,* 415–420.

Short, S.H., & Short, W.R. (1983). Four-year study of university athletes' dietary intake. *Journal of the American Dietetic Association, 82*(6), 632–645.

Simonsen, E. (1974). The influence of vitamin B complex surplus on the capacity for muscular and mental work. *Journal of Industrial Hygiene, 24,* 83–90.

Warren, M.P. (1983). Effects of undernutrition on reproductive function in the human. *Endocrine Reviews, 4*(4), 363–377.

Wason, S. (1982). Vitamin A toxicity. *American Journal of Diseases of Children, 136*(2), 174.

PART IV

Behavioral and Pedagogical Aspects of Dance Training

This section presents information on psychological and psychomotor aspects of dance training and depicts behavioral characteristics of teaching dance. The four chapters describe general mental, emotional, and psychomotor profiles of dancers.

Chapter 13 presents a comprehensive picture of the psychological makeup of dancers and the environment that spawns these characteristics. Information on dancers' perceptions of themselves, eating disorders, psychodynamic viewpoints, and the psychological effects of dance therapy is covered in detail.

Chapters 14 and 15 deal with psychomotor research on dance training. A general description of motor control parameters as related to skill acquisition is described in chapter 14, and chapter 15 presents specific data on the learning of certain dance skills. The information in these chapters is especially valuable for maximizing efficiency and effectiveness in the teaching of dance skills. It appears that time spent learning dance may not be as economical as dancers might expect.

Chapter 16 looks at the characteristics of the people who train the dancers. The criteria to measure successful performance as a teacher are described. Also, some recommendations are made concerning how to identify a good teacher and how teachers can evaluate their own performance.

Relative to the other topics in this book, the least is understood about the behavioral aspects of dance training. Few researchers are conducting studies in this area. Consequently, only selected behavioral topics are included. Nonetheless, the information should be helpful for those professionals who deal with the training of dancers as well as for the dancers themselves.

Chapter 13

Psychological Aspects of Dance

Jerome M. Schnitt
Yale University

Diana Schnitt
Connecticut College

The complete study of dance medicine requires more than a careful review of its mechanical and biological underpinnings; it also requires a close look at the psychological issues which affect dance and dancers. Western philosophy for the last three centuries has been heir to Descartes' idea that one's mind and body may be viewed separately. Dance does not always fit this concept well, because it, among other disciplines, requires an integration of mind and body. Feeling states, images, and thoughts are often simultaneously present in the dancer; the integration of these helps create a successful visual and emotional response in the observer. Some of these states we associate with the body (such as the kinesthetic feeling of spinning one's body through space or the sensation of muscles tensing and relaxing), and some we associate with the mind (such as the conscious thinking done by a dancer to maintain postural alignment during a *pirouette*).

Given some of the research findings presented in this chapter, it appears that many serious dancers either enter into or continue to dance in part because of the feeling states it evokes for them. Does this differentiate dancers from nondancers? How do dancers differ from the general population? Do they have a peculiar lifestyle, or unusual attitudes? Are they more creative, or perhaps are they in some way emotionally distorted or ill? Do they benefit from special therapeutic approaches to enhance their effective range of motion or postural alignment, or particular types of psychotherapeutic treatment? Certainly the literature describing the life-style of the serious ballet dancer suggests that it is one of extreme devotion, with disavowal of other needs and desires in preference for the discipline of enhancing self-control of movement and of body weight and alignment. Each of these issues has relevance when we consider the psychology of dance.

Psychology as a discipline seeks to understand human behavior and the forces underlying that behavior. The many subdisciplines of psychology focus on areas ranging from the neuropsychophysiological to the psycho-dynamic, with focus on such wide-ranging issues as the development of neuromuscular patterning, perceptual abilities, methods of learning, creativity, body image, self-esteem, and the relationship of psychodynamics to movement and expression. Dance is a complex type of multidetermined behavior, typically expressive of each of the above-mentioned issues. Given all this, one might then expect the study of the psychological aspects of dance and dancers to be an active discipline, with a considerable literature. This has not been generally true because of a number of factors, as Priddle (1978) has pointed out. First, expert scholars must typically be willing and able to cross disciplinary boundaries in order to interpret and make their knowledge available to the study of dance. Second, few dancers have had the necessary training in psychology to investigate dance from this perspective. Third, Priddle says that psychologists have been typically reluctant to investigate dance as a human behavior and have generally lacked interest in this area. Although still a nascent field of study, the situation Priddle described has improved somewhat in the last decade, especially with increasing interest in interdisciplinary collaboration and with the hard work of committed individuals and organizations such as the Congress on Research in Dance and others.

Accordingly, this chapter seeks to present significant findings from a widespread theoretical and experimental literature that touches on or directly addresses issues in the psychology of dance, much of which appears in special-interest journals, and which may not be easily accessible to students of other disciplines.

Effects of Dance on the Dancer

Dance has emotional impact on the dancer and on the observer; according to the comic strip beagle, Snoopy, "To dance is to live!" Dancing can evoke strong feeling states and may significantly change the mood of the dancer. Classes in dance have been shown to enhance a "sense of psychological well-being," decreasing anxiety and depression and enhancing the subjects' self-perceptions of creativity, confidence, relaxation, motivation, health, intelligence, excitation, and energy (Gurley, Neuringer,

& Massee, 1984); students taking dance classes not only felt better about themselves than a similar group who took an academic course, they also felt better about themselves than students who participated in active sports. Similar results were obtained in a large group of welfare-class young girls (Puretz, 1978). At the end of four months of either dance classes or a physical education program, Puretz found that both groups had improved their self-concepts; however, the self-concept of the dance students had improved significantly more than the other students' self-concepts.

Another study on the effects of dance on anxiety in 114 college students (Leste & Rust, 1984) found, over a three-month period, that subjects participating in modern dance classes showed significantly lowered anxiety, but that participants in other groups designed to control for the effects of the exercise and music components of dance (a physical education group, a music group, and a neutral, mathematics group) did not demonstrate similar decreases in anxiety when measured by the Spielberger State-Trait Anxiety Inventory.

Why did this happen? Is there something about dance itself that may cause people to feel better about themselves? Gurley et al. (1984) conclude that dance may promote these feelings differently than sports because of the cognitions and emotions specifically associated with dancing, and because of the dancer's emphasis on the expressive, creative, and aesthetic aspects of the activity itself. They view this in opposition to the sportsperson's goal-directed competitiveness: doing art as opposed to competing to win.

The studies just mentioned all focus on one area of clinically relevant material: What happens psychologically to the individual who enters the world of dance? Another highly related question involves which individuals decide to become dancers: Are certain types of people more drawn to serious dance than others? This type of question, although fascinating and quite relevant, is too global for a single project (or perhaps even for a single discipline) to answer. However, there is indirect evidence to suggest that dance does significantly affect its students' motor abilities, self-esteem, attitudes, and worldview, and that at least some of its students come into dance with certain psychological styles. Readers seeking a more complete picture of the psychology of dance are likely to be either disappointed by the early state of the literature or stimulated to begin to learn (and hopefully to investigate) questions they have in this area. Some areas have been more clearly researched than others. For example, the clinical disciplines of dance therapy and the body therapies have been the subject of little or no controlled research; by their very nature this research will be complex and difficut to conduct because of the range of variables involved in such projects. However, mention is made of these disciplines not only for the sake of completeness, but to encourage the reader to consider the potential usefulness of these concepts in the investigation of dancers' issues.

Because this volume surveys a broad range of issues in dance sciences, it is important in a chapter on the psychological issues of dancers to include material on what is normal for groups of dancers (shared attitudes, feeling states, and behaviors) and how this may differ from what might be considered normal in the larger culture. Although a difficult task, it is also important to provide data on what might be beyond the range of normal and into the range of illness or dysfunction. One theoretical paper proposes normal developmental phases for dancers (Schnitt & Schnitt, 1987). It should be said at the outset that in the authors' awareness there is no evidence for the existence of a dancer's personality. People with the full range of personality styles enter dance. Thus one can expect to encounter dancers with the full range of normal and abnormal thoughts and feelings that human beings experience. Similarly, one can expect to encounter the full range of psychopathology and illness. This does not mean that dancers' attitudes, feelings, and thoughts are randomly distributed across the general population. Indeed, when groups of dancers are studied, a remarkable number of group attitudes, beliefs, and feelings are often found. We simply wish to differentiate between a group finding and the assumption that the finding can be successfully applied to an individual without careful, individualized investigation.

The new arena of psychological research in dance is certainly an important one to dancers, dance educators, and clinicians interested in helping dancers if the field is to grow in the direction of self-awareness. If dancers come to know more about themselves and their peers, and about which of their attitudes and behaviors are shared with other dancers, their relationship to the larger culture may become more clear. Dance educators may benefit from a broader awareness of the diverse findings in this disparate area of study; the data may be useful both in advancing understanding of group phenomena among dance students and in individualized applications. Clinicians may also become more aware of the special psychological issues and needs of dancers who present themselves for diagnosis and/or treatment.

Locus of Control and Health Locus of Control

One interesting question regarding dancers involves their perceptions of themselves as individuals in the larger world, how much control they have over their abilities, and their interactions with others. This concept is termed the locus of control. The following section explains different strategies for control including self-control, control by outside factors, and the control over health maintenance.

Locus of Control

According to social learning theory, some persons believe strongly that the world is a place amenable to control, and that actions on the part of the individual can make a significant difference in that individual's life; they believe that self-control works. These persons are said to have an internal locus of control, because they believe their feelings and behavior tend to mold the world around them.

Other people believe that events in life are largely out of their control, that they are brought about by outside events beyond their personal influence. These persons are said to have an external locus of control because they believe their feelings and behavior are largely affected by outside forces.

Twenty years ago, Julian Rotter developed a locus of control scale (1966) to measure these beliefs. It was later modified by Levenson (1974) and by Reid and Ware (1974) to differentiate between two types of external beliefs. One type of belief was in fatalism: The outside forces determining control are actually chance events (not under anyone's control). The other type of belief was in social-system control: These outside forces are largely the result of actions and preferences of powerful other people.

One study (Dasch, 1978) suggested that well-trained dancers may exhibit a highly developed internal control orientation. Dasch gave the Levenson scale to 33 college undergraduates enrolled in dance classes and obtained mean (group average) scores which are significantly more oriented to internal control than is usually found in random samples, and somewhat more internally oriented than is usually found in college populations. That is, the dancers did not believe in chance (luck, fate) or in powerful others determining their life events; they felt that they were able (and responsible) to control their own lives to a greater degree than is usually found.

While obesity is not usually a problem for dancers, it is worth noting the contrast in locus of control findings between obese subjects and dancers. Thomason (1983) found that 20 obese college undergraduates scored more externally than did normal weight individuals on the Self-Control (internal locus of control) scale, and more external on the Social

System Control (powerful others) scale, but not more external on the Fatalism (chance) scale. These findings, that obesity correlates with an *external* locus of control with regard to powerful others but not chance, are in marked opposition to the findings with thin dancers and anorexia nervosa patients, who score high on *internal* self-control measures and low on external other-controlled or chance measures. This supports the notion that obese subjects have poor self-control and often suggest that weight problems are beyond their personal control. The strong difference in locus of control between obese subjects and dancers appears to support the notion that dancers desire and strive for greater self-control of their bodies.

Health Locus of Control

Another question on locus of control that is important to dancers involves the perception of how good health is achieved and maintained. One might assume that dancers believe that good health is largely a product of their own exercise and dietary habits. However, it may also be argued that many dancers look to powerful others to help them make decisions about how best to maintain their health; dancers deal with a variety of authorities, from diet books and exercise regimens to physicians' and teachers' prescriptions. Additionally, some dancers may believe that illness, and particularly some injuries, are the result of bad luck. A dancer who becomes ill with the flu or who injures an ankle after pushing too far with heavy exercise while eating an unbalanced but faddish diet could argue being the unfortunate victim of circumstance. Accordingly, it is helpful to know more about dancers' locus of control regarding health.

A recent study, Schnitt, Schnitt, and Del A'une (1987) investigated this question, using the Multidimensional Health Locus of Control Scales (MHLC Form B) developed by Wallston and Wallston (1978). These scales apply the locus of control questions to health, with the same three scales (Internal, Chance external, and Powerful others external) as the Levenson scale. Although some follow-up work (Stonley, Hyman, & Sharp, 1984) has suggested that the use of three scales rather than two (external and internal) may not be worthwhile, the results of this investigation were interesting.

Looking again at 72 modern dance students attending the American Dance Festival, Schnitt's group (Schnitt, Schnitt, & Del A'une, 1987) found the following group means for the MHLC scales: Internal, 29.5 (SD = 4.0); Powerful others, 13.2 (SD = 4.2); and Chance, 14.2 (SD = 4.4).

This group of modern dancers has a very strong belief in the internal control of health. When compared with different groups previously studied by others, the modern dancers have the highest scores for internal control and the lowest scores for the two other scales yet reported.

Although this work needs to be replicated among other dancers, especially ballet dancers, it would appear from these studies that serious modern dancers believe strongly in their ability to influence and control their health as well as the rest of their lives.

Eating Disorders

There are a number of eating disorders which may affect dancers. Certainly the most common involve loss of appetite and/or loss of weight. Eating disorders such as anorexia nervosa and bulimia have been heavily studied in the last decade. Diagnosable anorexia nervosa may be found in 1–2% of the population, and bulimia may be at least as prevalent (Crisp, Palmer, & Kalucy, 1976). Because these disorders are still not well understood, there are multiple schools of thought regarding the appropriate diagnostic features, causes, and treatment approaches.

One model of eating disorders which may be helpful as an overview suggests a continuum from normal weight (and normal eating attitudes) to abnormal states, with individuals placed at any point along this continuum who are able to move over time to different points. This model allows for various physiological, hormonal, behavioral, psychological, and social factors to interact in determining where on the continuum the individual sits at any point in time.

Dancers may be especially prone to these eating disorders, because anorexia nervosa and bulimia are overrepresented in populations of adolescent and postadolescent females from middle- and upper-class backgrounds. Some of the other relevant forces for dancers are discussed below.

Dancers are exposed to a considerable number of social pressures which may cause them to change their attitudes about eating and to change their weight. First are the usual societal and cultural pressures on American women to be slim; one extensive study found that 86% of the college women studied were either consciously dieting or restricting their intake of certain foods in order to remain or become thin (Jakobovits, Halstead, Kelley, Rae, & Young, 1977). Other studies have documented the obvious, that preferences for body styles and the ideal body image for an attractive person have changed in different eras, and certainly vary according to culture. Women in late-twentieth century America are ideally thinner than they were 50 years ago.

Ballet dancers, especially, are traditionally thin; the ideal body weight for a ballerina has been estimated at 75% of expected body weight (%EBW) (Lowenkaupf & Vincent, 1982). One study of 183 adolescent Canadian ballet students found that they averaged 86.7% %EBW (Garner & Garfinkel, 1980). The authors compared this group with modeling students (who have high expectations for thinness) and with music students from high performance expectation settings, and found the prevalence of anorexia nervosa and of abnormal eating attitudes was significantly higher in the ballet students. They concluded that "the pressure for thinness when augmented by high performance expectations is the ideal social medium for the expression of anorexia nervosa in vulnerable adolescents" (p. 655). Similar factors were hypothesized by Joseph, Wood, and Goldberg (1982) who found abnormal eating attitudes in college dance majors, which they attributed to a thin body ideal in the presence of social pressures to be thin and a rigorous exercise program.

Another author supports this contention, believing that students in competitive ballet schools are justified in their preoccupation with weight, given the school and peer pressures on them to be thin (Maloney, 1983). Calabrese et al. (1983) looked at some specific factors affecting dancers' weight and found that food faddism, low and abnormal caloric intake (low-energy and low nutritional density foods), and menstrual abnormalities abound in the population.

To achieve this degree of thinness purposely may take a great deal of effort. High exercise rates and reduction of caloric intake are the traditional means to this end, although bulimia introduces the purging element of vomiting recently-eaten food, which usually avoids weight gain (while introducing other physiological problems). Where dance aerobic classes use a high degree of stamina-inducing continual aerobic exercise as a fundamental principle, many ballet and modern dance classes do not contain a large proportion of aerobic exercise. Given all this, one might expect that the exercise program of a physical education major would contain as much or more aerobic exercise than the training of ballet and modern dance students, and that dancers and athletes might have similar eating attitudes. When one group (Joseph et al., 1982) investigated the eating attitudes of college dance, drama, English, and physical education majors, it found that the physical education majors had the most normal eating attitudes, whereas dance and drama students had the most abnormal. Clearly, something other than a love of, or commitment to, heavy exercise is more central to thinness and abnormal eating attitudes in dancers.

All of the aforementioned studies of dancers have focused on female ballet students. One study has been done with modern dancers (Schnitt,

Schnitt, & Del A'une, 1986); 62 female modern dance students were given the Eating Attitudes Test (EAT), a scale which has been shown to suggest anorexia nervosa with scores at or above 30. The group averaged 88% of expected body weight, and averaged 18.0 (SD = 10.8) on the EAT, compared to an age-comparative normal population's 15.6 (SD = 9.3). Eight of the modern students scored in the anorexic range, and another eight scored nearly as high. Interestingly, abnormal eating attitudes did not correlate with thinness in this group; three fourths of the group had normal eating attitudes yet were thin. The group as a whole was almost as thin as previously-studied ballet dancers, but had much more normal eating attitudes. It would appear that this group of modern dancers differed significantly from ballet dancers in their eating attitudes. The authors considered that this might be due in part to the more variable body image of the modern dancer; different schools and companies have differing ideals, and many are more tolerant of idiosyncratic body habit than are most ballet schools/companies. Other more psychological factors remain to be investigated.

A major unanswered question involves whether eating-disorder-prone individuals gravitate to dance, or whether dance, and especially ballet, help make dancers more prone to these disorders. That is, is the vulnerability inherent in the dancer, or does the environment of dance increase one's risk? Most likely, it is a combination of factors: genetic, biochemical, physiological, hormonal, intrapsychic, interpersonal, familial, subcultural, and cultural factors have all been hypothesized as playing an active part in determining whether one develops an eating disorder. Successful treatment models tend to take into account these factors, considering the individual's unique history and circumstances, and adapting treatment to these. A recent review covers these issues in greater depth (Schnitt & Schnitt, 1986).

Psychodynamic Viewpoints

The psychodynamic theoretical literature does not focus on the dynamics of dance. Rather, there have been extensive biographical and psychohistorical works focusing on individual dancers' psychological issues (such as Isadora Duncan's difficulty with her fading popularity over the years), or on their psychopathology (e.g., Nijinsky's decline and eventual institutionalization for schizophrenia). There is also a small clinical literature on groups of dancers.

Psychodynamics of Female Ballet Dancers

Several articles have been written by psychodynamically oriented clinicians who also address theoretical considerations. One group has studied female student ballet dancers at a major company school, at which in-depth interviews were undertaken with a small number of students (and with the school administrator); a larger number of students were given questionnaires on psychologically relevant issues (Druss & Silverman, 1979). Because of its uniqueness, this paper is reviewed in the paragraphs that follow; the authors, a psychiatrist and a pediatrician who manage an eating-disorders clinic, caution that their conclusions are impressionistic, but they are certainly among the most complete in print.

Their descriptive findings may sound familiar to ballet students; for the serious student, ballet training often begins at age 7 or 8. Academic work becomes less important over time, and may be markedly de-emphasized. Students at major company schools come from around the country, are usually from middle-class families, and are already the product of great competition for admission. Of approximately 10,000 applicants to major schools per year only 1000 are admitted; less than 5% of these are likely to make it to the stage at all, and less than 1% in a major role, a fact which is not hidden from the students. Crucial years of a student's career are ages 15–21; this is when major performers invariably are chosen. Weight and caloric intake are major preoccupations, with frequent attempts to diet to achieve a ballerina's look. Training and exercise programs take place six days/week, six hours/day, and are quite rigorous.

The training requires total dedication; other interests are wholly sacrificed. There is no social life; students perceive no time to get involved with others. Out-of-class time is spent doing chores or working. Life is cloistered, with students often labelling themselves as "nuns." Many of the students go through their teens and often their 20's without learning even rudimentary dating and social skills. Their focus on work prevents them from properly taking care of minor to moderate injuries, lest they fall behind due to missed classes.

The students interviewed were characterized as likeable, cooperative, and quite open. During the interviews there was much posturing and gesturing. There was a marked preoccupation with one's body, some wishing for unrealistic bodily changes (such as longer limbs), or for greater ability to perform a difficult maneuver. All wished to be thinner. They described themselves as friendly but not "huggy or physical." Some enjoyed sex, but did not describe a craving for physical closeness or being held; many said they did not like to be touched. They were very sensitive to criticism and were moody; moods were highly reactive to external feedback such as compliments or criticisms. The group tended to be non-cerebral and nonverbal, avoiding such interactions. They seemed to the authors to be following Balanchine's alleged remark, "Don't think dear, just dance."

The authors found patterns in their interviewees which may be less familiar to nonclinicians. The students all dismissed their thinness as entirely due to the requirements of being a ballet dancer. When questioned further about this, they often substituted a belief that they were pleasing a teacher; when this too was questioned (with the fact that the students were often thinner than what was demanded of them), they had no alternate explanations. To the authors, they seemed to be trying very hard to control their bodies and to deny any sensual pleasures. Eating, one of the earliest bodily pleasures, was prohibited in the extreme. Touching, skin contact, another of the first bodily pleasures, was thoroughly restricted and occurred only in the classroom. Intellectual sublimation was restricted; reading and going to movies or plays for personal enjoyment were self-refused.

The only available source of pleasure was kinesthetic: musculoskeletal. "The girls distrust words and concepts as much as the sensual, and speak best through body language . . . they are action-oriented."[1] The body distortions appeared to the authors to desexualize and defeminize the students; these adolescents seemed to be avoiding their young womanhood, remaining 10-year-old, presexual beings. To this end, the loss of menstrual periods (a frequent consequence of extreme thinness) was often welcomed with relief.

The girls strongly wanted to suppress impulses and desires. They appeared to regress from the emerging sexuality of adolescence to an earlier level, with real pleasure derived from control and mastery of the body, its movement, and perceptions, rather than from a broader range of intrapsychic and interpersonal sources.

In terms of family dynamics, the authors found that in opposition to "performance-minded obsessives, these girls [were] not fulfilling parental wishes for success." Rarely were the parents pushing their daughters; rather, the pressure came from within and appeared to have been learned early in life.

The hope of eventual success, which comes to few, was held dearly. Strikingly missing in the dancers were the usual athletes' motivations of excitement in competition and release of aggression through activity; rather, ritualistic practice took up most of the dancers' time. However,

---

[1]This is in line with Brown's report (1973) that action-oriented, physically fit, energetic people like dancers and athletes "may be emotionally crippled because they perceive their bodies as objects-of-use to be coerced into submission" (p. 104).

rather than complain of boredom, many of the students spoke of a pleasurable inner tranquility which arose from such practice and was beyond boredom.

Expectably, perfectionism was frequently encountered. The authors felt strongly that the desire for perfection was a crucial dynamic; "The desire to achieve the special momentary bliss accompanying the perfectness" (p. 119) was the powerful motivator. Being very good was not good enough.

Another project was reported in somewhat less detail (Lowenkaupf & Vincent, 1982). They studied 55 female student ballet dancers (aged 16–21) and found them not only to be quite thin but also to have eating patterns and hyperactivity consistent with anorexia nervosa patients. A major preoccupation was with food and weight; there was considerable misinformation and faddism in eating and dieting. Dating was infrequent; most were sexually inexperienced and had major doubts about their appearance and dancing ability. Dynamically, they rationalized their difficulties, minimized their own anorexic behavior but freely reported this in others. There was much group reinforcement for the abnormal eating and dieting behaviors.

These two reports are uncannily alike, presenting powerful portraits of the lives of the two groups studied. Generalization of these findings must be undertaken with caution, although it is made more plausible by the similarity of the reports. Regardless, major questions are raised by the authors of these studies: What are the developmental effects on elementary-aged and young adolescent girls of such intensive training? What happens to these young dancers when they grow up? Is there a way to help them develop better social skills and better attitudes toward dieting and treating injuries? Why were they continuing to diet beyond the demands of their teachers; was it truly a love of self-control, or perhaps an inability to limit the needs for self-control? Because the dancers in these studies were expert in and sensitive to kinesthetic experiences and musculoskeletal perception, is there a way to integrate this into other ways of perceiving, thinking, and feeling, so that they may develop more broad-based approaches to themselves and others during and after their prime dancing years (Schnitt, 1985a, 1985b)? Are there differences between ballet, modern, and jazz dancers? Most of these questions are open for future amplification and replication.

There is one discussion in the literature of the social structure of a ballet company (Forsyth & Kolende, 1966), which was seen as a unique social system. Extensive cooperation among the performers was seen in the development and presentation of group productions; this coexisted with a high level of competition, required for the attainment of high levels of skill and dedication for personal achievement, and required for successful placement in the pieces presented.

One potentially relevant footnote to the question of the effect of ballet training on its students is raised by Povey (1975) who examined the views of 30 leading British performers, asking if special schooling should be developed for gifted young musicians and dancers. Although most subjects were opposed to specialized schooling, preferring the ''. . . broad course of education not removed from normal life,'' successful members of ballet companies opted for special education in company schools similar to their own education. Apparently, at least those most successful in their ballet careers value their training.

Psychological Factors of Modern Dancers

One other group of authors did no interviewing, but looked at psychological profiles of 62 female modern dancers based on questionnaires and psychological tests (Schnitt, Schnitt, & Del A'une, 1986). The dancers in this project were 1 1/2 years older on average than the ballet students just mentioned, an inch taller and almost 9 pounds heavier. Only a third reported irregular menstrual periods in the modern group as opposed to over 3/4 of the ballet group. All had completed high school or were about to do so. Over 96% who were old enough to have finished two years of college had done so. This group was clearly different from the ballet sample in degree of thinness and of education.

They also began to study dance seriously later in life; only a third had studied for more than a decade. Two-thirds were in university dance programs, and a like-number saw themselves as primarily performers (the rest were usually primarily teachers—16%, or choreographers—8%). They spent almost six hours/day in class on just over five days/week. Three-quarters saw dance as their primary commitment. Having entered dance later in life did not diminish their willingness to devote time to their dance.

This series of studies found that, as a group, the dancers were not depressed; they scored in the normal range on the Beck Depression Inventory and on Depression scales of the MMPI. They also scored significantly below average (i.e., less symptomatic than a normal population) on the MMPI hypochondriasis, psychesthenia, and schizophrenia scales. Indeed, as a group their other mean scores were all within a standard deviation of normal (i.e., rather normal scores) with small variances in most of the subscales.

Given the findings previously mentioned on this group, that they have strong internal locus of control (with little belief in powerful others or in chance causality), and that 3/4 of them are relatively normal in their eating attitudes, they appear surprisingly different from their ballet peers. Of course, any comparison of these data must be undertaken with great caution because they were tested by different groups at different times.

Nonetheless, this seems a potentially fruitful area for further work, because there may be real differences, not only between ballet and modern dance subcultures, but also between the best approaches to students of these disciplines.

One hint of the possible differences comes in a paper by Paley (1975) who points out that no matter what the origins of dance in humans, by the beginning of the 20th century dance was far removed in technique, form, and content from its original natural expressions. She notes that the modern dance revolution brought about by Duncan and Graham ''. . . broke stereotypes and reestablished dance as a vehicle to explore and communicate human experience. Stilted movements were discarded and the body's own rhythms—contraction and release, fall and recovery—became the object of artistic concern'' (p. 81). Although Paley shows a bias against the formal movement language of ballet, she does point out a prime difference between these two schools of serious dance.

Several areas of dance have not been addressed here because of the apparent lack of a formal literature. However, jazz, tap, and ethnic dances, including some of the highly developed African and Asian forms of dance surely have their own subcultures and psychological issues which may differ from our own as markedly as do Western and Eastern philosophies and worldviews. Much work in related fields will be necessary to help round out our understanding of the psychological ramifications of these other dance forms. The disciplines of nonverbal communications, cultural anthropology, and sociology may all have something significant to say about such issues.

Dance, Play, and Sports

Dance and sports have often been seen as close relatives. The role of play in these fields has been underemphasized, although the psychology of play has been well-studied. The theoretical relationship to dance is subtle but crucial. Play has been defined as being consciously outside of ordinary life, as being not serious but simultaneously fully and intensely involving the player; it is a profitless experience, proceeding by fixed rules in an orderly way within boundaries of time and space; it causes exclusive social groups to be formed, groups which stress their differences from the outside world (Huizinga, 1950).

Early in his career Freud wrote that the pleasure of movement was inherently sexual, noting that ''modern'' education made much of games to replace sexual enjoyment by pleasure of movement (1955). Later on, he also pointed out that a central drive in play was the attempt at mastery;

playing became a way of dealing with psychologically traumatic episodes by repeating them in a simple, safe way. Menninger (1942) felt that play was most importantly a way to safely express aggression. Games are often battles or even one-on-one fights, with clear rules permitting and encouraging certain types of aggression.

Fenichel (1939) extended an earlier report of Deutsch's that had been based on the successful treatment of a highly inhibited ineffectual man who was paradoxically an able athlete. Deutsch had suggested that sports allowed individuals to express inner conflicts by transforming painful feelings into pleasurable ones. Fenichel agreed that without conscious intent, the psychological conflict is projected onto the sport, allowing a sense of mastery in that setting; this makes sport counterphobic.

Sacks (1979) has reviewed these findings in a paper on the psychodynamics of sport, extending these notions to focus also on the creative and transcendental aspects of sport, which may have application to dance. Sacks feels that a fantasy associated with sport allows the player to ". . . recapture the illusion of a subjective reality that is felt as intensely pleasurable and creative, despite his awareness that he is just participating in a sport." For Sacks, the subjective reality and illusion afforded by sport provide a highly pleasurable sense of omnipotence and fusion experiences similar to those of early childhood. He touches on one possible reason for the intense body preoccupations of athletes by noting that these omnipotence and fusion experiences and the repetitive movements in sport may provide further associations for the athlete to that early part of life when the individual's sense of "self" was largely a "body self," before the boundaries of one's body and one's sense of self and others were complete. During this period the outside world is seen as an extension of the self. Sacks believes that the athlete and the artist seek to return to this state, which Winnicott (1967) has described as an "intermediate area," partway between the objective reality of the adult and the subjective reality of dreams and fantasy.

This material allows us to raise further questions about the psychology of dance. One immediate question is the finding, reported above, of the absence of aggression and competition among the ballet dancers (Druss & Silverman, 1979). The noncompetitive ballet dancer may actually have a great deal in common with the solo athlete, who trains for mastery of the body, focuses attention on perfection of form, and may devote a lifetime to these tasks. The competitions may differ, in that the javelin thrower may have a fixed external measure of success (distance thrown) every time he throws, whereas the dancer may have a less visible external measure (teacher, peer, and/or audience approval; advancement in class; selection for more advanced performances), but are nonetheless working for the same goal of perfection.

Brennan (1980) found that dancers and gymnasts possessed similar characteristics of motor ability not shared with groups of other athletes and nonathletes. Given that the nonaerobic exercise patterns of dancers and gymnasts are similar, and that there is a clear need for mastery of one's musculoskeletal system in both, are there other similarities in, for example, body image and locus of control?

Jungian Perspectives

Jungian theorists look at the relationship of movement and dance to the historical development of civilization, providing a longitudinal view on how societal and cultural forces help determine our views of dance. Historically, dance was first a magical mimetic and intensely sacred experience; this sense of dance disappeared from Western culture long ago when dance became secularized (Spencer, 1984).

The concepts of *polarity* and the *transcendent function,* and the associated method of *active imagination* are important to the Jungian understanding of dance and the role of movement in the Jungian therapies. Perhaps the enormous appeal of Jungian concepts to some dancers may be partly explained by the interweaving of these concepts with movement. Polarity involves the presence of dynamic sets of opposites in all things: "Life is never 'either/or' but always the paradox of 'both/and'" (Whitehouse, 1975, p. 7). To move a limb (or to hold it still) one must have a dynamic tension between extensor and flexor muscle groups. This combination of polarities is inherent to all movement; even the Latin words for left and right express the polarity: right is the dextrous side; left is sinister. One must explore such polarities in order to move more freely, just as one must explore up/down, light/heavy. Only when these opposites are brought into conscious belonging can their movement become authentic. This is the transcendent function; an innate dynamic process which serves to unite opposite positions within the psyche and leads to a new level of being and a new situation (Smallwood, 1977).

For Whitehouse (Slusher, 1966), a crucial corollary in movement is the pair "I move" and "I am moved." The latter is defined as what happens when the individual lets go and stops trying to move, but lets inner bases for movement come forward. When movement is thus initiated, it carries with it an authenticity (a genuine, personally relevant meaning); in Jungian terms, when the ego gives up control and stops choosing, the self is allowed to take over and initiate the movement.

Active imagination is a process in which, while consciousness looks on, participating but not directing, cooperating but not choosing, the unconscious is allowed to speak whatever and however it likes. It appears as images which may change rapidly; there is no limit or necessary consistency. Active imagination is seen as particularly valuable in movement by involving people in their own fantasies and images, to provide raw material toward personal understanding. Through movement based on internal imagery, the person can grow.

Clearly, the focus here is on physical movement creating a situation wherein feelings and thoughts are brought to mind. The belief is that having conscious access to this material can not only allow further work to be done but also cause psychic change in the individual (Smallwood, 1977).

Although active imagination has been explored as a means to effectively enhance the range of movement and fantasy in dance therapy (Fay, 1977), another interesting and largely untested aspect of active imagination is its potential usefulness outside the therapeutic setting and in dance education (Schnitt, 1978). The expectation is that a trained teacher could enhance access to dancers' relevant personal material through the use of active imagination techniques. This remains to be explored.

Dance Therapy

Dance therapy is defined by its parent organization as the "psychotherapeutic use of movement as a process which furthers the emotional and physical integration of the individual" (American Dance Therapy Association, 1972, p. 1). To this end, it shares with the body therapies (such as those developed by Feldenkreis, Alexander, Rolf, and Bartenieff) the hypothesis that the capacity for growth, feeling, and change is limited by an individual's capacity for movement (Geller, 1978) and can be enhanced through the use of movement-oriented techniques which may allow for more rapid access to feeling states than do more traditional therapies. The dance therapies then, are a series of empirically-derived approaches (Whitehouse, 1980) to using movement in the service of healing or integrating the kinesthetic, emotional, and cognitive areas of a person, integrated to varying degrees with more traditional psychotherapeutic theories and techniques (Bernstein, 1979).

An approach initially developed in psychiatric inpatient settings, dance therapy has also become a means to help others increase awareness of bodily cues and emotions, gaining access to these through movement rather than discussion and conversation. As such, dance therapy is neither a formal extension of dance nor is it restricted to dance-like movements. To the contrary, the dance therapist must work from a framework of psychotherapeutic knowledge and skills, firmly integrated with a capacity to use movement and the emotional states it creates or uncovers to further the experiences of trust and growth in a safe environment. According to Smallwood (1977), a major decision with any individual is whether the immediate goal is to move to help the individual to open up and have more access to unconscious material, or to turn toward a more conscious, concrete reality (a technique more helpful with a psychotic or other disturbed individual). Accordingly, dance therapy has had a great deal to say about how psychopathology may be approached using movement (see Silberman, 1981 for an extensive bibliography); this often involves working with an individual patient by learning how to assist that person to express conflictual feelings through movement techniques (Sandel, 1980).

On a different front, dancers have often productively used dance therapy as an initial foray into a psychotherapeutic setting, because at the surface, the language of dance therapy is more closely aligned with the kinesthetic style of the serious dancer and may make a nonverbal dancer more comfortable with approaching difficult psychological material than would a more traditional therapy.

There is one principle of dance therapy (and many of the body therapies) that has importance in understanding the interrelationship between the individual psychological needs of a given dancer and his or her ability to adapt to a given dance technique. The principle is that certain patterns of holding groups of muscles or holding one's entire posture are related to, and indeed initially caused by, emotional experiences, whether pleasant or traumatic. These patterns are typical for the individual, and are in effect repositories of the memory of the initial experience. Called by a variety of names in different therapies (*muscle-memory, kinesthetic memory, muscle-holding*), the principle is best explained by Siegel (1975): ''The instinctive withdrawal or tightening by which we once protected ourselves from some specific threat becomes fixed in our body's repertoire and continues to govern the way we move long after the initial reason for it is gone'' (p. 6). Thus the dancer who is unable to grow beyond an idiosyncratic posture or movement pattern potentially may be demonstrating this principle; exhortatory approaches by teachers and even dedicated practice by the individual will not by themselves necessarily allow such a posture or pattern to markedly change. This opens a possible area for significant research: Can dancers change postural alignment and/or range of motion more readily after they have undergone dance therapy or the body therapies? As noted above, anecdotal evidence suggests short-term improvement. Rigorous controlled studies may be difficult but would be of great interest.

Related Issues

There are several issues that are related to the psychological aspects of dance training and should be addressed. These are dance and creativity, dance and perception, body imagery, and systems issues. Each topic will be discussed in the following sections.

Dance and Creativity

That dance is a creative art is undeniable. However, it can be argued that dance technique is not in itself creative, but is rather a schooling of one's body to achieve position, movement, and timing; from this viewpoint technique is a craft.

One question about creativity relevant to the psychology of dancers involves the possible relationship between creativity and madness. By extension to dance, the question reads: Are creative performers/choreographers likely to be emotionally disturbed, brittle individuals? The answer, the subject of a literature of its own, appears to be negative (Arieti, 1976). A review of the chronologies of highly creative individuals (including dancers) who were emotionally disturbed reveals that their most creative works were typically created prior to the appearance of their symptoms rather than to be a product of access to madness (Rothenberg, 1976). Additionally, many creative persons are not unstable, but are quite productive. Creative work often involves associations, stream of conscious, metaphor, analogy, distortion, and exaggeration. This kind of thought activity seems to lie at the interface of conscious and unconscious processes (Schnitt, 1978).

Dance and Perception

Most people agree that dance is an art form and that dancers are often creative, but do dancers see things differently than other people? Some of the literature on perception looks at dancers. Slusher (1966) studied

95 male football players, 22 college male dancers, and 65 male nonathlete nondancers who were given several difficult perceptual tasks requiring visual and depth perception of moving objects. The results failed to demonstrate consistent perceptual differences among the groups. Huff (1972) measured auditory and visual perception of rhythm, including motor response to both types, in 57 dancers and athletes and 21 controls. Dancers and athletes scored significantly better than controls in tests of motor response to both types of rhythms. Dancers also responded better to auditory rhythms than did a group of basketball players. Experience in dance or sports did not enhance the ability to perceive rhythm or perform rhythmically. This limited work apparently demonstrates that dancers either are naturally responsive or can be trained to respond to rhythm, but their perceptual abilities with regard to visual and auditory data do not automatically improve with dance training.

Priddle (1978) investigated the relationship between an individual's perception of spatial images and the creation of spatial images in movement. Giving seven subjects a test of creativity and perceptual abilities (the Welsh Figure Preference Test, with Art and Movement subscales), she established their relative degree of originality and artistic expression on the one hand, and an ability to perceive movement quality in geometric form on the other; she found a lack of correlation between the two. The subjects were then asked to present a three-minute movement sequence which was videotaped and analyzed, not only for specific movements and distances covered, but also (by skilled judges) for creativity and aesthetic quality. There was a high correlation between the judges' perceptions of creativity and the Art subscale's prediction of creativity in the individual subject. There was no such correlation between the Movement Perception subscale and creativity. The authors concluded that trained individuals can discern creative and aesthetic movement; creativity in movement can be perceived as well as predicted.

The larger body of writing on perception has bearing on the psychology of dance. Of particular relevance are the writings of J.J. Gibson (1966), who described a system of perception known as the *haptic system:* the sense of touch reconceptualized to include the entire body rather than merely the body's specific individual instruments of touch (such as the hands and skin). The haptic system includes physical touch of all kinds, as well as the larger perceptual experiences of the person, such as that of being inside a cathedral or of swallowing an ice cube. The haptic system involves feeling and doing simultaneously; thus the haptic sense of swimming is very different from observing someone swim.

It follows from the psychodynamic work on dancers (which, as reported earlier, emphasizes ballet students' preference for musculoskeletal expression over expression via emotions or thoughts) that part of the reason dancers dance may be to increase the frequency and intensity of kinesthetic experiences, to perceive (and perhaps to enjoy) the sense of movement; how this overlaps Gibson's haptic system is not yet clear. However, in modern dance there is a current performance emphasis on conveying the kinesthetic experience to the audience; dances are often discussed and criticized regarding their kinesthetic qualities.

The haptic system's application to dance is important: Jack Anderson (1974) says "Dance is not simply a visual art, it is kinesthetic as well; it appeals to our inherent sense of motion. As we watch dancers onstage, our own muscular systems react to the strain or relaxation of their movements. We not only observe what happens, we also, in some empathetic way, feel it" (p. 3). A recent technical refinement to this view stresses the importance of conceptual clarity when one looks at perception and questions whether an observer can fully perceive the kinesthetic experience of a performer (Anderson, 1974). That is, the audience's evoked reaction to the performance may involve the audience's musculoskeletal systems, but this reaction is different in crucial ways from the dancer's kinesthetic experience of actually moving on stage.

Body Imagery

Study of the eating disorders has enhanced interest in body image: How does the individual visualize or imagine herself, both currently and in the ideal? This interest in part results from the finding that many people with anorexia nervosa think of themselves as overweight even when obviously thin to the point of emaciation. However, this question also seems appropriate to dancers, because achieving an ideal body image in dance may produce personal satisfaction, is likely to produce praise from teachers, and appears related to potential vocational success.

Studies of body image in eating disorders, both anorexia nervosa and obesity, show a distortion of body image in persons suffering both disorders (Garner et al., 1976; Grinker, 1973). The typical distortion for anorexic patients is to overestimate body size by 10–20%, although one group showed that even normals will have a similar distribution of estimated self-size (Garfinkel, Molodofsky, Garner, Stancer, & Coscina, 1978).

Another factor in body image is height. There is substantial literature documenting the relationship between height and self-esteem in boys and men: taller persons are more often selected for leadership roles (Stogdill, 1974); taller men have even been found to have "prettier" girlfriends (Feingold, 1982). A recent report (Hensley, 1983) concludes that there is no such height preference for women, and that height has little role in the determination of a woman's self-esteem.

Height seems to have little to do with the dancer's ideal body image; it is weight that seems paramount, especially in ballet. In Druss and Silverman's study of student ballet dancers (1979), the preoccupation was entirely with weight. All students wished to be thinner than they were, even when they were already at or below the weight recommended to them by their teachers. Comments about evident weight loss were perceived as high compliments. Bodily changes due to training and dieting were significant; students developed "the typical ballerina's figure: overly muscular buttocks, thighs, and calves" (p. 118). While the authors were able to differentiate psychologically the group of student ballerinas from groups of anorexia nervosa patients on a number of measures, they noted great similarities in body imagery between the two groups.

Taking 21 modern dance (or music) classes over a seven-week period proved to have essentially no significant impact on changing distortions in body image in a group of 80 undergraduate females in a study by Jette (1981). This was despite personal testimonies by a number of students that the dance classes did have impact on them. The author believed that the period of study was probably too short for the impact to be seen on the Fisher Body Distortion Questionnaire and suggested further exploration.

Work on understanding the causes of disturbance in body imagery is in its early phase; a complex array of psychological, physiological, and perceptual factors is probably involved. Thus little about body image can be concluded other than what can be observed. Dancers, like models, are preferred thin; they may take on such a preoccupation with thinness as to make them sound like patients with anorexia nervosa, although most dancers do not suffer from this disorder.

A recent review and update of the general concept of body image both theoretically and clinically are provided by van der Velde (1985), who introduces the idea that an individual has more than one body image, because one's perceptual apparatus allows only partial perceptions of the body from any vantage point. One's notion of one's own body is thus a composite of innumerable body images. Van der Velde also differentiates one's own body image from the mental representations of others' appearance and behavior; he argues that how we see others is a crucial factor in how we see ourselves. This may be a highly relevant concept for dancers, inasmuch as seeing oneself and others work and perform is such a crucial part of dance training.

Another slant on body image comes from one of the body therapies, ideokinesis, which is the application of imagery to enhance postural and movement change and thus to alter the actual body appearance (which may affect the individual's perception of his or her body image), based on the work of Todd (1973), then Sweigard (1974), and now Dowd (1981). The idea is to use one of a group of images to imagine movement through one's body as if it were occurring in a specific location and direction without giving any voluntary muscular help (Papken, 1978). This active process addresses inefficiency in movement by recoordination of neuromuscular pathways.

Once again, this is an underresearched area whose success has been anecdotal; significant questions involve the use of ideokinetic principles on a sample population of dancers over time along with a matched control group of dancers taking similar classes except for the ideokinetic material. Comparisons of movement range and quality might be compared by blind raters; before and after photos or films might help create objective data on postural and range-of-motion changes.

Systems Issues in Dance

Because the psychology of dance and dancers is such a complex issue, it is no surprise that the developing fields of behavioral cybernetics and applications of general system theory have been able to make contributions. According to Hatch (1978), in a technical paper describing the dancer as a "control system," behavioral cybernetics provides both a philosophical and an attitudinal basis for a theory of how the dancer organizes and controls dance behavior. He presents a model based on system thinking, which emphasizes that dance behavior is more than a reaction to internal cues of feeling and instinct or to the external environment. Rather, it is the process of self-regulation and self-generation of stimuli by neuromuscular activity to control both internal and external. That is, dance behavior is the result of multiple determinants, integrated at a neuropsychological level. Using the concept of a closed-loop feedback controlled system, he points out that linear cause-and-effect models are insufficient to explain the phenomena occurring in a dance.

This type of model depends heavily on the language of body mechanics, emphasizing the role of the primary reactive components of motion and response (tremor, receptor articulation, posture, manipulation, contact, and transport). These components are integrated on the issues of space, time, and force feedback. Body tracking is an elaborate process whereby individuals self-guide themselves via homeokinetic mechanisms; various organ systems of perception and balance interconnect. In dance, the intersystem body tracking is crucial. The specific movement patterns of dance result from integrated closed-loop regulation of these components. In this type of model, creative behavior is the "responsive adaptation to the self-generated, system controlled, stimulus input representing the organism's internal and external environment interactions . . . due to an infinite variety of combinations of space-structured, direction-specific neurons" (Hatch, 1978, p. 6)

Codman (1978) has developed a heuristic model of the cognitive processes that occur in learning a dance, which she calls the "mental template." This is a mental pattern or model, a plan of action, which the individual adopts from a variety of perceptual and image-based, individual and cultural inputs. Because dance is a conscious activity, perceptions are structured in a manner that fits the template, unless the template is altered to accommodate new perceptions. Forming a mental template is a form of dynamic schematization, a regulative and directive process which structures past experiences and incoming data into meaningful patterns. For Codman, the schema serves as a guidepost against which the organism measures and compares new perceptual responses, and in dance, new motor responses.

Once a dance is learned, it is repeated by rote, potentially with the addition of some individual interpretation. The use of imagery (conscious mental visualization) is crucial to bring the material being recalled into sharp focus. Cues in recalling a dance can be visual, auditory, or kinesthetic. After a dancer experiences a particular dance style, *set,* or the tendency to expect that prior knowledge of a situation is predictive for dealing with the situation when it recurs, becomes important. For instance, given two advanced-level dancers, one a ballerina and the other a Cambodian court dancer, neither familiar with the other's type of dance, there is no question who would do better in the early phases of learning a phrase from Indian dance, or who would initially excel in performing Graham technique. The prior experience or set would make a significant difference. Body image, too, is relevant: How individuals interpret kinesthetic perceptions in relation to their bodies helps dictate how they will respond and what they will prefer.

Future Research

Clearly, the study of the psychology of dance and dancers is in its infancy. A highly multidisciplinary area, it has been touched on by writers from a variety of specialties. For clinicians, further work is needed to study specific forces, including questions about eating disorders, body imagery, locus of control, affective disorders, and the ranges of normality. There is as yet no clear way of conveying information to educators who are the best candidates for referral for psychotherapeutic treatments and who would benefit most from this modality. For dance educators, much is unclear about the special needs of subpopulations among dance students; male dancers, minorities, students of dance disciplines other than ballet, and modern dancers may all be expected to have particular sociological and psychological issues which are not fully elucidated. It may still be premature for comprehensive research into the best techniques for enhancing creativity and expanding students' capacity to comprehend the relationship of dance to the larger world.

A basic question remaining is first to understand in a prospective way who is attracted to dance. A second, related question involves what impacts the study of different forms of dance at different levels of intensity have on the psychological development of dancers.

References

American Dance Therapy Association. (1972). What is dance therapy really? In B. Govine & J. Smallwood (Eds.), *Proceedings of the 7th Annual Conference of the American Dance Therapy Association*, Columbia, MD.

Anderson, J. (1974). *Dance*. New York: Newsweek Books.

Arieti, S. (1976). *Creativity: The magic synthesis*. New York: Basic Books.

Bernstein, P. (1979). *Eight theoretical approaches in dance-movement therapy*. Dubuque, IA: Kendall/Hunt.

Brennan, M.A. (1980). Comparison of female dancers, gymnasts, athletes, and untrained subjects on selected characteristics. *Perceptual and Motor Skills*, **51**, 252.

Brown, M. (1973). The new body psychotherapies. *Psychotherapy: Theory, research and practice*, **10**, 98–116.

Calabrese, L.H., Kirkendall, D.T., Floyd, M., Rapoport, S., Williams, G.W., Weiker, G.G., & Bergfeld, J.A. (1983). Menstrual abnormalities, nutritional patterns and body composition in female classical ballet dancers. *The Physician and Sportsmedicine*, **11**, 86–98.

Codman, K.R. (1978). The mental template in dance. In R.E. Priddle (Ed.), *Psychological perspectives on dance. Dance research annual* (Vol. 11). New York: Congress on Research in Dance.

Crisp, A.H., Palmer, R.L., & Kalucy, R.S. (1976). How common is anorexia nervosa? A prevalence study. *British Journal of Psychiatry*, **128**, 549–554.

Dasch, C.S. (1978). Relation of dance skills to body cathexis and locus of control orientation. *Perceptual and Motor Skills*, **46**, 465–466.

Dowd, I. (1981). *Taking root to fly: Seven articles on functional anatomy.* New York: Contact Collaborations.

Druss, R.G., & Silverman, J.A. (1979). Body image and perfectionism of ballerinas: Comparison and contrast with anorexia nervosa. *General Hospital Psychiatry,* **1**, 115–121.

Fay, C.G. (1977). *Movement and fantasy: A dance therapy model based on the psychology of Carl G. Jung.* Unpublished master's thesis, Goddard College, Baltimore, MD.

Feingold, A. (1982). Do taller men have prettier girlfriends? *Psychological Reports,* **50**, 810.

Fenichel, O. (1939). The counterphobic attitude. *International Journal of Psychoanalysis,* **20**, 263–274.

Forsyth, S., & Kolenda, P.M. (1966). Competition, cooperation, and group cohesion in the ballet company. *Psychiatry,* **29**, 123–145.

Freud, S. (1955). Three essays on sexuality. In J. Strachey (Ed. and Trans.), *The standard edition of the complete psychological works of Sigmund Freud* (Vol. 7, pp. 203–212). London: Hogarth.

Garfinkel, P.E., Moldofsky, H., Garner, D.M., Stancer, H.C., & Coscina, D.C. (1978). Body awareness in anorexia nervosa: Disturbances in "body image" and "satiety." *Psychosomatic Medicine,* **40**, 487–498.

Garner, D.M., & Garfinkel, P.E. (1980). Socio-cultural factors in the development of anorexia nervosa. *Psychological Medicine,* **10**, 647–656.

Garner, D.M., Garfinkel, P.E., Stancer, H.C., & Moldofsky, H. (1976). Body image disturbances in anorexia nervosa and obesity. *Psychosomatic Medicine,* **38**, 327–336.

Geller, J.D. (1978). The body, expressive movement and physical contact in psychotherapy. In J.L. Singer & K.S. Pope (Eds.), *The power of human imagination.* New York: Plenum.

Gibson, J.J. (1966). *The senses considered as perceptual systems.* Boston: Houghton Mifflin.

Grinker, J. (1973). Behavioral and metabolic consequences of weight reduction. *Journal of the American Dietetics Association,* **62**, 30–34.

Gurley, V., Neuringer, A., & Massee, J. (1984). Dance and sports compared: Effects on psychological well-being. *Journal of Sports Medicine,* **24**, 58–68.

Hatch, F.W. (1978). The dancer as a control system. In R.E. Priddle (Ed.), *Psychological perspectives on dance. Dance research annual* (Vol. 11). New York: Congress on Research in Dance.

Hensley, W.E. (1983). Gender, self-esteem and height. *Perceptual and Motor Skills,* **56**, 235–238.

Huff, J. (1972). Auditory and visual perception of rhythm by performers skilled in selected motor activities. *Research Quarterly,* **43**, 197–207.

Huizinga, J. (1950). *Homo ludens: A study of the play element in culture.* Boston: Beacon.

Jakobovits, C., Halstead, P., Kelley, L., Roe, D., & Young, C. (1977). Eating habits and nutrient intakes of college women over a 30-year period. *Journal of the American Dietetic Association* **71**, 405–411.

Jette, N. (1981). The effect of modern dance and music on body image in college women. *American Corrective Therapy Journal*, **35**, 104–106.

Joseph, A., Wood, I.K., & Goldberg, S.C. (1982). Determining populations at risk for developing anorexia nervosa based on selection of college major. *Psychiatric Research*, **7**, 53–58.

Leste, A., & Rust, J. (1984). Effects of dance on anxiety. *Perceptual and Motor Skills*, **58**, 767–772.

Levenson, H. (1974). Activism and powerful others: Distinctions within the concept of internal-external locus of control. *Journal of Personality Assessment*, **38**, 377–383.

Lowenkaupf, E.L., & Vincent, L.M. (1982). The student ballet dancer and anorexia. *Hillside Journal of Clinical Psychiatry*, **4**, 53–64.

Maloney, M.J. (1983). Anorexia nervosa and bulimia in dancers: Accurate diagnosis and treatment planning. *Clinics in Sports Medicine*, **2**, 549–555.

Menninger, K. (1942). *Love against hate.* New York: Harcourt Brace Jovanovich.

Paley, A.N. (1975). Dance therapy: An overview. *American Journal of Psychoanalysis*, **34**, 81–85.

Popken, F.E. (1978). Efficiency in movement through ideokinesis (the Sweigard method). In R.E. Priddle (Ed.), *Psychological perspectives on dance. Dance research annual* (Vol. 11). New York: Congress on Research in Dance.

Povey, R.M. (1975). Educating the gifted. *Association of Educational Psychology Journal*, **3**, 1–4.

Priddle, R.E. (1978). A comparison between the perception of space images and the creation of spatial images in movement. In R.E. Priddle (Ed.), *Psychological perspectives on dance. Dance research annual* (Vol. 11). New York: Congress on Research in Dance.

Puretz, S.L. (1978). A comparison of the effects of dance and physical education on the self-concept of selected disadvantaged girls. In R.E. Priddle (Ed.), *Psychological perspectives on dance. Dance research annual* (Vol. 11). New York: Congress on Research in Dance.

Reid, W.J., & Ware, E.E. (1974). Multidimensionality of internal vs external control: Addition of a third dimension and non-distinction of self vs other. *Canadian Journal of Behavioral Science*, **6**, 131–142.

Rothenberg, A. (1976). Homospatial thinking in creativity. *Archives of General Psychiatry*, **33**, 17–26.

Rotter, J.B. (1966). Generalized expectancies for internal versus external control of reinforcement. *Psychologial Monographs*, **80** (1, Whole No. 609).

Sacks, M.H. (1979). A psychodynamic overview of sport. *Psychiatric Annals, 9*, 127–133.

Sandel, S.L. (1980). Dance therapy in the private psychiatric hospital. *Journal of Private Psychiatric Hospitals, 11*, 20–26.

Schnitt, D. (1978). *Jung's "active imagination" and the creative imagination of the artist/dancer: Their meaning and relevance to university dance training.* Unpublished master's thesis, Connecticut College, New London.

Schnitt, D. (1985a). *Dance and architecture.* Manuscript submitted for publication.

Schnitt, D. (1985b). *Dimensional space as reflections of complexity of thought.* Manuscript submitted for publication.

Schnitt, J.M., & Schnitt, D. (1986). Eating disorders in dancers. *Medical Problems of Performing Artists, 1*(2), 39–44.

Schnitt, J.M., & Schnitt, D. (1987). Psychological issues in a dancer's career. In A.J. Ryan (Ed.), *Dance medicine.* Chicago: Precept Press.

Schnitt, J.M., Schnitt, D., & Del A'une, W. (1985). Health locus of control in modern dancers. Manuscript submitted for publication.

Schnitt, J.M., Schnitt, D., & Del A'une, W. (1986). Anorexia nervosa or thinness in modern dance students: A comparison with ballerinas. *Annals of Sports Medicine, 3*(1), 9–13.

Siegel, M.B. (1975). *Please run on the playground.* Hartford, CT: Connecticut Commission on the Arts.

Silberman, L. (1981). *Dance therapy bibliography.* Columbia, MD: American Dance Therapy Association.

Slusher, H.S. (1966). Perceptual differences of selected football players, dancers and nonperformers to a given stimulus. *Research Quarterly of the American Association of Health and Physical Education, 37*, 424–428.

Smallwood, J.C. (1977, June). Dance therapy and the transcendent function. Paper presented at the First Regional Congress of the International Association for Social Psychiatry, Santa Barbara, CA.

Smyth, M. (1984). Kinesthetic communication in dance. *Dance Research Journal, 16*(2), 19–22.

Spencer, M.J. (1984). Amplification: The dance. *Journal of Analytic Psychology, 29*, 113–123.

Stanley, R.O., Hyman, G.J., & Sharp, C.A. (1984). Health locus of control: Support for recent multidimensional developments. *Psychological Reports, 54*, 329–330.

Stogdill, R.M. (1974). *Handbook of leadership.* New York: Free Press.

Sweigard, L.E. (1974). *Human movement potential: Its ideokinetic facilitation.* New York: Dodd, Mead and Co.

Thomason, J.A. (1983). Multidimensional assessment of locus of control and obesity. *Psychological Reports, 53*, 1083–1086.

Todd, M.E. (1973). *The thinking body.* New York: Dance Horizons.

van der Velde, C.D. (1985). Body images of one's self and others: Developmental and clinical significance. *American Journal of Psychiatry, 142,* 527–537.

Wallston, K.A., & Wallston, B.S. (1978). Development of the multi-dimensional health locus of control (MHLC) scales. *Health Education Monographs, 6,* 160–170.

Whitehouse, M.S. (1975). *C.J. Jung and dance therapy: Two major principles.* Houston, TX: C.G. Jung Institute.

Whitehouse, M.S. (1980). *Physical movement and personality.* Houston, TX: C.G. Jung Institute.

Winnicott, D.W. (1967). The location of cultural experience. *International Journal of Psychoanalysis, 48,* 368–372.

Chapter 14

Selected Motor Learning Applications to the Technique Class

Margaret Skrinar

Is learning to dance more difficult than it need be? It probably is, especially for beginning and intermediate dancers. There is evidence suggesting that dance is taught inefficiently, with perhaps greater expenditures of time and energy than is necessary. Because of this inefficiency, potential dancers and choreographers may be lost to other mediums and fields of endeavor. As with any learning process, avoidance is the natural tendency when learning is made difficult at early stages.

No data exist on how many children take dance classes, but one would expect that the numbers compare with those of specific popular sports. Most towns have at least one dance studio for the training of dancers. The concern of this chapter has to do with the reason why, of the many students who have filled those studios, a large portion of them do not continue with dance classes and do not go on to perform and choreograph even with small companies. Is dropping out the nature of art? Do musicians, actors, and painters drop out at similar rates? Many factors are intervening in dance: aging in the western art form that panders to youth, narrow aesthetic standards which dictate where and how dance is accepted, a waning yet prevalent cultural acceptance of relative inactivity among women, and poor teaching. Although all of these, as well as others, contribute to the attrition rate of young dancers, poor teaching is one of the major factors that may discourage dancers from continued study.

This chapter focuses on a specific poor teaching trait: lack of information about what and how dance skills are learned. This discussion reveals how application or misapplication of selected motor learning principles by the teacher may influence each student's ability to learn and perform any dance skill. The results of documented psychomotor dance studies have indicated that a teacher's lack of information could erode rather than augment a student's ability to learn and perform a specific skill. Based on these studies, this chapter examines psychomotor (neuro-logical and muscular) information that teachers need to know and apply in order to facilitate each student's learning and performance of a skill.

How movement is learned falls under the aegis of motor learning. Motor learning is the study of the psychomotor experiences which enhance or decay learning of a motor skill. These experiences occur as external and internal messages to the dancer. Some forms of the experiences are practice, instruction, transfer, feedback, and retention. Both this chapter and the one that follows are not meant to serve as texts on motor learning for dancers. It would be impossible in this space to discuss each area of study in motor learning accurately and thoroughly. (For fundamental reading on the subject see Cratty, 1973.)

Identifying the Problem

Before surveying the research in this area, this chapter first must identify why psychomotor principles of motor learning generally have not been applied in dance class. Dance has rarely been taken seriously by the general public; thus the teaching of dance has been allowed to go unchecked. To the public, unfortunately, dancers fall into two categories: Little girls in *tutus* walking on tiptoe or entertainers dancing in time to rock music. In contrast, activities deemed valuable to the public have been developed and refined. Aerobic dance to promote fitness is an example: After only 15 years since its inception, considerable research has been conducted which has led to shoe design and redesign as well as changes in training methods.

The existing studies of dance training frequently are mistrusted by dancers because research requires systematic quantification and, to dancers, quantification demeans art. But quantification of how the instrument of dance, the body, is most efficiently and effectively trained is necessary and healthful. Further, it can be done without imposing on aesthetic preferences. Dance teaching can be systematically examined without an estrangement of the teaching from the art.

The never-ending change in aesthetics, a factor setting dance training apart from sport, makes it difficult for teachers to reexamine and redesign classes perpetually. In general, dancers are trained as they have been for many years whereas major changes have occurred in choreography regularly. Teachers simply are not prepared to adjust training to fluctuating aesthetic demands. Consequently, dance training is not keeping pace with dance as an art form.

In summary, the teaching of dance technique is not what it should be, in part because the field is not extensively questioning why or what is being done, and in part because training procedures are not keeping pace with the continually changing aesthetics. What can be done? Although not a panacea, the field of motor learning can provide some answers.

Isolated research has supported the notion that motor learning could be a means of updating and increasing effectiveness and efficiency in dance training. In this chapter the motor learning dance research has been classified into four areas of focus: perception, learning, instructional cue use, and transfer. Taken together, these four classifications form a picture of the psychomotor make-up of dancers and their training.

Perception

Two of the greatest difficulties in learning to dance are perhaps that teachers know neither how skills are learned nor what actually needs to be learned. This is a strong indictment, which suggests that many potentially talented, hardworking dancers may have been misdirected. For example, many dance teachers believe that while learning to dance perceptual skills like rhythm and timing are enhanced (Lockhart & Pease, 1977). Two studies indicated that, rather than perceptual skills development, a self-selection process may be at work. Gruen (1955) administered four perceptual tests (three written, one physical) to 60 professional dancers (30 females and 30 males) from major ballet, modern, and Afro-American dance companies in New York City. He also administered the perceptual tests to 99 nondancer controls. Gruen found that, with one exception, dance experience was not a factor regarding increased perceptual abilities. Balance was the only differentiating factor; dancers were better balancers than nondancers. Differences among dancers were not found. Coupling that latter finding with the fact that there were professional dancers with as little as one year of dance experience, Gruen concluded that balance had to have been developed within the first year of dance training. In contrast, teachers believe that dancers must continually refine balance skills throughout their career (Shick, Stover, & Jette, 1983).

Gruen's study indicates that perceptual skills like hand-eye coordination, rhythm, spatial and visual discrimination, and body control were not learned in dance class, but were either acquired elsewhere at an earlier age or genetically inherited. Yet it is likely that most teachers believe these perceptual skills are developed through dance training. If it is true that classes, rehearsals, and performances do not develop the perceptual skills that Gruen measured, then what has been learned in their place? The answer is unclear.

Contradictory data on the perceptual ability of field dependence/ independence is an example of how little is understood about the skills necessary for success in dance. Three opposing studies (Barrell & Trippe, 1977; Bowman, 1971; Gruen, 1955) on the topic have respectively found dancers to be more field-dependent, more field-independent, and no different from the general population.[1] These contradictory findings are an example of how little is known about either the natural perceptual skills students bring into the class or the influence of training on the enhancement of perceptual skills. Dance training needs to be adjusted according to the identification of what needs to be learned and what is actually being absorbed in current training practice.

Learning

Bowman's (1971) study of beginning dancers' learning schemes implies that their training may not focus on the dance skills which need the most attention. She found that, in learning a dance phrase, the dancers committed most errors with lateral locomotor movement as well as timing. These results indicate that, at least for beginners, significantly more time should be spent on side-to-side movements and temporal problems rather than on stationary and forward-backward movements taught at half-speed. Typically more than half of every dance class is spent on non-locomotor movement (Gray & Skrinar, 1984) whereas new material is frequently taught at half- or quarter-speed.

Related to the theme of learning, some research has shown that men may learn dance more efficiently than women. Three studies of professional and college dancers spanning over 30 years have established that males study five to six years less than their female counterparts (Gruen, 1955; Hellerman & Skrinar, 1984; Skrinar & Zelonka, 1978). Whether motivation, movement history, sex biases, or some other factor has made the difference is not clear. One study which paired males and females in the same technique classes according to technical skill suggests that the different movement histories of males and females is likely an intervening factor (Hellerman, Skrinar, & Dodds, 1983). Researchers should continue to

---

[1]At one end of a continuum, field-independence measures one's skill for discriminating items from outside the expected context. Conversely, field-dependence indicates an inability to identify items when they are outside the expected setting. One may be field dependent/independent with any, all, or none of their senses. Common visual screening tests for this have been childrens' hidden picture games which have asked them to locate something like ten parrots in a setting of clouds.

study why these gender differences are occurring in order to understand and/or perhaps prevent further waste of female dancers' training time.

From the results of the studies of Gruen (1955); Bowman (1971); and Hellerman, Skrinar, and Dodds (1983) the question arises: Which is more valuable, a general or a conventional skills-specific approach to training. That is, should skill learning focus on general skills like balance and lateral locomotion rather than on specific skills like *pliés, tendus,* leaps, and turns? Clarkson, Kennedy and Flanagan (1984) studied the reaction times of dancers and found that consistency of movement patterns is one skill that dancers have and nondancers lack. If that skill is one that is developed in dance training, it would behoove teachers to focus greater attention on it rather than on specific steps. Mastery of specific skills in dance may be the means rather than the ends. If this is so, students in classes (not rehearsals or performances) need to know that being consistent in movement patterns, rather than learning dance steps, is the ultimate goal.

Motor learning research has found that when students have a clear understanding of their final goal, skill acquisition is more efficient and effective (Cratty, 1973). In general, the majority of dance teachers never mention short-term goals for daily classes, let alone long-term goals like movement consistency. If final goals are general skills like consistency of movement or balance then they deserve attention.

In the future, critical skills learned in the studio must be identified and distinguished from those skills acquired from other environmental or genetic sources. The preliminary evidence suggests that critical skills developed in technique classes may be of a more general nature. For example, among teachers there are several different idiosyncratic elements in a movement as basic as the *tendu*. Timing, dynamics, tilt of head, gesture of hands, and so on, all vary widely. Consequently, talented dancers have in common general skills like balance and movement consistency but not inclinations of the head or gestures of the hand. It is possible that, at least in the early learning stages, if general skills were the primary focus, then specific skills would be more easily acquired in subsequent class, rehearsal, and performance situations.

Instructional Cue Use

The learning of movement skills is influenced by the type of instructional cues provided. Cuing can occur visually, verbally, kinesthetically, or with any combination of these three. The literature indicates that teaching methods that combine all types of cues are more effective than those using only one type (Cratty, 1973). Furthermore, for efficient skill acquisition, each ability level has its own cuing needs (Cratty, 1973; Newell,

Morris, & Scully, 1985; Shick, Stover, & Jette, 1983). Three studies indicate that regardless of level, idiom, or class purpose, verbal cues dominate instructional time. Visual/verbal cues are used considerably less with the occurrence of little or no kinesthetic, kinesthetic/visual, kinesthetic/verbal, or visual instructions (Borelli & Skrinar, 1982; Cheffers, Mancini, & Martinek, 1980; Lord, 1980).

Borrelli and Skrinar (1982) found that the use of verbal instruction was significantly greater (p < .05) than all other forms, whereas visual/verbal cues were used significantly more (p < .05) than the remaining types of cues. Lord (1980) and Cheffers et al. (1980) found similar results between types of classes. Verbal instruction time dominated both technique and composition classes. Cheffers et al. found that students spent 65.7% of technique class time listening to verbal teacher instructions and 52.1% in composition class. In classes where movement and observational instruction time (visual and kinesthetic cues) should prevail, it is disconcerting to see how few opportunities are available for these. How can dancers efficiently or effectively learn to move if they do not spend significant amounts of time doing and watching? All teachers must become more aware of how much time they spend talking, as well as realizing the detriments of excessive talk. Is it possible that this emphasis on verbal cues explains why it takes females five or six more years than males? That is, can males, who have developed a more generalized movement vocabulary from previous sports participation, more easily apply verbal cues than their female classmates?

Transfer

The use of transfer as an instructional tool may be inefficiently utilized in dance classes. Transfer suggests that the learning of one task may positively or negatively influence the learning of other tasks. Negative or positive transfer is effected by the degree of similarity in the stimulus and response elements of each task. Negative transfer occurs when the stimulus elements for each task are identical but the response elements are dissimilar (Cratty, 1973). Associated with negative transfer is a diminished, skill-acquisition ability. During technique class the stimulus elements are relatively constant; the setting, the teacher, the accompaniment, and so on, are unchanged. Yet the response elements between the warm-up and dancing phases of class can be quite different. For example, in a ballet warm-up students stand at a *barre*, often sideways to a mirror, and alternately work one leg at a time in essentially a unidirectional facing. During the center dancing phase the students, using some skills from the warm-up, face the mirror, stand away from the *barre,* and execute movement which quickly and frequently changes directions and shifts legs. Practice of skills during the warm-up could be negatively transferring to the center work. That is, warm-up theoretically could erode dancing ability.

Gray and Skrinar (1984) indirectly examined how use of the center of gravity transferred from warm-up to dancing phases of modern dance and ballet classes. Using beginning, intermediate, and advanced college classes for dance majors, they determined the frequency of use for six different sized bases of support (very narrow, narrow, medium, wide, grounded, and in the air). They found that warm-up for classes within an idiom varied significantly from the dancing phase (p < .01). As cited in chapter 11 they found that ballet's and modern's use of base supports were significantly dissimilar during warm-up and similar in the dancing phases of class. A disproportional use during warm-up of very narrow bases in ballet and grounded bases in modern were contrasted with a relatively even distribution of base support use while dancing in either idiom. Future research needs to determine whether there is an erosion of skill due to negative transfer from warm-up to dancing and whether similar negative transfer may be occurring within and among classes, rehearsals, and performances.

Further research needs to examine if there are ways to more efficiently use warm-up time. If time were spent more economically, professional ballet dancers might not need to spend eight to ten hours per day, six days per week in classes, rehearsals, and performances (Skrinar & Zelonka, 1978), nor would females need to study five to six more years than males.

Summary

Unfortunately motor learning research on dance is not readily available to dancers, and what exists is inconclusive. The accessible documentation suggests that dancers may not be provided optimum opportunities for successful psycho-motor skill development. The art form is demanding more movement expertise each year, yet the most effective ways to meet these demands are not always being applied.

Until more abundant evidence becomes available dancers must rely on related information from sport, physical education, general education, and industry. The application of findings in these areas to the physical training of dancers may mean greater efficiency and effectiveness. That is, less time may be needed in class and rehearsal in order to glean today's levels of skill in performance. That economy would mean more available time and attention to choreography. An often neglected point is that ultimately dance exists not for training dancers but for making dances.

Dancers may learn how motor learning can further serve them by seeking out a specialist at a nearby college or university. Motor learning professionals are usually in the physical education department. Talk with them about dance training procedures, conditions, and habits. Invite them to observe classes. Follow their list of recommended readings, and/or enroll in an introductory course.

Training for dance needs to be thoroughly examined and probably revised. Becoming a skilled dancer could be a hit or miss situation whereby skill acquisition hinges more on luck rather than talent, motivation, or training. Research on skill acquisition may serve to dilute the luck factor and refine the technique of dance classes.

Note: Portions of this chapter are excerpted from Skrinar, M. (1985). Motor learning may help the dancer. In C. Shell (Ed.), *The dancer as athlete* (pp. 187-194). Champaign, IL: Human Kinetics.

References

Barrell, G., & Trippe, H. (1977). Field dependence and physical ability. *Perceptual and Motor Skills, 41,* 216–218.

Borrelli, G., & Skrinar, M. (1982). Instructional cue use in two dance idioms. *Kinesiology for Dance, 5*(1), 6.

Bowman, B.A. (1971). *Learning experiences in selected aspects of a dance movement sequence.* Unpublished doctoral dissertation, University of Michigan, Ann Arbor.

Clarkson, P.M., Kennedy, T., & Flanagan, J. (1984). A study of three movements in classical ballet. *Research Quarterly for Exercise and Sport, 55*(2), 175–179.

Cheffers, J.T.F., Mancini, V., & Martinek, T. (1980). *Interaction analysis: An application to nonverbal activity* (2nd ed.). St. Paul, Minnesota: Paul S. Amedon and Associates.

Cratty, B. (1973). *Teaching motor skills.* Englewood Cliffs, NJ: Prentice-Hall.

Gray, M., & Skrinar, M. (1984). Base support use in two dance idioms. *Research Quarterly for Exercise and Sport, 55*(2), 184-187.

Gruen, A. (1955). The relation of dancing experience and personality to perception. *Psychological Monographs: General and Applied, 69*(14), 1–16.

Hellerman, A., & Skrinar, M. (1984). Relationship of technical skill rank to age, gender, and number of years in dance training. *Research Quarterly for Exercise and Sport, 55*(2), 188–190.

Hellerman, A., Skrinar, M., & Dodds, P. (1983). *Gender differences in dancers' acquisition of a novel movement pattern.* Unpublished manuscript, Physical Education Department, University of Massachusetts.

Lockhart, A., & Pease, E.E. (1977). *Modern dance* (5th ed.). Dubuque, IA: Wm. C. Brown.

Lord, M.C. (1980). The teaching of dance: A characterization of dance? University level. *Dissertation Abstracts International,* **40a,** 5778.

Newell, K.M., Morris, L.R., & Scully, D.M. (1985). Augmented information and the acquisition of skill in physical activity. In R.L. Terjung (Ed.), *Exercise and sport sciences reviews* (Vol 13). New York: Macmillan.

Shick, J., Stover, L.J., & Jette, N. (1983). Relationship between modern-dance experience and balancing performance. *Research Quarterly for Exercise and Sport,* **54**(1), 79–82.

Singer, R.N. (1980). *Motor learning and human performance* (3rd ed.). New York: Macmillan.

Skrinar, M., & Zelonka, N.H. (1978). A descriptive study of ballet and modern dancers at three levels of training. Unpublished manuscript, School of Education, University of Pittsburgh, PA.

Chapter 15

Psychomotor Research and the Dance Teacher

Susan Puretz
State University of New York
College at New Paltz

Many questions face the dance teacher when initially choosing a teaching method. Unfortunately, much of the exciting psychomotor research, with its implications for dance skill acquisition, never reaches the new teacher. As a result, the novice often uses traditional teaching methods which, for the most part, do not incorporate the newest research. A perfect example is the continued use of the *grand plié* in ballet classes despite recent findings (Hamilton, 1985) of its detrimental nature.

This chapter will examine studies and look at some of the current psychomotor research, specifically in the areas of motor memory and bilateral transfer, and relate them to pedagogical techniques. Two studies in particular (Puretz, 1983, 1986) have examined complex motor patterns comprised of a series of movements linked together—sequences typical of dance classes. The use of the complex motor pattern in these studies has corrected one of the major problems with transferring the results of motor research to the dance studio. That is, up until this point, the overwhelming majority of the psychomotor studies have used simple and short motor patterns whereas dance classes use complex movement patterns.

Bilateral Transfer of Motor Skills

Bilateral transfer involves the transfer of motor patterns from one side of the body to the other through practice on only the one side (Underwood, 1966). The theoretical question of bilateral transfer was addressed as early as 1903 by Woodworth who suggested that the bilateral transfer phenomenon existed because a) hands are always innervated together and thus specifically are involved at the same time, and b) eye movements and total bodily coordination might be common elements. In a research paper by Woodworth and Marsh (1905), the authors reported that the performance of an individual on different tests with the same hand did not yield as high a positive correlation as the performance of the person's right and left hand on the same test. Studies (Goldstein & Braun, 1974; Laszlo, Baguley, & Bairstow, 1970; Singer, 1968; Tsuji & Ide, 1974) have supported the theory of bilateral transfer, although some research (Dunham, 1977; Lurcat, 1971–1972) has refuted it. (For a more extensive review see Weig, 1923 and Ammons, 1958.)

Interestingly, positive transfer exists not only from hand to hand but from hand to foot (Bray, 1928; Cook, 1934). This finding might account for the phenomenon frequently observed in dance studios of marking out a movement sequence, whereby the dancer goes through the movement pattern standing still, except for the use of the hands to indicate what the feet are doing.

Although research did not address the issue of the bilateral transfer of dance skills until 1983 (Puretz, 1983), an observation of dance classes prior to that time would have shown that most teachers were conducting their classes as if bilateral transfer were a proven fact. In those classes, warm-up, technique, and locomotor patterns have been demonstrated and then taught to the dancer's right side, the expectation being that dancers will transfer the motor information to the left without further practice time. Although there has been no study indicating that the movement replication is not as proficient on the left (in the case of right-handed subjects, nonpreferred) side, most would agree that this is so. The explanations for this lack of proficiency have been conjectural but would include lack of sufficient practice, lack of bilateral transfer, or merely the fact that the left is the nonpreferred side.

In a recent study (Puretz, 1983), I addressed the question of whether the current dance practice of teaching complex patterns to the preferred side and expecting transfer without practice to the nonpreferred side—because of bilateral transfer—is correct; and if so, whether it is the best of possible teaching techniques. The study examined the factors of ability (naive/experienced), direction of transfer (preferred to nonpreferred side/nonpreferred to preferred side), and transfer of learning (one-trial/practice). The subjects, college students, were grouped according to experience or naivete in dance. Each subject learned two different eight-count movement sequences. The videotaped performances of each subject were scored by dance authorities.

The significant new finding of the research was that direction of transfer was important: Transference is best from nonpreferred to preferred side. This result was not expected, because the results from studies on the effects of hand preferences (Ammons, 1958) indicated greater positive transfer from preferred to nonpreferred side.

The discrepancy could be accounted for by the fact that bilateral transfer studies had heretofore used simple tasks, and this study used complex movements (because dance teaching relies on complex movements rather than the simple tasks or movements used in the psychomotor laboratory.) Thus the results on the direction of transfer call into question the conventional dance studio wisdom of teaching to the right (the preferred side) and expecting quality replication on the nonpreferred side. Clearly, the more effective approach seems to be to teach to the nonpreferred side because that side will improve through the practice effect while at the same time the dancer's preferred side will efficiently maintain a high level of skill performance by way of transference.

A future research direction that evolves from this study would be extending the defined population from naive and experienced dancers to include professional dancers, and then replicating the study with these new subjects. In this study, the experienced dancers were defined as anyone with some dance training, from a six-month college modern dance course to no more than four years of dance training, whereas the naive dancers had never danced before. It is possible that professional dancers (a term which would have to be carefully defined), because of their superior neuromuscular skills, would constitute a special class for whom these current findings would not be applicable.

In summary, dance teachers who, in order to save time, have used a teaching methodology which relies on the assumption of the validity of bilateral transfer, whereby they analyze a complex movement in detail on only one side and expect dancers to affect the transference themselves, are correct according to this research. But it may be that if they were to teach to the nonpreferred side, that side would significantly improve (through practice), and the quality of the bilateral transfer of the movement would be noticeably better.

Long-Term Memory and Recalling Dance Movements

A question that follows quite naturally from the discussion of bilateral transfer is how movements, once learned, are retained in memory, and further, how the memory traces are then recovered in order to replicate the motor movement? Recent research (Fox, 1983) has pointed to the possibility that there are two biologically and physically distinct memory systems that reside in different structures of the brain and may be under different biochemical controls (Lynch & Baudry, 1984). One system controls the assimilation of facts, which is known as *declarative knowledge*, whereas the other system controls assimilation of skills, or *procedural knowledge*. This latter system would be active in dance activities, which are the focus of this book.

Learning a dance skill is a multistep process that begins with the presentation of the material and ends with its replication immediately, or several hours, days, or months later. In the interim between the actual learning and the replication, the material is encoded and stored in long-term memory. This discussion deals with recall (the response initiation— including retrieval cues and strategy) from long-term memory and its outward manifestation in the motor product that is recreated as a result of the act of recall.

The process of recalling a motor pattern from long-term memory involves some type of retrieval strategy. One such retrieval strategy uses rehearsal in order to generate the movement stimulus. Rehearsal as discussed here is not the process that originally encodes the material but rather the process that recovers it. The literature is scant about the differential effects of mental or physical rehearsal on recall situations. Rehearsal can be divided into overt and covert rehearsal. Overt (physical) rehearsal involves active replication of the movement, and covert (cognitive) rehearsal is mental rehearsal of the criterion movement. Although there have been several studies (Decaria, 1977; Jeffrey, 1976) that compared overt and covert rehearsal on acquisition and retention of motor skills, they have dealt with rehearsal as a central mechanism by which information is transferred from short-term store to a more permanent, long-term store. The results of these studies have supported covert (cognitive) rehearsal as being as effective as physical practice. These results have reconfirmed early observations of this phenomenon by Vandell, Davis, and Clugston (1943) who demonstrated that mental rehearsal was as effective as physical practice in improving performance at dart throwing and free-throw basketball shooting.

The explanation to account for those observations was that mental rehearsal involved minute contractions of the muscles in patterns similar to those in actual physical practice, and this was demonstrated as early as 1931 by Freeman (1931). It can be hypothesized that mental rehearsal utilizes processes that are known to be a part of the motor task in its early stages and thus establishes appropriate strategies for both coding and subsequent recall.

In a dance class, a movement pattern is presented and practiced until some criterion is reached and, presumably, encoding has been completed. Regarding encoding, it has been agreed that successive replications of the original item result in both improved short-term retention (Dark & Loftus, 1976; Meunier, Kestner, Meunier, & Ritz, 1974) and long-term memory (Modigliani & Seamon, 1974) for verbal and motor items. Atkinson and Shiffrin (1968) hypothesized that rehearsal (during the initial learning) gives coding and other storage processes time to operate. It can be argued, however, that in the processing of a dance movement, which can be considered of more than minimal complexity and load, some type of perceptual organization other than mere active physical replication of the movement is necessary. Perceptual-motor organization (Diewart & Stelmach, 1978) and premovement organization or strategy formations (Keele & Ellis, 1972; Stelmach, 1973; Stelmach & Kelso, 1977) have both been considered potent factors. Further work done by Thompson, Wenger, and Bartling (1978) has emphasized the importance of the encoding process in increasing the availability of items to be recalled. Nacson, Jaeger, and Gentile (1972) and Shea (1977) have found that verbal labels or knowledge of movement relationships given to subjects resulted in improved reproduction performance as well as differential performance patterns.

The studies discussed above begin to provide some characteristics of and preliminary answers to some issues facing motor researchers. However, the primary focus of psychomotor research has been on simple motor movements. The few studies that have dealt with recall of more complex motor movements have used physical education activities.

I have addressed the question of how dance rehearsal strategy provides for maximum recall (see Puretz, 1986). In my study an experimenter-presented organization was used: The experimenter presented a movement which was then repeated by the subjects until a criterion was reached. This teaching methodology is typical of traditional dance classes. The subjects do not have to select their own organizational plan; they need only observe what organization is present, store it and transmit the structure to recall to facilitate performance. In the experiment the subjects were instructed to recall the previously learned movement using several different rehearsal strategies (physical versus mental practice) and temporal periods (one-half hour, two days, and one week later). Videotapes taken at retest were compared with those taped at the time of initial criterion learning.

There were two striking results from this experiment. First, there is no difference between the various rehearsal strategies for recovering dance movements from long-term memory. This supports other studies (Decaria, 1977; Jeffrey, 1976; Vandell et al., 1943), which found that cognitive rehearsal is as effective as physical rehearsal in retrieving movements, and extends the findings from the general motor literature to now include complex dance movements. The implications for dance classes are that precious class time does not have to be used physically practicing a previously learned dance sequence; mental rehearsal will provide the same quality of movement reproduction.

Second, there is no significant decrement of dance movement replication up to periods of one week later. This finding corroborates recent research (Fox, 1983) on the two memory systems which claim that procedural knowledge (which includes motor and cognitive skills), once learned, is rarely lost or forgotten. The results of this experiment confirm that a dance movement pattern, once entered into the long-term memory store, can be physically recreated despite a lapse of several days without practice.

Differences between two-day and one-week conditions indicated that motor memory declined after two days and then returned. This diminution in recall followed by a rebound effect supports the early studies by Hull (1952) on inhibition and reminiscence. According to Hull, responses have some degree of inhibitory potential that is cumulative with each response and leads to performance decrements. This reactive inhibition accumulates with work and dissipates with rest and accounts for increments in performance following rest.

This study's findings are of particular value to the dance teacher because they provide options. First, the teacher can now choose to structure a lesson using either physical or mental rehearsal to facilitate recall of dance sequences that were learned previously. Second, the teacher can, with more assurance, now teach a movement sequence with the expectation that the dancer will recall it sometime in the future. This is not really a new option because it is a long-standing practice in dance classes; but now there are data to support the practice.

The confirmation of the expectation that dancers can recreate previously learned movements has implications for dance historians as well as teachers. Many dances have been brought back into a dance company's repertory after a lapse of many years, and there is sometimes a question as to the accuracy of the dance. Some of these dances are pieces that were created by the same choreographer who is now reviving the dance whereas others are dances that the reviver had danced in many years earlier. Further research might indicate whether these individuals can accurately recreate dance pieces of many years ago.

Although this study only used a time-span of one week, the findings confirmed that movements can be accurately recreated. It would be beneficial to duplicate this study's methodology to test for longer memory retention of movement sequences—thus extending the time period to, for example, six months, one year, five years, or longer. These findings would be most helpful to dance reconstructionists and dance historians.

Summary

In addition to offering the dance teacher new options discussed previously, this research provides the scientific underpinnings for two practices that have been followed for years as a matter of course. The expectations that a) movements transfer from one side of the body to the other, and b) that dancers will be able to recreate dance sequences previously learned are ones that are held in dance studios. An interesting future study would be to discover if there is any relationship between the bilateral transfer phenomenon and long-term memory retrieval.

The psychomotor study (1986) combined with the one on bilateral transfer (1983) has important ramifications for the dance studio because they point towards new ways of teaching, which will maximize efficiency and performance. However, as psychologists have already pointed out, habits are hard to change, and it will take a motivated dance teacher to incorporate these findings into teaching techniques.

References

Ammons, R.B. (1958). Le mouvement [Movement]. In G. Seward & J. Seward (Eds.), *Current psychological issues: Essays in honor of R. Woodworth*. New York: Holt.

Atkinson, R.C., & Shiffrin, R.M. (1968). Human memory: A proposed system and its control processes. In K.W. Spence & J. Spence (Eds.), *The psychology of learning and motivation* (Vol. 2, pp. 90–195). New York: Academic Press.

Bray, C.W. (1928). Transfer of learning. *Journal of Experimental Psychology,* **11**, 443–467.

Cook, T.W. (1934). Studies in cross education: Kinaesthetic learning of an irregular pattern. *Journal of Experimental Psychology,* **17**, 749–762.

Dark, V.R., & Loftus, G.R. (1976). The role of rehearsal in long-term memory performance. *Journal of Verbal Learning and Verbal Behavior,* **15**, 479–490.

Decaria, M.D. (1977). *The affect of cognitive rehearsal training on performance and on self-report of anxiety in novice and intermediate female gymnasts.* Unpublished doctoral dissertation, University of Utah, Salt Lake City.

Diewart, G.L., & Stelmach, G.E. (1978). Perceptual organization in motor learning. In G.E. Stelmach (Ed.), *Motor control: Issues and trends* (pp. 241–265). New York: Academic Press.

Dunham, P., Jr. (1977). Effect of bilateral transfer on coincidence/anticipation performance. *Research Quarterly, 48,* 51–55.

Fox, J. (1983). Memories are made of this. *Science, 222,* 1318.

Freeman, G.L. (1931). The spread of neuro-muscular activity during mental work. *Journal of General Psychology, 5,* 479–494.

Goldstein, S., & Braun, I. (1974). Reversal of expected transfer as a function of increasing age. *Perceptual and Motor Skills, 38,* 1139–1145.

Hamilton, W. (1985, April). *Problems of the knee and hips.* Paper presented at the PACH (Performing Arts Center for Health) Seminar, Dance Health '85, New York, NY.

Hull, C.L. (1952). *A behavior system: An introduction to behavioral theory concerning the individual organism.* New Haven, CT: Yale University.

Jeffrey, R.W. (1976). The influence of symbolic and motor rehearsal in observational learning. *Journal of Research in Personality, 10*(1), 116–127.

Keele, S.W., & Ellis, J.C. (1972). Memory characteristics of kinesthetic information. *Journal of Motor Behavior, 4,* 127–134.

Laszlo, J., Baguley, R., & Bairstow, P. (1970). Bilateral transfer in tapping skill in the absence of peripheral information. *Journal of Motor Behavior, 2,* 261–271.

Lurcat, L. (1971–72). Study of graphic activity of two hands: Model from one hand reproduced by two. *Bulletin de Psychologie, 35*(18), 1022–1034. (*Psychological Abstracts,* 1973, *49,* Abstract No. 8310)

Lynch, G., & Baudry, M. (1984). The biochemistry of memory: A new and specific hypothesis. *Science, 224,* 1057–1063.

Meunier, G.F., Kestner, J., Meunier, J.A., & Ritz, D. (1974). Overt rehearsal and long-term retention. *Journal of Experimental Psychology, 102*(5), 913–914.

Modigliani, V., & Seamon, J.G. (1974). Transfer of information from short- to long-term memory. *Journal of Experimental Psychology, 102*(5), 768–772.

Nacson, J., Jaeger, M., & Gentile, A. (1972). Encoding processes in short-term motor memory. In I.D. Williams & L.M. Wankel (Eds.), *Proceedings of the Fourth Canadian Psychomotor Learning and Sports Psychology Symposium* (pp. 158–162). Ottawa, Canada: Department of National Health.

Puretz, S.L. (1983). Bilateral transfer: The effects of practice on the transfer of complex dance movement patterns. *Research Quarterly, 54*(1), 48–54.

Puretz, S.L. (1986, April). *Retrieval of movements from long term memory: Two views of a collaborative process.* Paper presented at the Researching Dance Through Film and Video conference sponsored by the Human Studies Film Archives of the Smithsonian Institute and the Congress on Research in Dance, Washington, DC.

Shea, J.B. (1977). Effects of labelling on motor short-term memory. *Journal of Experimental Psychology: Human Learning and Memory, 3*, 92–99.

Singer, R.N. (1968). *Motor learning and human performance.* New York: Macmillan.

Stelmach, G.E. (1973). Feedback—a determiner of forgetting in short-term memory. *Acta Psychologica, 37*, 333–339.

Stelmach, G.E., & Kelso, J.A.S. (1977). Memory processes in motor control. In S. Dornic (Ed.), *Attention and performance* (Vol. 6, pp. 719–739). Hillsdale, NJ: Erlbaum.

Thompson, C.P., Wenger, S., & Bartling, C. (1978). How recall facilitates subsequent recall: A reappraisal. *Journal of Experimental Psychology: Human Learning and Memory, 4*(3), 210–221.

Tsuji, K., & Ide, Y. (1974). Development of bilateral transfer of skills in the mirror tracing. *Japanese Psychological Research, 16*, 171–178.

Underwood, B.J. (1966). *Experimental psychology* (2nd ed.). Englewood Cliffs, NJ: Prentice-Hall.

Vandell, R.A., Davis, R.A., & Clugston, H.A. (1943). The function of mental practice in the acquisition of motor skills. *Journal of General Psychology, 29*, 243–250.

Weig, E. (1923). Bilateral transfer in the motor learning of young children and adults. *Child Development, 3*, 247–267.

Woodworth, R., & Marsh, H. (1905). Motor correlations. *Psychological Bulletin, 2*, 49.

Chapter 16

Who's Teaching the Dance Class?

Margaret Skrinar
Nancy H. Moses
Boston University

Earlier chapters have addressed physical problems encountered by dancers in the training of their bodies. Teachers, as vehicles for that training, are key figures in a dancer's accomplishments. Their methods of guiding and selecting students can facilitate or thwart the physical, psychological, sociological, and spiritual development of students, irrespective of class purpose or level. Although the selection of a dance teacher is a critical decision, the majority of dancers/parents are unable to make informed determinations of whether teaching is truly safe, valid, effective, and worthwhile.

Physical aspects of what should and should not occur in the dance class are the realm of other chapters. At issue in this chapter is how students' total development is related to (a) how dance is taught and (b) what factors qualify teachers to teach dance.

Research on personal characteristics, class management procedures, success, and training of dance teachers is sparse. The popular literature says little about who teaches and how they were trained but does imply that effective teaching is equated with the number of professional dancers developed (Tobias, 1981). Most published methodologies only describe what to teach by suggesting activities for classes. These are indirect denials of a relationship between how material is taught and the accomplishments of the dancers. The denials imply limited capabilities for developing well-qualified dance teachers.

This chapter is a consumers' guide to selecting and evaluating teachers. As such it is able to recommend to teachers preparatory elements necessary for designing and conducting classes that meet a broad range of student needs. The focus of the chapter is on traits of teacher behavior and education, which may, according to research, optimize total development in dancers.

While reading this chapter keep in mind that the information presented outlines ideal teaching/learning conditions. Finding or becoming the ideal teacher is unlikely if not impossible. Most of the following recommendations should be viewed on a relative scale. The guidelines are intended to help the reader find the best available dance teacher and/or become a more effective teacher.

Teacher Behavior: How Teachers Conduct Their Classes

How teachers conduct their classes will greatly influence the student's ability to learn. In this section three aspects of classroom management will be described. These are (a) authoritative behavior, (b) poor time management, and (c) distribution of feedback.

Authoritarian Behavior

In the past ten years teacher behaviorists have attempted to discover what kind of person teaches. It seems that teachers in general are quite authoritarian and verbal. They tend to control the class situation through direct verbal commands and instructions as opposed to indirect questioning and acceptance of student ideas.

Dance teachers appear to be no different from other kinds of teachers. Lord (1980) and Cheffers, Mancini, and Martinek (1980) found teachers of technique and composition classes to be quite verbal: Lord found them to be direct and inflexible as well. Dance classes are typically run under the control of a single teacher who defines a majority of the following class conditions:

1. Nature of the wearing apparel
2. Color of apparel
3. Acceptable physical qualities of the student
4. Hair style
5. When to begin and end class
6. Where students stand (individually and collectively)
7. Where to hold class
8. Class content
9. When students move and stop
10. How students move
11. Acceptable aesthetics

According to Mosston (1966) these are all qualities of authoritarian teaching.

Authoritarian behavior is very important when skill acquisition is the primary focus. When the development of creativity or independent thinking is valued, this form of direct teaching becomes an interference. The art form would flounder without creativity and independent thought. Yet as will be discussed later, the authoritarian qualities of the dance teacher may be thwarting that growth.

Authoritarian behavior dominates the class to such a degree that dance teachers talk at the expense of visual and kinesthetic instruction (Borrelli & Skrinar, 1982). It has been found that modern and ballet teachers tend to overuse verbal instruction and drastically underuse visual and kinesthetic forms. At the same time, teachers appeared to talk far more to beginning than to advanced dancers. Motor skill acquisition research on the ideal frequency of instructional cue use indicates that although beginners profit from considerable visual and kinesthetic instruction and advanced dancers handle verbal cues more effectively, every class should use all three forms with relatively similar frequency (Cratty, 1973; Singer, 1980). No research has been completed in dance on the ideal frequency of the three types of instructional cues. Until such work is done, it is recommended that dance classes be taught using verbal, visual, and kinesthetic cues on a fairly equal basis.

Theoretically every dance class contains familiar, not-so-familiar, and unfamiliar material. Familiar material is that which would be considered at or near the mastery level. Such material does not require visual or kinesthetic input; verbal instruction efficiently imparts feedback to the student. For new or unfamiliar material, kinesthetic and visual cues are critical because the dancer has not developed a verbal vocabulary of the movement elements. That vocabulary develops as skill develops. For not-so-familiar skills the degree of verbal, kinesthetic, or visual cues should vary with each skill depending on where the class and/or student are along the familiar-unfamiliar continuum. That is, lots of practice and observation in the early learning stages are necessary with greater amounts of verbal instruction as they approach mastery.

Poor Time Management

The excessive talking of an authoritarian teacher is an example of inefficient use of time. Poor time managers do not necessarily start or end class late. Rather, they may minimize the time spent on activities directly related to the goals of the class. If a dancer wants to learn movement, excessive listening could be counterproductive.

Gray and Skrinar's (1984) research on base-support[1] use may be a further indication that poor time management occurs in other forms during dance class. They found the warm-up for college ballet and modern technique classes to be significantly different from the dancing phase with regard to the size of base-supports used. Two examples from their findings were that for the average (mean) modern warm-up dancers spent 34% more time working the on-the-floor[2] position than dancing on the floor. Meanwhile, in ballet no time was spent jumping during warm-up whereas 15% of dancing was spent jumping. These differences represent conflicting ways of using the body's center of gravity between warm-up and dancing in class. According to Cratty's (1973) references on motor skill acquisition, the more similar a warm-up to final demands the greater the learning. Direct evidence about the relationship of warm-up to performance of a phrase, section, or entire dance is lacking. Until such research is completed, Cratty's recommendations may be the safest guide. That is, classes consisting of several unrelated activities may be poorly organized, thus using the students' learning time less efficiently.

BACK OF ROOM

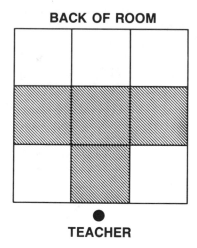

TEACHER

Figure 16.1   Patterns of teaching feedback in the technique class. Shaded blocks indicate areas of the room in which students received significantly more feedback (p < .01) than dancers in the non-shaded areas.

---

[1]Base-support here is defined as the area, generally between the feet, over which the weight is placed.

---

[2]On-the-floor'' is one of six base sizes examined by Gray and Skrinar. It is defined as having a weight-bearing body part on the ground outside the area of the feet.

Distribution of Feedback

A study completed by Samaro and Skrinar (1982) detailed in which areas of the room a teacher gave the most feedback to students. Dancers to the immediate right and left and back positions of the room received the least teacher input, front-center and right and left-center received the most (see Figure 16.1). A surprising result of the research indicated that, regardless of position in the room, dancers who stood in a location other than that of their typical location were likely to receive eight times more feedback than those standing in their usual places. The results suggest that teachers and/or students need to move about the room during class in order to distribute teacher input to students more evenly.

Teacher Education: How Dance Teachers Are Trained

How dance teachers are trained will influence their ability and capability to teach. The credentials of a dance teacher are examined in the following section. Also presented is a discussion of formal education for dance instructors and how teaching methods may be influenced by the education of the instructor.

Common Teacher Credentials

From what we have learned about teacher behavior there may be discrepancies between what should be and what is occurring in dance classes. Perhaps one reason is the way in which dance teachers are prepared to teach. Currently, anyone may open a dance studio. Frequently used credentials are that the teacher has a) studied with a famous teacher or at a well-known school, b) studied for a notable number of years, c) performed with a well-known company, d) choreographed a number of dances, and/or e) taught multiple forms of dance. Each of these factors should be considered when selecting a teacher. Examination of the merits of each credit is necessary.

Who are the teachers with whom a teacher has studied? What kind of examples did the mentor's behavior set? How were the mentors' teachers trained? What did they know of the basic principles of teaching? And, what of their teachers' mentors? Strong or weak links to the past may have been established which often can never be evaluated. A conversation with the prospective teachers about the nature and circumstance of their training may indicate whether or not you can evaluate these points.

How long the teacher has studied dance is almost minor, primarily because infinite years of study does not necessarily guarantee a talented teacher. The more important objective question is to what degree did they train? The level of involvement in dance is critical. Weekly classes for ten years may be less effective than daily classes for three years. Further, a good teacher has likely seen a great deal of dance, presented regular concerts, and in general become entrenched in dance activities at least at the local level.

The teacher's having performed with a well-known company does suggest a high level of sophistication about the art form. That person has probably seen and danced a wide variety of material, all of which influenced his or her perspective of dance. But will that outlook match the needs of the student? How effective is that former performer in a class of children with varying interests? Are the teacher's goals focused on professional development of physical skills? Is there a strong concern for mental, psychological, and spiritual development? In addition, the teaching skills of the performer/teacher must be considered. Being a high-level performer does not always mean that the teacher understands the rudiments of effective material simplification which optimize the success of the whole class, especially at the beginning levels.

What if the teacher has choreographed extensively? The next question must be, what is the purpose of the class? The choreographer quite likely understands composition but may be no better prepared to teach technique than the performer is to teach composition.

Finally, there is the teacher who professes to teach everything from tap, ballet, jazz, and Hawaiian to fire baton-twirling. Watch out! That is like saying that swim coaches can teach springboard diving, scuba diving, water ballet, and water polo equally well. Certainly a school may offer a broad curriculum, but that material should be taught by specialists in each idiom.

Without available research on the role a teacher's training, performance and pedagogical experiences play in teacher success, it is difficult to weigh one against the other. Skilled teachers develop in many different ways. What is important is that thoughtful attention be given to each of these considerations. If questions are not asked about the quality of the background, the ability to choose or evaluate a teacher may be remiss.

Teaching Methods

Some decisions as to the quality of a teacher's credentials can be made from the aforementioned factors. As well, decisions as to the conditions of a dance teacher's training are possible using the results of general education research. For instance, it has been established that supervision during practice teaching can be valuable when the supervising teacher has been well-trained in various teaching methodologies. Training in methods or styles of teaching develops an awareness of the connection between class purpose and teacher behavior.

For example, if creativity and independent thinking were primary goals for the class, a nonauthoritarian, indirect style of teaching would be needed. If development of social skills were the intention, a more student interactive style would be appropriate (Mosston, 1966). Experts in the field have established from seven to eleven teaching styles appropriate to respective class goals (Mosston, 1966; Joyce & Weil, 1972). Supervising teachers are better able to assist practice teachers when they realize the value of linking teaching behaviors to the goals of a class and/or sections of a class.

Formal Teacher Preparation

One of the few studies of dance teacher education was completed by Conroy (1973). She surveyed 25 public school modern dance teachers in Los Angeles County. All the teachers had a bachelors degree with 16% having a masters; 84% had done nondegree graduate work. Most of the teachers had majored in dance. The average college credits taken in dance were 15.6 (4–5 courses): 60% of the teachers had less than 12 credits (3–4 courses), and 40% had between 12 and 55 credits in dance! Some of these teachers may have spent as little as one year studying dance. The average time spent in outside private dance lessons was 10.6 years; 84% reported having had private instruction.

Conroy compared training characteristics of dance teachers to the variety of dance activities taught and the methods of teaching they used. She found that (a) the more private dance training the teachers had, the more curricular activities they conducted and the greater variety of teaching methods they used; and (b) the more college credits in dance the teachers had earned, the more advanced-level classes they taught. The suggestion is that dance students should seek teachers with a thorough combination of private and academic dance training.

Few, if any, dance curricula require adequate teacher training programs for students. Curiously, most dancers will be teachers although their training stresses performance and choreography (Skrinar & Zelonka, 1978). Consequently, even the teachers with considerable training and breadth of experience are likely ill-prepared to teach.

Summary

So far, bleak pictures have been painted of dance teachers' training as well as their behavior in class. Certainly many teachers are doing commendable work with students. Just how outstanding teachers are conducting classes and being trained needs to be documented. Until then, benefits for dance students can be maximized if students/parents

- pinpoint their reasons for taking dance,
- match their reasons with the teacher's purpose,
- observe various classes taught by the same prospective teacher,
- inquire about the prospective teacher's training.

Teachers can become better at what they do as well as maximizing benefits for dance students if they

- design class procedures according to the daily, monthly, and ongoing goals of the class;
- respect their own abilities and limitations to teach dance; if a student's needs can not be met, they should refer them to resources who can;
- teach classes which meet the specific needs (physical, social, psychological, and spiritual) of each student.

Certainly, there is no teacher in the world who matches the ideal mold. If there are teachers to choose from in your community, use these guidelines to make the best available choice. In communities where there are no teachers with the qualities discussed in this chapter, the prospective dancer has two choices: make the effort to travel to a qualified school, and/or locally become involved in a wide variety of sport and artistic activities.

References

Borrelli, G., & Skrinar, M. (1982). Frequency and type of instructional cues used in dance technique classes. *Kinesiology for Dance*, **5**(1), 6.

Cheffers, J.T.F., Mancini, V., & Martinek, T. (1980). In *Interaction analysis: An application to nonverbal activity* (2nd ed.). St. Paul, MN: Paul S. Amidon and Associates.

Conroy, M. (1973). Curricular activities of the secondary school modern dance teachers. *Dissertation Abstracts International*, **33a**, 6158.

Cratty, B. (1973). *Teaching motor skills*. Englewood Cliffs, NJ: Prentice-Hall.

Gray, M., & Skrinar, M. (1984). Support base use in two dance idioms. *Research Quarterly for Exercise and Sport*, **55**(2), 184–187.

Joyce, B., & Weil, M. (1972). *Models of teaching.* Englewood Cliffs: NJ: Prentice-Hall.

Lord, M.C. (1980). The teaching of dance: A characterization of dance teacher behaviors in technique and choreography classes at the university level. *Dissertation Abstracts International,* **40A,** 5778.

Mosston, M. (1966). *Teaching physical education.* Columbus, OH: Charles E. Merrill.

Singer, R.N. (1980). *Motor learning–human performance* (3rd ed.). New York, Macmillan.

Samaro, A., & Skrinar, M. (1982). *Location of feedback in the dance class.* Unpublished manuscript, University of Massachusetts, Department of Dance, Amherst.

Skrinar, M., & Zelonka, N.H. (1978). *A descriptive study of ballet and modern dancers at three levels of training.* Unpublished manuscript, University of Pittsburgh, School of Education.

Tobias, T. (1981, March). Stanley Williams: The quality of movement. *Dance Magazine,* pp. 74-83.

Index